QUALITATIVE
METHODS IN
AGING RESEARCH

OTHER RECENT VOLUMES IN THE
SAGE FOCUS EDITIONS

QUALITATIVE
METHODS IN
AGING RESEARCH

Jaber F. Gubrium
Andrea Sankar
editors

SAGE PUBLICATIONS
International Educational and Professional Publisher
Thousand Oaks   London   New Delhi

For information address:

SAGE Publications, Inc.
2455 Teller Road
Thousand Oaks, California 91320
E-mail: order@sagepub.com

SAGE Publications Ltd.
6 Bonhill Street
London EC2A 4PU
United Kingdom

SAGE Publications India Pvt. Ltd.
M-32 Market
Greater Kailash I
New Delhi 110 048 India

Printed in the United States of America

Library of Congress Cataloging-in-Publication Data

Main entry under title:

Qualitative methods in aging research / Jaber F. Gubrium, Andrea
    Sankar, editors.
        p.   cm. — (Sage focus editions; vol. 168)
    Includes bibliographical references and index.
    ISBN 0-8039-4943-X (cl). — ISBN 0-8039-4944-8 (pb)
        1. Old age—Research. 2. Gerontology—Research. I. Gubrium,
    Jaber F. II. Sankar, Andrea.
    HQ1061.Q35   1994
    305.26'072—dc20   93-21401
                                                                       CIP

96 97 98 99 00 01 10 9 8 7 6 5 4 3

Sage Production Editor: Yvonne Könneker

Contents

Introduction

ANDREA SANKAR
JABER F. GUBRIUM

Gerontology is the study of old age and aging. It also is the study of health policy focused on old age, the care and treatment of the frail and those who care for them, and many collateral issues. We can attempt to understand the subject matter in two ways: (a) through the profiles, trends, and associations produced by surveys and statistical analysis and (b) through the patterns of meaning, context, language, and culture revealed by qualitative approaches.

This book presents the nature, range, and uses of qualitative methods in aging research. The strength of qualitative research lies in the richness of its data and its decided attention to complexity, process, and meaning. The contributors emphasize the types of situations that call for this approach and methodological issues specific to its conduct and forms of analysis.

What Is Qualitative Research?

Qualitative research starts from the assumption that one can obtain a profound understanding about persons and their worlds from ordinary conversations and observations. Its empiricism is grounded in the everyday data of experience. Despite linguistic and cultural differences, we can recognize grief, joy, sadness, anger, and other strong emotions from the gestures and talk of strangers. We can tell a great deal about our own culture and its variable attitudes and sentiments by paying attention to dress, body language, accent, mannerisms, and spatial arrangements. In someone we know well, a simple look speaks volumes. These data are available to us through our interactive and interpretive sensibility, based on shared understandings—most distantly as strangers, more intimately as friends and family members.

Qualitative research acknowledges the considerable native ability people have to know things about their own lives, one another, and their respective worlds. It proceeds to advance beyond a basic empirical grasp of the situation through the use of expressly mundane methodologies such as in-depth interviews, participant observation, and documentary analysis, procedures that do not deny the practical grounds of experience. This in turn is anchored in diverse perspectives: phenomenology, structuralism, ethnomethodology, critical theory, constructionism, feminism, structural-functionalism, and practice theory.

Qualitative research acknowledges the researcher's role in obtaining the facts of experience, as Lucy Rose Fischer touchingly describes in Chapter 1. This stands in contrast to statistically based approaches that seek to minimize the researcher's role in order to standardize and replicate data. Qualitative research not only accepts the researcher's working ability to know, but also proceeds to theorize about and respond to what the researcher brings to the research context. Ethnomethodological and feminist studies, for example, have established that "science" cannot be separated from the traditions, beliefs, prejudices, and world views of its practitioners (Harding, 1987; Jordonova, 1987; Knorr-Cetina & Woolgar, 1983; Latour & Woolgar, 1979). In Chapter 4, Dale Jaffe and Eleanor Miller extend the connection to status differences, cautioning us not to overlook the relative descriptive advantage the researcher can have over the researched. As Ann Dill shows in Chapter 15, this even extends to written reports.

Qualitative research seeks to understand the multifaceted and complex nature of human experience from the perspective of subjects. Drawing on cultural theory, it assumes that experiences of life vary significantly and that one cannot interpret the nature of those experiences by mechanically assigning subjects to groups such as African-American or Caucasian, male or female, young, old, or oldest old. Although these categories must be taken into account, we need to understand how their respective experiences form and change.

Experience in all of its ordinary complexity remains in the foreground of the research (Gubrium, 1992). For example, in Chapter 3 Neil

Henderson shows how ethnicity and race intruded on what seemed to be a straightforward intervention project. Of course, the experience of old age is further segmented by gender and class. We also should add sexual orientation, a factor of growing importance to the experience of aging for future generations.

Qualitative researchers turn us to practice, taking bottom-up rather than top-down views, to argue that however "sophisticated" research descriptions eventually become, their source is everyday life. In seeking to understand meaning, the focus is on the taken-for-granted and commonsense understandings that people have about their lives. Research treats these understandings and experiences as something to be examined and explained rather than second-guessed. Qualitative research makes the often invisible, unreflected aspects of life explicit. It gives voice to the ordinary. For example, qualitative research examines how families experience the caregiving role (Gubrium, 1988, 1991). It explores how the incontinent elderly manage their condition (Mitteness, 1987) and how frail elderly use strategies to remain independent (Rubinstein, Kilbride, & Nagy, 1992). By focusing on practice, the qualitative researcher treats study participants as active agents in their own lives.

Study participants remain on center stage through all phases of the research. Qualitative research must be true to the study participant's meanings and experience. It seeks to represent the participant's reality as faithfully as possible. This requires close attention to the frames of reference of both the researcher and research participants as well as the context in which the research is conducted. For example, in Chapter 7, Jennie Keith describes the difficulties of comparing data gathered in one cultural context to those gathered in another and emphasizes the consequences for research of the systematic study of differences between groups as well as analyzing their areas of similarity. She points out that simple research instruments such as a pile sort, which is designed to elicit people's understanding of life-stage development, do not apply in cultures that do not recognize the concept of the linear progression of life. Using this instrument to establish comparable data across cultural settings will not work unless one appreciates native meanings. The validity problems inherent in crosscultural research are also present among groups distinguished by race, ethnicity, class, or gender within a single culture. The forced-choice format of most survey instruments does not allow the researcher to appreciate how these "variables" affect participants' understandings of questions or researchers' understandings of responses.

Qualitative research is a distinct orientation, with its own analytic traditions and methodologies, and it cannot be reduced to or understood as a precursor to quantification. Projects combining both approaches work when their separate strengths and contributions are recognized (see Rubinstein, Chapter 5; Mitteness and Barker, Chapter 6; and Keith, Chapter 7). Qualitative methods can suggest hypotheses for later testing. The use of quantitative methods in combination with qualitative can make findings more compelling, as in the strategy of *triangulation*, or when quantitative methods are used to perform such tasks as experimentally confirming patterns in the data and establishing relationships among variables in larger data sets. But basic and applied research that also applies qualitative procedures is likely to be more effective.

Special Uses of Qualitative Research

Although qualitative research is a general orientation method, it also has special uses. In situations where variables are unknown, where cultural issues are key, where it is important to understand the texture of differences within the study population, where the focus is on the dynamics of a situation or the development of a relationship, or where the very meaning or definition of the issues under study is unknown or not agreed upon, then qualitative research can bring clarity and understanding through its attention to meaning, process, and context. In particular, its flexibility and sensitivity to process allow it to respond to issues and directions that emerge in the course of the research. This includes attention through all stages of the research, from design to analysis to the interaction between researcher, informant, and research context as a source of data.

Meaning

One clear strength of qualitative research is its ability to detect, represent, and explicate the meaning of something from the viewpoint of the actors involved. Philosophers use the example of the twitch of an eye to illustrate the diverse significance and variability of meaning. A twitch can have several meanings in different contexts. It can reference a shared secret. It can indicate interest, often sexual, in another person.

It might be an involuntary, nervous tick or the eye's response to a piece of grit. If one is to understand the twitch, it is necessary to seek its meaning, perhaps ask the subject about it. The answer, however, may only be partial. To appreciate fully the twitch, especially in the first two cases, will require extensive knowledge about such areas of the subject's culture as the significances of interaction, assignation, gender roles, privacy, body language, demeanor, and decorum. Knowing behavior without understanding its meaning to the actors and its shared significances provides little useful or reliable information, as Mark Luborsky in Chapter 12 argues in discussing the dual folk and analytic life of "themes." To appreciate the meanings that the subjects express, we must understand the context of both the behavior and its interpretation.

Meaning operates on many levels. Actors use a broad range of significances to assign meaning to specific actions, which together might be referred to as the *cultural patterning* of the actions. These contexts and their categories provide frameworks within which people act and make sense of themselves. Understanding what categories people use and how these categories operate is an important goal of qualitative research, as demonstrated by Sharon Kaufman in Chapter 8 (in-depth interviewing), Brandon Wallace in Chapter 9 (life stories), Mark Luborsky in Chapter 12 (themes), Harry Berman in Chapter 13 (personal journals), and Emily Abel in Chapter 14 (historical perspective).

Caregiving research provides an important example. Policy makers tend to worry about what is called the *substitution* or *woodwork* effect, the idea that, given increased access to formal services, family members will reduce the amount of care they provide to an older person. Researchers have established, however, that this issue is not relevant or meaningful to caregivers, who instead tend to see their caregiving actions as relational, as growing out of their ties to the person for whom they are caring, not as a simple fund of services (Kaspar, in Sankar, 1993). For that matter, many "caregivers" resist the label altogether and do not see themselves in that role—as Jaber Gubrium and James Holstein show in Chapter 11.

Policy makers and caregivers may place the work of caregiving in different categories (Sankar, 1993). Policy makers tend to see caregiving as a series of discrete tasks, similar to the model of labor associated with industrial production, and thus categorize the work as distinct and separable from those who perform it. Caregivers, in contrast, often see the work as embedded in relationships and categorize it as an expression of the emotions that characterize the relationship, such as love, hate, affection, respect, and shame. Meaning should be understood both as generated by the individual actor and structured by the actor's context.

The Centrality of Cultural Issues

When research involves issues that are cultural, qualitative methods are needed to establish what the research variables mean in general to the study participants and to distinguish their meaning from those assigned by the researcher. This is broadly the case in crosscultural research when even subtle, taken-for-granted concepts such as space and time differ significantly between groups and peoples. Qualitative research is also needed when core issues in the researcher's own cultural context such as age, sex, gender, race, and class are the focus. Each of these areas is subject to cultural elaboration and interpretation, and one cannot assume that any particular research topic or research question will retain a stable meaning across the divisions within any particular society.

The role of culture in shaping our research extends to the questions we ask (Luborsky & Sankar, 1993), even to the issue of what is properly askable (see Kayser-Jones and Koenig, Chapter 2). Qualitative research explores not only the effect of the participant's culture on the experience of aging, but also the structuring role of culture on how the researcher conceives of gerontology and of the relevant issues and problems therein. For example, the use of *life satisfaction* as an outcome variable in numerous gerontological studies posits happiness as a desirable and widely held value. This value is not shared by all cultures or groups, nor do all people in our own culture consider it a desirable criterion against which to judge one's life (Gubrium, 1993; Sankar, 1993). This observation leaves us with the question of what is being measured with life satisfaction instruments (see Gubrium & Lynott, 1983).

Process

We sometimes need to know not only what has happened or what the nature of an experience is; we need to know *how* it took place. Attention to process in qualitative research operates on two levels: the methodological and the empirical. The first entails an awareness of how the interview process affects the quality of the data that we gather. The second concerns the dynamics of the subject matter under consideration. For example, the focus on the nature of the interview includes attention to establishing a narrative flow, which might preferably resemble a natural conversation. One might argue that the more one approximates a natural conversation the greater the validity and, hence, the less likely it is that subject and researcher will misunderstand each other (Mishler, 1986; Suchman & Jordan, 1990). Unlike "normal" conversation, however, this "active listening" requires the researcher to look beyond the surface of the conversation for implicit analytic questions, alternative frames, and the content of categories created and used by the informant.

Qualitative researchers habitually study the processes by which an attribute or status comes into being: for example, the process of becoming a caregiver or the process by which a definition such as *senile* is constructed (see Gubrium, 1986). Two ways of approaching the study of process are participant observation and the analysis of talk and interaction. In participant observation, which is described by Karen Lyman in Chapter 10, the researcher becomes directly engaged in the research context. The researcher is part of the data-collection and analysis process. The researcher uses her or his own sense data—the impressions and feelings picked up in the research process through interaction with study participants—as a source of information about the subject of study.

The way in which meaning is constructed in talk and interaction is another approach to the study of process (see Gubrium and Holstein, Chapter 11). As Mark Luborsky discusses in Chapter 12, *how* something is said just as much as *what* is said defines the nature of an experience. Themes and patterns in talk embody both the personal and the social aspects of experience. This type of analysis emphasizes talk as much as the stock-in-trade focus on interaction by participant observers.

Casting a Broad Net

In exploring uncharted terrain whose details and dimensions are unclear, it is necessary to cast a broad net in order to attend to issues not obviously suggested by the topic at hand. Relatively unstructured approaches such as open-ended interviews and participant observation as well as more formal in-depth interviews and focus groups permit subjects to set the frames for their responses or actions and so introduce topics or dynamics possibly unknown or poorly understood by the researcher. As such, topics unanticipated in research plans are allowed to emerge from the research process and evaluation can be undertaken with the diversity of subjectivity in mind, as Shulamit Reinharz illustrates in Chapter 16.

Qualitative Research as Science

Lest assertions about the relevance of the researcher's basic knowledge of experience be taken to suggest that just any reportage of conversation or observation constitutes qualitative research, it is important to be explicit about the scientific status of qualitative research. Criteria for evaluating qualitative research as science are located in diverse arenas, reflecting the complex, multifaceted nature of the approach.

Briefly, first, qualitative research recognizes that all research on experience deals with perspectives. It thus attends to the potential influences—social, cultural, and political—that affect how the researcher perceives the research process and its outcomes. Attention is also paid to the way subjects themselves structure the research encounter and to related native factors that frame the research process. Second, because qualitative research concentrates on actors in contexts, the researcher must be aware of and attend to relevant detail and particularity in representing participants' experience. Third, concern for and attention to ethical issues must be present throughout the research process, not just at the start. Qualitative research relies on the ability of the researcher to establish rapport with research participants. A characteristic kind of mutual trust is involved that allows the researcher to gather personal, sometimes intimate, information about the subjects' lives. This creates a continuous ethical obligation on the part of the researcher to ensure that the research does not harm the participant and that the privileged position of access granted the researcher will not be used to the participant's detriment, as Kayser-Jones and Koenig amply describe in Chapter 2.

Attention to meaning is far more complex than simply asking open-ended questions and allowing participants to speak extemporaneously. It requires a heightened sense of self-awareness about the researcher's personal understandings, beliefs, prejudices, and world view. Researchers bring to the research encounter considerable social, historical, and cultural baggage (Gubrium, 1992; Harding, 1987; Keller, 1985). The researcher is situated in his or her own context and proceeds to engage in science from that standpoint. The use of the decontextualization methods of "hard" science do not erase the situated nature of research, as many historians and philosophers of science have demonstrated (Latour & Woolgar, 1979). A so-called hard science is soft indeed that does not attend to this aspect of research practice.

Attention to what the researcher brings to the research process is not meant to underestimate the subject's ability to shape the interview. Respondents engage in an interview for their own reasons (see Behar, 1990). Further, the respondent or informant controls what he or she chooses to disclose and thus plays his or her part in structuring the portrait that emerges from the research process. Self-censorship by participants is an issue for all social scientists, which any hard science also must consider. Qualitative researchers are expressly concerned with the issue as they focus on the subjectivity of respondents.

Qualitative research involves a special responsibility on the part of the researcher. Because the unstructured, intimate nature of the research often places the researcher in close contact with the participant, the researcher perennially encounters ethical issues arising from his or her status as participant in the research context. This is especially crucial when the researcher deals with the elderly, who may be vulnerable, frail, or incapacitated (Reinharz & Rowles, 1988).

All in all, it is a deliberate attention to the concrete and practical conditions and subjectivities of the research encounter that makes qualitative research equal to other scientific modes of investigation. Lack of rigor comes in not attending to subjects' worlds, meanings, and differences from *their* points of view. This is the unique contribution of qualitative research.

Organization of the Book

We invite you to consider these issues in the following chapters, in which several seasoned qualitative researchers discuss aspects of the research process in relation to specific sites where they have worked. All of the sites present aging and old age as an experience, and the researchers develop their *analysis* in the context of the topics. They also consider *method,* the proverbial nuts and bolts of research procedure. The linkage between analysis and method is characteristic of the best qualitative research: working close to the experiential ground, while attuned to broader concerns of meaning, complexity, and process.

The book is organized roughly in terms of the steps taken in conducting a study. Part I, "Thinking Ahead," addresses the spectrum of issues that must be considered as a researcher looks forward to working with people; these range from how to think about the enterprise as a whole to ethical and interpersonally political matters.

Part II, "Planning," addresses concrete research organization. The important questions here are: How is the project to develop? What difference will the scale of the project make for its management? How will culture affect the interpretation of meaning? Although we have introduced these as analytic issues, the authors of these chapters address them equally as matters of procedure.

Part III, "Data Collection," shows ways in which qualitative researchers gather their empirical material, from in-depth interviewing and narrative studies to participant observation. Again, all three chapters in this part present method as more than technique, referencing the important interactive elements of the research process.

Part IV, "Forms of Analysis," teaches us about various ways that we can interpret qualitative data. The range is remarkable, from the use of literary frameworks and phenomenological orientations to fine-grained attention to talk and interaction.

Part V, "Writing and Recommending," reminds us that we are not done when we have finished gathering and analyzing our empirical material. There still is the matter of presenting it to an audience. The way this is done—writing itself—is part and parcel of being sensitive to research as a social process. We are in some sense always recommending as we choose a style of presentation, even while we can expressly offer policy advice based on our findings.

References

Abel, E. (1991). *Who cares for the elderly: Public policy and the experiences of adult daughters.* Philadelphia: Temple University Press.

Behar, R. (1990). Rage and redemption: Reading the life story of a Mexican marketing woman. *Feminist Studies, 16,* 223-258.

Gubrium, J. (1986). *Old timers and Alzheimer's: The descriptive organization of senility.* Greenwich, CT: JAI.

Gubrium, J. (1988). Family responsibility and caregiving in the qualitative analysis of the Alzheimer's disease experience. *Journal of Marriage and the Family, 50,* 197-207.

Gubrium, J. (1991). *The mosaic of care.* New York: Springer.

Gubrium, J. (1992). Qualitative research comes of age in gerontology. *Gerontologist,* *32*(5), 581-582.

Gubrium, J. (1993). *Speaking of life: Horizons of meaning for nursing home residents.* Hawthorne, NY: Aldine de Gruyter.

Gubrium, J., & Lynott, R. J. (1983). Rethinking life satisfaction. *Human Organization,* *42*, 30-38.

Harding, S. (1987). *Feminism and methodology.* Bloomington: Indiana University Press.

Jordanova, L. (1987). *Sexual visions: Images of gender in science and medicine between the eighteenth and twentieth centuries.* Madison: University of Wisconsin Press.

Keller, E. (1985). *Reflections on gender and science.* New Haven: Yale University Press.

Knorr-Cetina, K. S., & Woolgar, S. (Eds.). (1983). *Science observed.* Beverly Hills, CA: Sage.

Latour, B., & Woolgar, S. (1979). *Laboratory life: The social construction of scientific facts.* Beverly Hills, CA: Sage.

Luborsky, M., & Sankar, A. (1993). Extending the critical gerontology perspective. *Gerontologist, 33*(4), 440-445.

Mishler, E. (1986). *Research interviewing: Context and narrative.* Cambridge, MA: Harvard University Press.

Mitteness, L. S. (1987). The management of urinary incontinence by community-living elderly. *Gerontologist, 27,* 185-193.

Reinharz, S., & Rowles, G. (1988). *Qualitative gerontology.* New York: Springer.

Rubinstein, R., Kilbride, J., & Nagy, S. (1992). *Elders living alone: frailty and the perception of choice.* Hawthorne, NY: Aldine.

Sankar, A. (1993). Culture, research, and policy. *Gerontologist, 33*(4), 437-438.

Suchman, L., & Jordan, B. (1990). Interactional troubles in face-to-face survey interviews. *Journal of the American Statistical Association, 85,* 409.

PART I

Thinking Ahead

1

Qualitative Research as Art and Science

LUCY ROSE FISCHER

Doing qualitative research is both art and science. Art always involves decisions about how much to "tell"—with brush strokes, musical notes, or words. For a painter, being able to apply paint to paper largely requires technical expertise; creating a work of art is knowing when to stop painting. It is his or her unique sensibility and taste that guide the artist. In a similar sense, a good qualitative researcher understands how much to disclose—how much data to collect, how much to report, and how to present narrative findings—based on previous experience as a researcher, sensitivity to the issues being studied, and an intuitive understanding of the "art" of qualitative research.

Qualitative research as a "science" has several issues of disclosure. We have questions of accuracy. How much detail should we gather? Obviously, any interview has limitations on what we are told—both because of self-censorship by respondents and because we do not always know what to ask. We always have more to learn. How do we decide that we have enough information?

Certain questions of context exist. An advantage of qualitative research is that we gather in-depth information about individuals, groups, or institutions. Even so, as we focus on our topic of interest, how much do we understand about the environment that shapes individual experience? How do we interpret contextual factors in our analysis?

Thorny questions about selection bias also present themselves. Some people talk more and tell better stories. Some stories are more interesting and dramatic than others. We are always making choices in qualitative research. Which examples will we report? Which respondents will be given voice? Selection entails not only interpretation, but also potential bias—ignoring some issues, emphasizing others.

Finally, certain ethical questions are associated with what to disclose in qualitative research. Social research holds out the promise of anonymity for respondents, but detailed individual stories may violate this promise. Having done several qualitative studies in gerontology, I am sometimes haunted by issues of disclosure—both pragmatic and ethical. In many of my projects, the participants have a special vulnerability because of my research. For example, my associates and I have interviewed elderly parents and their adult children and children-in-law. In the privacy of their living rooms, they have told us stories about their family relationships, sometimes revealing feelings or actions that they have not told one another. Their stories are the heart of our research. How do we report these findings?

In the pages that follow, I will discuss dilemmas confronted in qualitative research. I will draw examples mostly from my own qualitative research in social gerontology. This is an exercise in self-reflection on both ethical and methodological issues. What are the hazards of qualitative research as both art and science? What are the special considerations of such research on topics in aging?

Issues of Accuracy

Several years ago, I found myself on the other end of the microphone: I was the subject of a qualitative study in the social sciences. About 10 years later, the author was kind enough to send me a copy of her book in which I was one of some 20 respondents. My participation in the study was illuminating. It was, as I recall, a rather long interview—more than two hours. I was interested in her methods, and I replicated some of her techniques in my subsequent studies, but mostly it was useful to note my own sensations as a respondent. I was both flattered and wary. It is not often that someone had been so interested in me. I felt exposed under the scrutiny of her questions, and all during the interview I kept thinking, "So this is what it feels like to them when I am the interviewer." At the same time, I was aware that I had control over what I did or did not say: I was self-censoring. The interviewer had no way of knowing about experiences that I did not share.

When the book came, I read it piecemeal—first reading the parts about myself and then reading the rest. I was impressed. I thought the author had interesting insights. In one or two places, I disagreed with her—especially concerning my own interview. I thought she missed certain details and nuances. These "inaccuracies" did not undermine her overall analysis, but they indicated that her information about me, in particular, was incomplete and perhaps misleading. It made me wonder: How accurate are my own data?

Issues of accuracy generally are subtle and murky. Occasionally, however, we know that we are missing critical pieces of information, the qualitative equivalent of "missing data" in survey research. In the research for my book *Linked Lives: Adult Daughters and Their Mothers* (Fischer, 1986), I found myself in such a situation. In one of my daughter interviews—with an unmarried woman in her 20s—I was asking about an incident from her teenage years. The daughter alluded to a serious problem in her relationship with her mother. But when I probed for details, she said, "I'm not going to tell you about that!" As I sat with this answer thrown in my lap, I knew that what she was censoring was important information about her relationship with her mother. After a few more tentative questions around the edges of that issue, I also understood that she would not tell me anything more. I went on with the rest of the interview.

In retrospect, the setting of the interview might have partly explained her reticence. When I called potential respondents to set up the interviews, I always asked to do the interview in a private place. Even so, other people occasionally were around. In this case, I interviewed the daughter in the living room of the apartment she shared with several other people. Although we were alone for most of the interview, sometimes others walked through or near that room. Whether she did not trust me to keep the information confidential or whether she did not want to reveal her secrets to her housemates was not clear.

More commonly, we have no way of guessing what we are not being told. Self-censorship by respondents may be a primary reason for inaccurate data in any kind of social science research, quantitative or qualitative. The "social desirability" factor is well known in survey research—that is, respondents try to present a positive image of themselves. Potentially, the detail and depth of information in qualitative research ought to mitigate the social desirability problem. In a long interview, for example, the respondent may "give off" information that counters or adds complexity to the respondent's presentation of self.

Ironically, however, the actual existence of a relationship between interviewer and respondent may exacerbate the social desirability factor.

Self-censorship in an interview is not necessarily a problem. We cannot and do not want to hear every detail about a person's life and experiences. But what do we do when respondents refuse to reveal information that is central to our study? Our only way to confront this issue is by the range of our questions and our ability to ask probing questions. As interviewers, we need to be aware of small and large issues that are hinted at but not fully explained. We need to keep asking more, testing the limits of what we know and understand. That is, quite simply, the best that we can do. Even with in-depth qualitative interview or observational data, our accuracy and understanding have limits.

Understanding the Context

My research has spanned a rather broad range of topics in gerontology: intergenerational family relationships, caregiving, home health care, volunteerism, senior housing, and health services. Because most of my studies are in applied gerontology, I have interviewed and consulted with practitioners in various fields—nurses, physicians, social workers, home health aides, directors of home health agencies and nursing homes, volunteer coordinators, and program planners in governmental agencies. As a researcher, I am an outsider. Even if I have done a competent review of the research literature, I am not an expert in any of these professional fields.

My most recent book, *Older Volunteers: A Guide to Research and Practice,* is based on a synthesis of research on volunteerism and case studies of exemplary programs for older volunteers (Fischer & Schaffer, 1993). Based on our research findings, my coauthor and I have been conducting workshops in which we train volunteer professionals. Many of the attenders at these workshops have had years of experience as volunteer coordinators, and several have developed innovative and creative programs for older volunteers. At the beginning of our workshops, we tell them that they are the experts and that we are just offering them our research as a tool to help them learn from one another and stimulate new ideas.

Nonetheless, outsider status offers an important vantage point for qualitative social research in several ways. First, as outsiders, we ask naive questions. Recently, I was designing a descriptive evaluation of a new program for pharmacists. The director of the program told me that she appreciated my involvement—not only because of my expertise in research, but also because I am not an expert in pharmacy: "You keep asking questions, and that's good."

Second, being new, we notice things that insiders tend to take for granted. In *Living and Dying at Murray Manor,* Jaber Gubrium (1975) revealed how a nursing home has different meanings for both patients and staff at different levels. Similarly, in a study of elderly hospital patients, I analyzed the contrasting perspectives of hospital staff, patients, and family members (Fischer, with Hoffman, 1984). These kinds of analyses provide an overview of institutional relationships that come from the outsiders' view.

Third, being an outsider adds some measure of objectivity because we do not have the particular loyalties to the organization or the profession that we are studying. This is not absolute objectivity, of course. What we notice and how we interpret what we observe are shaped by our personal values and biases. Moreover, we also face interpersonal factors and emotional reactions. In several of my studies, I have been enormously impressed with some of the people I have interviewed, including home health aides, service coordinators, volunteer coordinators, social workers, and other professionals. When I write up my reports, I think of their faces and their voices. I am writing about people, not just "systems."

In some ways, being an outsider is a problem. If I ask naive questions, it may be because of my ignorance. My failure to take things for granted may largely result from my naivete. Sometimes I make mistakes in interpretation, terminology, and so forth. Recently, for example, I wrote a report on service coordination in senior housing (Fischer, 1992). Staff members at the agency that had hired me to do this study objected to the way I was using certain terms such as *case management* and *care coordination* that have formal definitions within social work. Misusing terminology may be symptomatic of a larger problem: misunderstanding the environment and professional context.

I think it is useful to view both respondents and other professionals in the field being studied as colleagues in the research process. One benefit of qualitative research is that respondents can share their insights. It is also important to have professional experts (not just fellow researchers) review reports before they are published. This can avert embarrassing inaccuracies. Nonetheless, thorny issues exist: If a researcher and a participant do not agree, how should differences in interpretation be resolved? How sensitive does a researcher have to be to peoples' feelings—especially, if some portions of a report might be viewed as negative or critical? I have no easy answers to such questions. In my own experience, I have at times walked a fine line, listening to critique, usually following suggestions, but retaining my own right over editorial decisions.

Extraordinary Stories

As every qualitative researcher knows, some respondents are more interesting than others. The stories they tell are more vivid or more conceptually useful. Certain stories also impress us and stimulate our thinking. I have found myself developing entire theoretical frameworks from interview stories.

One afternoon while doing research for *Linked Lives,* I was taken aback when one daughter echoed my own feelings about my relationship with my mother. This daughter said she was determined never to learn to play bridge because her mother was a bridge player and she believed that bridge clubs just "kill time." Instantly, I recognized the similarity. I also did not play bridge. I had a bridge-playing mother, and I had resolved to have a different kind of life because I thought my mother's life was a waste. This daughter's story suggested to me the concept of *negative identity,* or defining oneself as the converse of another's image. As I reviewed my daughter interviews, I found that most of the daughters, in a variety of individual ways, talked about wanting their lives to be different from their mothers'. It was the bridge-playing story—which was interesting to me personally—that sparked the insight about negative identity.

But vivid stories also can be misleading in qualitative research. In my research on mothers and daughters and mothers-in-law and daughters-in-law, I was always more aware of negative or problematic accounts than positive portrayals of relationships. Some daughters talked about painful struggles with their mothers, especially when they were teenagers. One daughter said she hated her mother and had not spoken to her in several years. Several daughters-in-law complained bitterly about their mothers-in-law, and two daughters-in-law were barely on speaking terms with their mothers-in-law.

These problematic relationships were not "typical" in that the negative or problematic qualities represented a small minority of mother-daughter or in-law relationships. In fact, the stories are striking because they are different. But sometimes anomalous or extraordinary stories can help to illuminate underlying relational structures and themes.

For example, I listened to several accounts of *role-reversal* relationships in which young daughters felt emotionally and psychologically responsible for their mothers. When one daughter was a teenager, her mother confided in her about sexual and other marital problems:

> My mother told me that he [the father] was masturbating upstairs and they hadn't had sex for a long time. That, of course, was none of my business but I mentioned to my father that I thought there were an awful lot of Kleenexes in the laundry lately. . . . My mother was complaining that she had to do all the handkerchiefs. . . . She washed them and she ironed them and my father was using them to masturbate upstairs and then he'd throw them under the bed and she'd have to clean them up. I didn't think that was her job. So when she told me I got angry with my father. I didn't confront him directly . . . but I let him know that I knew. (Fischer, 1986, p. 30)

In some ways, the intimacy between this mother and daughter reflects a common theme: their "linked lives." Nonetheless, this daughter was aware that her experience was unusual and that she was violating family boundaries by knowing and commenting on her parents' sexual relations ("That, of course, was none of my business"). What is unusual—and dysfunctional—in this family is the particular triadic structure: a mother who has an unhappy marriage with the father and who allies with her daughter as a protector. In my analysis of the mother and daughter interviews, I discovered that role reversal seems to be associated with a particular kind of family triangle: That is, daughters tend to become protective of their mothers when problems develop with fathers. Although most young daughters said they confided in their mothers (at least to some degree), the daughters with alcoholic, philandering, or mentally unstable fathers were especially likely to become confidantes and advice givers to their mothers (see Fischer, 1986, p. 37). The daughters with problem fathers counseled their mothers to divorce or their mothers asked them to intercede with their fathers on their behalf. These mother-daughter relationships were exceptional because of their negative alliance against the father.

Sometimes in qualitative research it is useful to count cases. A quantitative analysis can help to resolve the problem of "extraordinary" respondents. By coding and counting, we address research questions (or test minihypotheses) with our data. Is negative identity an underlying theme in mother-daughter relationships? Yes. Can we always find strain in relationships between mothers-in-law and daughters-in-law? No, but there is likely to be both more involvement and more tension after the birth of grandchildren.

Thus extraordinary respondents sometimes reveal important themes or common patterns. Often, however, the insight is more subtle. The story is noticeable because it is not typical. Most teenage daughters do not have role-reversed relationships with their mothers; most young women like their mothers and their mothers-in-law. But these atypical stories can nonetheless be revealing. In my research, the critical question was, Why is this relationship different from other relationships? Thus the core of the analysis was to examine underlying relational themes and the factors that make some relationships diverge from these patterns.

How Much to Disclose

When I begin a study, I generally write letters to potential respondents, tell them about the study, and invite them to participate. In virtually every letter, I promise that no names will be used in reports and publications and that the information will be confidential. In qualitative research, when detailed individual stories are reported, this assurance of confidentiality may be compromised. In many of my studies, I have been haunted by the potential for harm.

As I write this chapter, my most recent book, *Older Volunteers: A Guide to Research and Practice* (Fischer & Schaffer, 1993), has gone to press with one quote that makes me particularly uneasy. *Older Volunteers* is based on a synthesis of research on volunteerism and case studies of exemplary and innovative programs for older volunteers. In Chapter 7, I discuss the dilemma of quality versus compassion. I begin the chapter with the following vignette:

> Our volunteers have to read for two hours and for some people as they get older the quality of their voice declines. We have one man who is 87—he's our oldest volunteer—his voice is not of sufficient quality anymore to use his

tape. So we let him read and then we erase what he has read. He comes a couple of times a week, and he doesn't have much else to do. He's the sweetest man. We don't have it in our hearts to tell him, because doing this work is so important for him. But our core group is aging, and we are going to have to find other ways of dealing with this problem. (Fischer & Schaffer, 1993, p. 120)

I used this story from an organization that records books for blind persons, because it so vividly captures the quality versus compassion dilemma. The work for volunteers in this program requires special skills. Two volunteers work together in two-hour sessions, one reading and the other monitoring the taping equipment. If the quality is not good, the taping has to be partially or completely redone. What is particularly remarkable about this story is the cost: Another volunteer (the one doing the monitoring) spends four hours a week and has his or her time wasted when the tapes are erased.

The quote makes me uneasy because I could not find a reasonable way to disguise the setting. Anyone familiar with volunteer associations is likely to identify this organization (that is, they would know, at the least, the national organization, not necessarily the local affiliate). This organization was chosen because it has an exemplary program for older volunteers. It provides a critical service, does high-quality work, and has intense loyalty from its volunteers, many of whom are retirees. Unfortunately, this story presents a rather critical view on an organization that would generally be assessed very positively.

Volunteer professionals who have read the manuscript or have heard me presenting this material at workshops react intensely to this story. They often get angry at the deception. I have chosen to present this story, however, because it shows, in extreme form, a common theme: That volunteer managers feel obliged to treat volunteers with special consideration (because they offer no monetary or material incentive for the work), that an inherent tension exists between compassion and work-performance standards, and that even among exemplary volunteer programs very few have policies for discharging volunteers.

The stories that are the most ethically difficult are also those that are the most useful analytically. They are rich in detail. They offer an opportunity to examine the dynamics of organizations or interpersonal relationships. In my research for *Linked Lives,* I included a case study from one of the more interesting interviewees. Her stories, which were detailed and dramatic, revealed inherent tensions in family relationships. One story was about a bed:

> I had picked out—at a tag sale—a really nice wicker headboard for Michael's bed when he was going to have his bed. I loved it. And Donald's mother had gone and bought Michael a bed that was a beautiful gift and very expensive. But I was heartbroken because I really wanted this bed. I couldn't tell her because she was so happy to be buying this bed for Michael. It was almost worth it to let her be happy and me not . . . little things like that—I don't want to hurt her. (Fischer, 1986, p. 134)

The point of telling this story was to illustrate the particular quality of in-law relationships—that a mother-in-law is both kin and stranger. A mother-in-law is like family: She has a blood relationship with the grandchild and therefore has a right to be involved in family affairs (like buying her grandson a bed). But she is a stranger because there is no long history of intimacy that allows familiarity in interpersonal exchanges. Even in this generally harmonious and affectionate relationship with a mother-in-law, some strain is found simply because a daughter-in-law is unable to be as open with her in-law as with her own parent.

Unlike the colleague who sent me a copy of her book because I agreed to be interviewed for her study, I did not extend such a courtesy to the hundred or so daughters, mothers, and mothers-in-law who participated in my project. I had no budget to purchase such a large number of books. But the book was published by a trade press. It is likely that at least some of the participants read the book. Even without names, the stories carry identities.

I can imagine this mother-in-law reading the story of the bed. Assuming she remembered buying a bed for her grandson (by the time she read the book, the bed incident would have been old history), she would wonder, "Did my daughter-in-law resent me because of that bed?" She might have called her daughter-in-law and asked, "I was reading the book by that researcher. Did you tell her about my getting a bed for [the first grandson]?" The daughter-in-law might have said, "Well, yes. . . ." And assuming that they still had a good relationship, which by now would have had a fairly long history, they might have both laughed. Or maybe the mother-in-law would read the story and fret, but not wanting to confront her daughter-in-law she would say nothing. Or maybe the daughter-in-law divorced the mother-in-law's son long ago and the mother-in-law would have no way of checking out the story.

Overall, I do not believe that the breaches of confidentiality in my reports have had horrific consequences. I also am aware that most participants in my studies will never see my publications, most of which are in professional journals. But what is worrisome is that I will never know what harm I might have done.

Issues of Art and Science in
Qualitative Gerontology

The issues of qualitative research as art and science are not really particular to qualitative research in gerontology. Even so, there are special concerns in studies of vulnerable populations—minorities, the elderly, women, disabled persons, and so forth. As a researcher in social gerontology, I find that the subjects of my studies often fit one or more of these categories of vulnerability. Many of the people I have interviewed are frail, poor, or physically or mentally ill. Do these respondents see my research assistants and me as able-bodied, middle-class intruders in their lives? What if we are inaccurate in our analyses because our understanding is limited by our personal background?

Research on institutions that involve the elderly have similar complexities. Case studies inevitably have limited information. What if we are wrong in our interpretations because we do not fully explore the context of particular situations?

In this chapter, I have described some of the problems, limitations, and dilemmas associated with qualitative research. I am not suggesting, however, that all qualitative research is inaccurate, ethically problematic, or valueless. Qualitative studies that have rich, descriptive data offer insights that are not available with survey research alone. Practitioners and policy makers in aging often find good qualitative studies invaluable for evaluating established programs and developing new programs and policies. In our reports in social gerontology, we sometimes speak on behalf of persons who are old, frail, and poor. We may be their only voice. We need to be aware of both the special trust in this responsibility and the limitations of our data.

If qualitative research is art as well as science, this is particularly apt for the topic of aging. Science may purport to be objective; art is subjective. When we try to understand aging, we are both researchers and the subjects of study. Doing qualitative research is the ultimate test of our sensitivity to our own aging.

References

Fischer, L. R. (1986). *Linked lives: Adult daughters and their mothers.* New York: Harper & Row.

Fischer, L. R. (1992). *Minnesota age-in-place project: The on-site coordinator study.* Report for Minnesota Board on Aging, Department of Human Services, St. Paul, MN.

Fischer, L. R., with Hoffman, C. (1984). Who cares for the elderly: The dilemma of family support. In M. Lewis & J. Miller (Eds.), *Research in social problems and public policy* (Vol. 3, pp. 169-215). Greenwich, CT: JAI.

Fischer, L. R., & Schaffer, K. B. (1993). *Older volunteers: A guide to research and practice.* Newbury Park, CA: Sage.

Gubrium, J. (1975). *Living and dying at Murray Manor.* New York: St. Martin's.

2

Ethical Issues

JEANIE KAYSER-JONES
BARBARA A. KOENIG

Ethnographic or qualitative research with the elderly presents an array of ethical dilemmas for both the novice and experienced researcher. Some of these issues are common to any type of research with human subjects and include ensuring the voluntary cooperation of research subjects through careful informed-consent procedures, balancing the risk of research participation against the potential benefit of the research, and ensuring that vulnerable populations are not bearing the burden of research without the possibility of benefit (Marshall, 1991; Rynkiewich & Spradley, 1976). These concerns correspond to the fundamental ethical principles of (a) autonomy or respect for persons, (b) beneficence or nonmaleficence, and (c) justice (Beauchamp & Childress, 1989).

Qualitative research, however, raises issues unique to the specific techniques of ethnographic fieldwork. The strong reciprocal bonds that develop between researcher and informant create both obligations and potential hazards for the researcher. True voluntary participation becomes an ideal that is difficult to evaluate in practice; subjects and researcher may become interdependent. And intimate daily contact with informants may expose the research scientist to conflict-of-interest situations. Qualitative research with the elderly intensifies these funda-

AUTHORS' NOTE: The research reported here was supported by the National Institute on Aging, Grant No. AG 05073.

15

mental problems because of the vulnerability of many populations studied, such as the institutionalized elderly or those living in poverty.

In this chapter we will outline the major ethical dilemmas that qualitative investigators face in planning and conducting ethnographic research.

Biomedical Background

In his review of the social origins of the modern bioethics field, Rothman (1991) dates the recent interest in protection of human subjects to a key 1966 *New England Journal of Medicine* article by Henry Beecher. In this paper, Beecher, a noted medical researcher, revealed an alarming list of 22 instances in which human subjects had been egregiously abused. Many of the abuses listed in Beecher's controversial paper have become well known, including the Willowbrook incident in which mentally retarded children were injected with live hepatitis vaccine (Rothman, 1991, p. 74).

As a social historian, Rothman documents how the publication of Beecher's paper signalled the need for significant change in the researcher-subject relationship. His 22 examples were not aberrant. They were conducted by well-known researchers at reputable institutions, including the National Institutes of Health's clinical center.

Beecher's goal was not to limit research, but to expose past abuses in order to protect good science. Of course, earlier abuses of research subjects, such as the Nazi experiments with humans, had resulted in a general outcry. The Nuremberg Code of 1947 was used as a set of standards in evaluating war crimes by scientists and physicians (Marshall, 1991). But this episode was seen as aberrant and beyond the conduct of normal science. Beecher's paper revealed how even well-intentioned researchers at major U.S. medical schools might allow the goals of research to override the interests of research subjects.

Beecher's exposé—along with the public outcry brought about by Chester Southam's injection of live cancer cells into demented elderly patients in the early 1960s (Rothman, 1991)—led to the first federal regulations to protect human subjects in research (published by the Public Health Service in July 1966).

In 1974, the National Research Act established the President's Commission for the Protection of Human Subjects of Biomedical and Behavioral Research. This commission published numerous influential reports, including *The Belmont Report*, which outlined the basic principles of research with human subjects (President's Commission, 1978).

The end result is a fully institutionalized national system designed to protect human subjects, which requires that each institution sponsoring research—whether biomedical, social, or behavioral—have an institutional review board (IRB) examine all prospective projects. Because of the notoriety of many abuses of research subjects, the same guidelines were applied to all types of research; social and behavioral research projects were required to undergo the same review as biomedical studies.

Professional Codes of Ethics

Although the original movement to protect human subjects arose from abuses in biomedical research, it soon became evident that other forms of research also posed hazards to subjects, often subtle but significant. In the late 1960s, for example, anthropologists were forced to deal with the potential negative impact of their ethnographic work on local populations in politically volatile areas such as Southeast Asia and Latin America (Jorgensen, 1971). As a result of an increasing awareness of the potential negative effect of seemingly harmless field research, codes of research ethics have been promulgated by professional groups.

In 1971, the American Anthropological Association first adopted a code of professional responsibilities for researchers (AAA, 1990); this code has recently been updated (Marshall, 1991). In 1983, the Society for Applied Anthropology issued a *Statement on Professional and Ethical Responsibilities*. The professional associations of psychologists and sociologists responded similarly (American Psychological Association, 1974, 1982; American Sociological Association, 1971).

Although these efforts are extremely useful in raising awareness, the codes themselves do not provide solutions to many of the problems encountered by qualitative investigators. These codes emphasize the researcher's primary ethical obligation to protect the welfare of all research subjects. For example, a government's desire for information about a population to aid a war effort should always be secondary to the researcher's responsibility to his or her primary informants. In complex research settings, this ideal goal is difficult to implement. In research conducted in a nursing home, for example, the interests of staff and residents may conflict, and yet all are technically subjects of the ethnographer's research. What is the researcher's responsibility, for example, if a resident informant in a nursing home reveals that a particular nurse or administrator (who is also participating in the research) has seriously abused the patient? Codes that simply state the primacy of a researcher's obligation to informants do not solve such commonly encountered dilemmas. Although useful, codes are not a panacea; the fundamental principles expressed are not always easily applied to unique fieldwork situations.

Ethical Issues in Qualitative Process

Review by IRBs

The development of IRBs and other forms of formal review procedures have been a reasonable response to past abuse of subjects. However, the regulations that the U.S. Congress enacted were primarily a response to biomedical research; social and behavioral research added to the mandate of IRBs. Although such modifications as an expedited review process have been implemented to make the review process more appropriate to nonbiomedical research, problems remain. In qualitative research projects, differences with more traditional proposals must be explained carefully. In qualitative research, for example, the consent process is sometimes a prolonged negotiation between researcher and informants rather than a formalized moment at one point in time when a consent document is signed by an informant.

Observational research or participant observation presents other difficulties. Many IRBs now recognize that observation in public settings requires no special review. Research involving the observation of public behavior is considered to have exempt status, unless it includes the following:

1. Observations are recorded in such a manner that human subjects can be identified.
2. The observations recorded could, if they became known outside the research, place the subject at risk of criminal or civil liability or be damaging to his or her financial status or employability.
3. The research deals with sensitive aspects of the subject's behavior, such as drug use, sexual behavior, or the use of alcohol (University of California, San Francisco, Guidelines, 1991).

Defining what constitutes a *public* space, however, can be problematic. Is the dining room of a nursing home public in the same way that a suburban shopping mall is public? Perhaps not, given that nursing home residents may not have a choice about whether to attend meals or even about their primary place of residence. On the other hand, observational research often presents few risks (other than invasion of privacy) to the population under study, and it might actually be more burdensome for the researcher and informants constantly to interrupt ongoing social interaction in order to get permission from each individual in a room.

Other elements to be included in an IRB protocol include assessing the risk to informants, informed consent, decisional capacity, the right to privacy or confidentiality, and when to intervene or act as an advocate on behalf of a research subject. Although not composing an all-inclusive list, these are among the most important ethical issues in conducting qualitative research with the aged.

Assessing Risk Versus Benefit

When developing a qualitative research project, an initial concern should be assessing the potential harm to informants and considering methods to minimize or eliminate that harm. The ultimate benefits of the research—for example, increased knowledge—must be balanced against the potential harm to subjects. With frail elderly populations, even participation in an interview may be more harmful than with a younger individual; techniques may need to be modified to avoid fatigue.

Informed Consent

When conducting research that involves elderly subjects, informed consent is paramount. The key elements of informed consent are providing information about the research, comprehension of the information by potential subjects, voluntary participation, and freedom to withdraw at any time without adverse consequences (Faden & Beauchamp, 1986; Marshall, 1991). The purpose and intent of informed consent is violated if any part of the process is flawed. True voluntary participation by an elderly person may be jeopardized by many factors, including coercion by more powerful individuals or a desire for human contact (even with a researcher) as a result of social isolation.

Because the techniques of qualitative research often involve developing a long-term, reciprocity-based relationship with an informant, the ideal of informed consent is quite different than in survey or biomedical research.

In participant observation, consent is negotiated formally when first entering into the field. Thereafter, however, the researcher must engage in an almost daily process of obtaining "informal" informed consent, constantly reexplaining his or her activities and presence and creating meaningful social bonds with the subjects. Once developed, these bonds may make withdrawal from the research difficult for an elderly informant, and one must deal with the consequences of severing ties when the project is completed.

Decisional Capacity

Before obtaining informed consent, decisional capacity must be assessed. Decisional capacity has been defined as (a) the ability to comprehend information relevant to the decision, (b) the ability to deliberate about choices according to one's personal values and goals, and (c) the ability to communicate with others verbally or nonverbally (Hastings Center, 1987).

The term *decisional capacity* is preferred to *competence* to emphasize that the ability to make decisions is not an absolute; individuals may maintain the capacity to make certain choices even in the face of significant incapacity (President's Commission, 1982). An elderly individual who is unable to manage his finances or to perform independently the tasks of daily hygiene may still retain the capacity to make many choices, including whether to participate in a research interview. Because of the high level of cognitive impairment, particularly among the institutionalized elderly, assessing decisional capacity is crucial to obtaining informed consent.

Privacy and Confidentiality

The right to privacy implies that individuals have control over when and how communication about themselves is given to others, and confidentiality suggests that an agreement has been made that limits access to private information (Sieber, 1982; Westin, 1968). Maintaining anonymity for subjects and concealing the identity of the research setting is an ideal that is sometimes difficult to achieve in social science research.

Advocacy and Intervention

Clearly, the issue of advocacy is controversial. Some theorists believe that the anthropologist must be an advocate, especially in the area of applied research and policy development. They suggest that advocacy is part of the anthropologist's responsibility and that once data analysis indicates a course of action, action must be taken (Marshall, 1991). Intervention, however, carries with it grave responsibilities on the part of the investigator and consequences for the recipients of advocacy as well as for other informants in the study.

A brief case study along with other data from a research project conducted by Kayser-Jones that investigated the treatment of acute illness in nursing homes (National Institutes of Health, ROl AG05073) will be used to illustrate some of the difficulties an investigator can experience in striving to adhere to ethical principles.

The Case Study

Mrs. Smith, an 85-year-old Caucasian woman, was a widow with one son who lived in a nearby affluent suburb. She was admitted to the nursing home with a diagnosis of Alzheimer's disease, arthritis, and hypothyroidism. Despite the diagnosis of Alzheimer's, Mrs. Smith was active socially and functionally independent. She participated in social activities in the nursing home, enjoyed outings, and had developed a close friendship with a male patient with whom she had lunch daily. Each day, they could be seen walking hand in hand in the corridors of the nursing home. Mrs. Smith needed minimal assistance with personal grooming, was continent of bowel and bladder, could carry on conversations with others, and was generally alert, although confused at times.

Four years after Mrs. Smith had first been admitted to the nursing home, her condition suddenly changed. She complained of a sore throat (demonstrating this by placing her hand on the right side of her neck) and said that she had difficulty talking and swallowing. She had a 100° fever. The nurse called Mrs. Smith's physician to notify him of her condition; he ordered oral antibiotics and medication for pain. The following day Mrs. Smith refused food; she drank only a few sips of juice, she could not swallow her medication, and her temperature rose to 102 degrees. The nurses encouraged her to drink, but she said, "I just can't swallow—my throat." The nurses again called her physician. He advised them to encourage her to take fluids and said he would visit the following day.

Three days after the initial onset of Mrs. Smith's acute illness, she was still unable to swallow, was restless, and her chest was congested. The nurses again called the doctor; he left an order for Mrs. Smith to be transferred to an acute hospital. A few minutes later, however, the doctor called back and canceled the order for transfer, saying the family did not want her moved.

The doctor visited Mrs. Smith the next day, observed that she could not eat or drink but did not order intravenous fluids or medication for the infection. At this point, purulent secretions were draining from her mouth. The nurses asked the physician if he had tried to persuade the family to send Mrs. Smith to an acute hospital for treatment. The doctor reaffirmed the family's wishes, saying they did not want to do anything "heroic" for her. The nurses had tried unsuccessfully to reach the family by telephone. They left messages on the answering machine, but their calls were not returned.

Because this research was being conducted in three nursing homes, we could not be in each setting every day. One research assistant (RA) (a doctoral nursing student) first became aware of Mrs. Smith's condition in the evening on the fourth day of her illness. When she found Mrs. Smith in a semicomatose condition, she asked the staff why this woman was not receiving intravenous fluids and antibiotics. They replied that the family did not want heroic measures taken; they just wanted her to be kept comfortable. The RA called the first author in the late evening to inform her of the situation, and she went to the nursing home the next morning. The principal investigator (PI), Kayser-Jones, approached the director of nursing service (DNS) and inquired about the management of Mrs. Smith's care, stating that she was gravely ill and needed immediate treatment. The DNS replied that the family did not want Mrs. Smith treated, and, in fact, they wanted her to die. Because it appeared that the family and Mrs. Smith's personal physician were not acting in her best interests, the PI suggested that the DNS call the medical director of the nursing home, whose responsibility is to intervene in such cases. Reluctantly, the DNS called him; but he also refused to take any action.

The following morning, six days after the initial onset of the infection, a concerned staff nurse (after urging by members of the research team) agreed to call the doctor after the DNS was off-duty. She persuaded him to order intravenous fluids for Mrs. Smith; however, some two hours after the intravenous fluids were started, Mrs. Smith died.

When conducting this research, we used three research strategies to obtain data: in-depth interviews, participant observation, and event analysis. We therefore had detailed and comprehensive data that involved a large number of people who were interacting professionally with one another and with the investigators. For example, before her illness, we had interviewed Mrs. Smith, her physician, and members of the nursing staff, and we had observed the medical director as he managed other residents' care.

Maintaining Confidentiality

Maintaining confidentiality for all subjects became a challenge; it also made it difficult for us to intervene. When interviewing Mrs. Smith's physician, for example, we had asked if he would treat an acute illness if the patient were mentally impaired. He responded that he usually went along with the family's wishes. If the family did not want the patient treated, he would not treat him or her. We had also observed that the medical director philosophically did not believe in treating mentally impaired patients when they became acutely ill. In one case in which he had withheld treatment, the resident was treated only because her granddaughter went over the head of the physician and arranged transfer to an acute care hospital. Yet to maintain the confidentiality of staff members we had interviewed, we could not disclose this information to the DNS in trying to convince her to persuade the physician to treat Mrs. Smith.

Fortuitously, we had interviewed Mrs. Smith some months before she became acutely ill. Initially, we had planned to interview only mentally unimpaired residents. A member of the nursing staff, however, had suggested to an RA that Mrs. Smith would be a good resident to interview. When the RA realized that Mrs. Smith was severely impaired, she did not want to offend her by discontinuing the interview, so it was completed. When Mrs. Smith was asked during the interview if she would want to be treated should she develop an acute illness, she replied, "Yes." She also said that she would agree to surgery if it were necessary. In her notes, the RA wrote, "It is interesting that even though this patient was generally confused, she was very clear about wanting to be treated if she became ill and wanting to be tube fed if necessary." Also of interest is that when asked to define quality of life, Mrs. Smith responded, "Your children make life worth living," She also remarked, "It is important to have confidence in the person treating you." These two statements took on added meaning when she later became acutely ill and neither her son nor her physician acted in her best interest.

Informed Consent and Decisional Capacity

It is useful at this point to ask not only if Mrs. Smith's responses were valid, but whether it was legitimate to interview her. Is it possible to obtain informed consent from people who are cognitively impaired? As mentioned above, we had planned in our initial research design to interview only mentally unimpaired residents. From the physician interviews, however, we learned that when considering whether to treat an acute illness in nursing homes, mental status was one of the most important variables in their decision-making process. This factor, along with having obtained meaningful data when interviewing Mrs. Smith, prompted us to make a theoretical decision to change the research design and interview a small number of residents with severe cognitive impairment to obtain their points of view.

With these residents, we carried out the informed-consent procedure as we had done with the cognitively unimpaired interviewees. When it appeared that they understood the purpose of the research and what was involved in the interview, and if they willingly consented, then we conducted the interview. If we had any doubts, we did not interview them. Some residents could not respond to certain questions, but on the whole, the interviews generated useful and relevant data.

The concern about informed consent and whether cognitively impaired residents should be included in research studies must be addressed. First, because participating in an interview presents minimal risk, obtaining proxy consent from a legally appointed representative of the patient or institution is not necessary. For research that presents significant risk, it would be essential to have a third party involved in the informed-consent process to protect the subject from the investigator's misjudgments.

The voluntary participation of nursing home residents, however, may be compromised not only by the presence of dementia but also by the institutional setting. Many elderly people know that when they enter a nursing home, they will be there for the rest of their lives. Because for many it is a permanent residence, they may fear that refusal to participate in research may compromise their medical and nursing care, despite assurances to the contrary (Abrams, 1988; Berkowitz, 1978).

Furthermore, many residents are very lonely. One severely impaired woman whom we interviewed began to cry when we asked her if she would like to discuss future treatment with her family. "Why don't they come to visit me?" she inquired. When an RA asked another patient if it was a convenient time to interview her, she replied affirmatively, saying that to talk with the RA made her "feel human instead of being treated like an animal," and that the effect of having someone to talk to lasted for hours. If people are lonely, do they consent to be interviewed because of the social interaction it provides them? If so, does this violate the principles of voluntary participation?

In addition, can we be sure that the cognitively impaired residents whom we interviewed understood the purpose of the research? Should they be included in research studies? Cassel (1988) states that for the 60% of people in nursing homes who suffer from some degree of cognitive impairment, informed consent is an extremely problematic issue. The National Commission for the Protection of Human Subjects acknowledged that it had not begun to examine in depth all of the problems of conducting research with institutionalized populations. These problems, they concluded, were so serious and complex that the commission's recommendations were simply to limit research to that which was very low risk and would have a direct chance of helping the subject in some clinical way (Cassel, 1988).

Efforts to justify research that involves cognitively impaired nursing home residents have focused primarily on risk-benefit analyses. The degree to which the proposed research is likely to benefit the person is compared to the extent to which the risk can be tolerated (Abrams, 1988). Others would more readily allow research that poses minimal risk to the individual but that potentially will benefit society through its contribution to knowledge (Drane, 1984; Melnick, Dubler, Weisbard, & Butler, 1984). If this perspective is taken, then cultural and psychosocial research, which would seem to present little risk to the subject, would be more acceptable than invasive pathophysiological or psychopharmacological studies (Abrams, 1988).

When conducting research, however, in addition to a risk-benefit analysis, other issues such as burden and protection of a person's rights and dignity also must be considered. Before we obtain informed consent, a person's decisional capacity should be assessed. Sometimes the nursing staff is asked to identify residents who can participate in research, but the use of a mental-status examination is common.

The use of such questionnaires, however, are not without consequences. In one study in which we used a brief and one of the least demanding mental-status questionnaires (Kahn, Goldfarb, Pollack, & Peck, 1960) to assess mental status, an elderly African-American woman began to cry as questions were posed that she could not answer. "I'm educated too," she poignantly cried. In another case, an 88-year-old woman who was being assessed in a physician's office could not remember the name of the city and state in which she lived. The following morning her family found her crying. "I know I didn't do well on that test yesterday," she said. "I'm just a dummy. It would be better if I were dead."

When conducting research, we are obligated to protect not only our subjects' bodily integrity and confidentiality, but also their dignity. Here we are faced with a dilemma. To determine if a person is capable of giving informed consent, decisional capacity should be assessed, yet the tests that are used to assess decisional capacity may cause anguish and be an affront to personal dignity.

Investigators also must recognize that decisional capacity is not an all or nothing situation, as the President's Commission (1982) emphasized. A range of abilities exist, and decisional capacity can fluctuate over time and in different circumstances. An elderly person who was mentally alert at home, for example, may become mentally confused to some degree when admitted to an acute hospital.

Thus when we determine decisional capacity, we must pay careful attention to timing and other circumstances such as the setting, anxiety over being tested, medications, pain, acute infections, and depression. The woman described above, for example, who could not recall the name of the city and state in which she lived was found on examination to have a duodenal ulcer and a fractured rib. Moreover, it was learned that a home health-care aide was giving her repeated doses of a nighttime medication that contained 25% alcohol and an antihistamine along with a sleeping tablet. When the use of these medications was discontinued and the woman was informed that the pain in her chest was the result of a broken rib rather than a heart condition, her mental status improved.

Dubler (1987) proposes that many elderly people, even those of diminished or declining ability, are not only legally competent but also capable of providing acceptable consent. This depends, of course, on the complexity of the research. A person may be able to consent effectively to participate in an observational study but not in a Phase 1 drug trial. Our experience supports Dubler's position, and judging from the responses we have obtained from interviewing the cognitively impaired elderly, much has yet to be learned from them that will benefit the elderly and society.

Privacy and Confidentiality

Each informant's right to privacy and confidentiality accentuated the wrenching ethical dilemmas experienced by the investigators in the case described above. Before beginning the research, we had promised anonymity to the nursing homes and guaranteed them that we would strictly adhere to the principles of confidentiality of data and anonymity of participants.

In the case study presented here, we had unsuccessfully attempted to intervene by asking the DNS to call the medical director and ask for assistance. At this point, we had not violated any ethical principles of research. The next probable course of action would have been to report the case to the local ombudsman office or to a legal authority such as the district attorney's office.

If we reported the case, the identity of the nursing home and the names of the nursing staff and the physicians would be made public, thus violating the principles of confidentiality and anonymity. Furthermore, our concern for Mrs. Smith must not ignore the complexity of the situation. By definition, an ethnographer has an obligation to *all* participants—in this instance, including the physicians (the attending physician and the medical director), the staff, and the nursing home administration. The physicians may have actually believed that by respecting the family's wishes, they were acting in Mrs. Smith's best interests. Moreover, reporting the staff to regulatory authorities would clearly be damaging to the staff members and the nursing home itself, and also might jeopardize further research by the investigators.

In retrospect after Mrs. Smith died, the adverse consequences for the informants (physicians and nurses) and the nursing home seem far less important than Mrs. Smith's death. The research team members experienced feelings of guilt, and we discussed at length how we might have handled the situation to Mrs. Smith's benefit.

Advocacy and Intervention

Although theoretically morally laudable, advocacy in practice can be difficult to effect and may produce problematic results. In this case, for example, when we asked the DNS to call the medical director for assistance, we thought he would respond immediately with a course of action. Instead, he said he would discuss the patient's care with the attending physician and call back. Wanting to be there when the physician called back, the PI waited in the nursing home for more than an hour, but the physician did not call. Having to teach a class at the university, the PI had to leave the research setting. Later in the day, the DNS informed the PI that the medical director decided not to go against the wishes of the attending physician.

PIs have many responsibilities in addition to conducting research, and sometimes carrying out a plan of action in a crisis situation that needs immediate attention is difficult. Furthermore, anticipating that such events might occur, the PI had discussed these issues with the medical consultant (geriatrician) before data collection began. He emphasized that it was not the PI's professional responsibility to diagnose or make treatment decisions. Although we knew that Mrs. Smith was very ill, we could not predict that she would die from the infection.

Perhaps the greatest ethical dilemma occurs when the investigator confronts a situation in which a decision must be made about whether to intervene in a situation or act as an advocate for an elderly person needing assistance. In the case presented above, what should the qualitative investigators have done about the patient's acute illness? Was their behavior ethical? Did it conform to accepted standards of research ethics?

In quantitative, positivistic research, intervention in the events or process under study is viewed as a "contaminant" that renders the research invalid (Ramos, 1989; Robinson & Thorne, 1988). The investigators had IRB approval; they had carefully negotiated entrée with the nursing homes under study, including provisions for confidentiality, and they had obtained informed consent from staff and residents in the facility.

Elsewhere, using the case presented here, we have discussed the role of the nursing staff as patient advocates (Kayser-Jones, Davis, Wiener, & Higgins, 1989) and other advocacy issues (Kayser-Jones & Kapp, 1989). The issue of advocacy is especially problematic for investigators who are also clinicians, such as nurses, physicians, and social workers. Nonclinicians may not have the skills necessary to recognize, for example, that a patient in home care is seriously dehydrated; or that a nursing home resident, who is being tube fed while lying flat on her back, is at risk for aspiration pneumonia; or, as in the case above, a patient has a life-threatening illness that requires immediate action.

Fowler's (1988) position on the ethics of intervention is unequivocal: "The nurse researcher, though dedicated to research, remains dedicated to the patient first; the role of nurse supersedes that of researcher." At the other end of the continuum are investigators who assert that one must avoid intervening and therefore contaminating data (Davis, 1968), an assumption shared by most researchers working from a positivist paradigm. In the middle are those who believe that from time to time one must intervene because ethical obligations take precedence over research interests (Archbold, 1986; Davis, 1986). Despite the various viewpoints, no guidelines serve all eventualities (Robinson & Thorne, 1988).

When conducting anthropological research in nursing homes, the question of intervention is exceedingly difficult. Nearly every day a problem presents itself that cries out for intervention. Because qualitative investigators spend long hours and many months in a research setting, they frequently grow close to their informants. Establishing rapport facilitates data collection, and intimacy has traditionally been recognized as increasing the data's validity and richness (Golde, 1970; Pearsall, 1965). As one becomes attached to informants and listens to their stories, it becomes increasingly difficult to ignore these problems; yet if one attempts to resolve every problem, it is impossible to conduct research.

The very relationships that make qualitative research unique, improving the depth and meaningfulness of data, also make the dilemma of advocacy more intense for the researchers. And it can be argued that unless one can continue to investigate the natural conditions and dynamics of the nursing home culture, solutions will not be forthcoming. Thus the long-term goals of the research—improving the quality of care for the institutionalized aged—may be seriously damaged by taking an advocacy stance.

Certain strategies, however, may be helpful. In the research project discussed, the investigators developed an understanding with the administrator and the DNS that any serious problem observed by the research team would be reported immediately. Other conditions, such as staff inefficiency that does not directly endanger residents, can be included in a written report or at a staff conference (Kayser-Jones, 1990a).

Conclusion

Each situation encountered during fieldwork with the elderly will be unique, the application of moral principles dauntingly complex. Anticipation is the key. When planning research, the investigator must consider the central issues of balancing risks and benefits, protecting confidentiality, and ensuring an informed-consent process that is tailored to the varied levels of decisional capacity found among elderly persons.

Should obligation to vulnerable elderly residents override obligations to other informants such as administrators? In each instance, the researcher must balance the ultimate value of the research against the immediate needs of residents. The need to document the failure to provide adequate treatment for residents such as Mrs. Smith in order to effect policy change is an important justification for not intervening in her care. Investigators have no easy answers when confronted with conflicting values: protecting informants versus improving the care of elderly nursing home residents. The inevitable dilemmas of fieldwork, however, can be lessened if anticipated. Although no specific rule can stipulate when intervention is justified, each investigator can make sure that decisions will be made based on serious reflection and careful balancing of potential benefit and harm, rather than hasty responses to problems that could have been foreseen.

References

Abrams, R. (1988). Dementia research in the nursing home. *Hospital and Community Psychiatry, 39*(3), 257-259.

American Anthropological Association. (1990). *Professional ethics: Statements and procedures of the American Anthropological Association.* Washington, DC: Author.

American Psychological Association. (1974). *Standards for educational and psychological tests.* Washington, DC: Author.

American Psychological Association. (1982). *Ethical principles in the conduct of research with human participants.* Washington, DC: Author.

American Sociological Association. (1971). *Code of ethics.* Washington, DC: Author.

Archbold, P. (1986). Ethical issues in qualitative research. In W. C. Chenitz & J. M. Swanson (Eds.), *From practice to grounded theory: Qualitative research in nursing* (pp. 153-163). Reading, MA: Addison-Wesley.

Beauchamp, T. L., & Childress, J. F. (1989). *Principles of biomedical ethics* (3rd ed.). New York: Oxford University Press.

Beecher, H. J. (1966). Ethics and clinical research. *New England Journal of Medicine, 74,* 1354-1360.

Berkowitz, S. B. (1978). Informed consent, research, and the elderly. *Gerontologist, 18,* 237-243.

Cassel, C. K. (1988). Ethical issues in the conduct of research in long term care. *Gerontologist, 28*(suppl.), 90-96.

Davis, M. Z. (1968). Some problems in identity becoming a nurse researcher. *Nursing Research, 17*(1), 166-168.

Davis, M. Z. (1986). Observation in natural settings. In W. C. Chenitz & J. M. Swanson (Eds.), *From practice to grounded theory: Qualitative research in nursing* (pp. 48-65). Reading, MA: Addison-Wesley.

Drane, J. F. (1984). Competency to give an informed consent: A model for making clinical assessments. *Journal of American Medical Association, 252,* 925-927.

Dubler, N. N. (1987). Legal judgments and informed consent in geriatric research. *Journal of American Geriatrics Society, 35,* 545-549.

Faden, R. R., & Beauchamp, T. L. (1986). *A history and theory of informed consent.* New York: Oxford University Press.

Fowler, M. D. (1988). Ethical issues in nursing research: Issues in qualitative research. *Western Journal of Nursing Research, 10*(1), 109-111.

Golde, P. (Ed.). (1970). *Women in the field.* Berkeley: University of California Press.

Hastings Center. (1987). *Guidelines on the termination of life-sustaining treatment and the care of the dying.* Briarcliff Manor, NY: Author.

Jorgensen, J. G. (1971). On ethics and anthropology. *Current Anthropology, 12*(3), 321-334.

Kahn, R. L., Goldfarb, A. I., Pollack, M., & Peck, A. (1960). Brief objective measure for the determination of mental status in the aged. *American Journal of Psychiatry, 117,* 326-328.

Kayser-Jones, J. S. (1990a). *Old, alone and neglected: Care of the aged in the United States and Scotland. With a new epilogue.* Berkeley: University of California Press.

Kayser-Jones, J. S. (1990b). The use of nasogastric feeding tubes in nursing homes: Patient, family and health care provider perspectives. *Gerontologist, 30*(4), 469-479.

Kayser-Jones, J. S., Davis, A., Wiener, C. L., & Higgins, S. (1989). An ethical analysis of an elder's treatment. *Nursing Outlook, 37*(6), 267-270.

Kayser-Jones, J. S., & Kapp, M. (1989). Advocacy for the mentally impaired elderly: A case study analysis. *American Journal of Law and Medicine, 14*(4), 353-376.

Marshall, P. A. (1991). Research ethics in applied medical anthropology. In C. E. Hill (Ed.), *Training manual in applied medical anthropology* (pp. 213-235). Washington, DC: American Anthropological Association.

Melnick, V. L., Dubler, N. N., Weisbard, A., & Butler, R. N. (1984). Clinical research in senile dementia of the Alzheimer type: Suggested guidelines addressing the ethical and legal issues. *Journal of American Geriatrics Society, 32*(7), 531-536.

Pearsall, M. (1965). Participant observation as role and method in behavioral research. *Nursing Research, 14*(1), 37-42.

President's Commission for the Protection of Human Subjects of Biomedical and Behavioral Research. (1978). *The Belmont report: Ethical principles and guidelines for the protection of human subjects research.* Washington, DC: Government Printing Office.

President's Commission for the Study of Ethical Problems in Medicine and Biomedical and Behavioral Research. (1982). *Making health care decisions: The ethical and legal implications of informed consent in the patient-practitioner relationship* (Vol. 1). Washington, DC: Government Printing Office.

Ramos, M. C. (1989). Some ethical implications of qualitative research. *Research in Nursing and Health, 12*(1), 57-63.

Robinson, C. A., & Thorne, S. E. (1988). Dilemmas of ethics and validity in qualitative nursing research. *The Canadian Journal of Nursing Research, 20*(1), 65-76.

Rothman, D. J. (1991). *Strangers at the bedside.* New York: Basic Books.

Rynkiewich, M. A., & Spradley, J. P. (1976). *Ethics and anthropology: Dilemmas in fieldwork.* New York: John Wiley.

Sieber, J. E. (Ed.). (1982). *The ethics of social research: Surveys and experiments.* New York: Springer Verlag.

Society for Applied Anthropology. (1983). *Statement on professional and ethical responsibilities.* Washington, DC: Author.

University of California, San Francisco. (1991). *Guidelines for research involving human subjects.* San Francisco: University of California.

Westin, A. F. (1968). *Privacy and freedom.* New York: Atheneum.

3

Ethnic and Racial Issues

J. NEIL HENDERSON

Dissecting the cultural mix of life requires sensitive tools and analytic techniques. Nowhere is this truer than with elderly ethnic minorities experiencing health needs. The multiple statuses of advanced age, ethnic-minority membership, and health failure combine to create a vulnerable late life experience. Very old ethnic-minority elders experience persistent effects of racial and ethnic prejudices to which is added their highest lifetime risk for financial and health difficulties. This presents a challenge to coping skills precisely when these are at their most precarious. The comforting routines of life achieved by most people may no longer be adaptive. Life has new rules that few are able to readily adopt. Paradoxically, increased need may produce increased retreat from help in an effort to shield oneself from further harm.

Explicating the varied beliefs, values, and concepts of an elderly ethnic-minority cultural domain is difficult beyond belief. First, culture is always changing because of the need to adapt to new environments and experiences. Second, culture reflected in behavior is at times implicit, abstract thought that must be inferred from behavior and conversation. Because beliefs and values are not always conscious, special observational techniques are required to identify the cultural factors because they cannot explicitly be verbalized. This is in part why qualitative research involves not only verbal-text data collection but also observation.

The qualitative researcher working with ethnic-minority elders also is confronted with several sources of ethnocultural variation. For example, the unit of research, whether individuals or groups, needs to be assessed in terms of the acculturation continuum. The extent of involvement among ethnic minorities in the majority culture can be seen as a continuum ranging from minimal involvement or participation to assimilation. Also, intracultural variations within ethnic-minority groups should be expected. The in-depth involvement of qualitative research in ethnic-minority life will highlight the artificial and nearly arbitrary nature of historical and government-generated rubrics such as "American Indians." The researcher is challenged to understand each subject in the context of the larger elderly American Indian population on a national scale and also finds it mandatory to bring specific detail to the particular ecological and regional grouping out of which the subject's culture grew, the political climate in which this group exists, its status as a subgroup of a larger "tribal" community, specific language groups and dialects within the larger group, and, if relevant, specific lineage and clan organizational structures.

Qualitative research among ethnic-minority elders must include sensitivity to detect situational variation in the amount of personal culture revealed to the researcher. Ethnic-minority elders adapt to life in a multicultural society by revealing their ethnic culture in certain situations and concealing it in others. The choice to conceal one's ethnic identity is affected by the penalizing experience of being perceived as different. Moreover, cultural overlap can be observed when the majority group and the minority group have independently used similar behaviors. The trick for the researcher is to determine the variable context from which these superficially similar behaviors derive. Also, cultural overlap can occur when two different cultures borrow from each other to adapt to changing conditions. As a result, they come to share values and behaviors. The sharing, however, does not necessarily mean that the two cultures are interpreting the common behavior or belief the same way.

Cultural overlap reveals subtle but significant elements that can be crucial in understanding elderly ethnic-minority behavior patterns. For example, older ethnic-minority elders who grew up in a pre-Civil Rights era now have adult grandchildren who grew up in a post-Civil Rights era. The difference in cultural eras results in ethnic-minority elders who are less likely to seek and use services than their younger relatives even while both reside in the same national context.

The Case: Ethnic-Minority Alzheimer's Disease Support Groups

The purpose of this chapter is to present qualitative research as a fitting tool for delineating the ethnic-minority life experience under the stimulus and duress of health needs. Beliefs, values, and concepts that influence thinking and behavior must be understood in the context of the ethnic-minority elder subjects. This will be discussed in relation to a two-year community health intervention project in African-American and Hispanic populations in two Southern cities, only one of which will be featured here. The project was designed to discover a means by which to introduce Alzheimer's disease support groups in ethnic-minority communities for the benefit of ethnic-minority caregivers. To highlight specific points of the ethnic-minority health-intervention project, the case will be presented in segments. Each segment will relate to specific issues of qualitative research among ethnic-minority elders.

A community health-intervention program was designed to test the hypothesis that ethnic minorities' minimal use of Alzheimer's disease support groups on a national basis is a function of sociocultural disincentives and not the lack of cases of Alzheimer's disease or the presence of fully functioning family groups obviating the need for intervention (Henderson, 1987, 1990; Henderson & Gutierrez-Mayka, 1992; Henderson, Gutierrez-Mayka, Garcia, & Boyd, 1993). This project demonstrated that community health interventions such as Alzheimer's disease support groups can be successfully introduced into African-American and Hispanic populations when ethnocultural factors are adequately identified, understood, and meaningfully integrated into the intervention plan.

Elderly Ethnic-Minority Culture and Qualitative Research

Failure to adequately incorporate the fundamentals of the ethnic-minority culture has led to the failure of other attempts at developing ethnic-minority Alzheimer's disease support groups. The perception that ethnocultural variables would be central to the successful implementation of this project led to the selection of qualitative research methods that could penetrate to the heart of the ethnocultural system to discover the basic building blocks of its broader structure.

All too often, professionals trained in general social science or administrative services do not fully appreciate the ubiquitous, permeating nature of culture. In fact, culture can be essentially invisible because of its implicit nature. For example, each society has its own unwritten rule specifying the distance to be kept between two conversing people although neither maintains an explicit awareness of such rules. Violation of these rules, such as standing too close, produces genuine discomfort. The origin of such rules are out of consciousness for the actors. They probably could not state how they learned the rules that they judiciously practice. The symbolic and ever-changing adaptive nature of culture creates a moving target difficult to capture in static form. People are creative beings who respond to changing environments of thought and nature. Consider the evolving terms used to refer to African-Americans as a reflection of changing perceptions, each with its own time period of acceptance, social and political context, and variation in usage by the African-American community and the majority population.

The failure to account for ethnic-minority culture between health-care providers and ethnic-minority patients is well recognized and serves as a model for larger-scale intercultural difficulties. For example, cohort effects pertain when the clinician and patient are of different generational groups that hold variant beliefs about gender roles (Garcia, Cuervo, Kosberg, & Henderson, 1989). A young Anglo male clinician may suggest that an elderly Hispanic woman tell her husband that she will not prepare meals too high in fat content. Such advice is predicated more on a clinician's relatively recent cohort learning regarding women's generally greater assertiveness and quality of life. However, the elderly Hispanic woman may feel as if she has no right to go against the wishes of her husband in this case. In another instance, the stigma of mental health crises are more apparent for elders than today's young adults. Mental health was once handled by state institutions, which were perceived as prisons for punishing the weak (Ho, 1987; Levine & Padilla, 1980). When older ethnic-minority members have greater adherence to traditional cultural values than younger cohorts, they avoid the helping services until very serious need occurs or a younger ethnic-minority member assists the elder in getting services (Maldonado, 1975). There also may be a reluctance to maximize the use of community helping resources (Cox & Monk, 1990; Wood & Parham, 1990). Ethnic-minority elders are likely to show subjugated role behavior in the presence of clinical authority figures (Haug, 1981).

Although usually unacknowledged, cosmopolitan health-care practitioners likewise have learned what is actually a health-care belief system. Kuhn (1962) and other historians of science and health care have demonstrated that clinicians perceive their professionally derived knowledge as fact when actually it is part of an evolving belief system. When a professional belief system is acknowledged, the structural dynamics of the clinician-patient encounters are more balanced. No one has the edge on possessing the ultimately correct data set. In an egalitarian atmosphere, the clinician does not act condescendingly to the patient's "magical" folk beliefs, nor does the patient achieve enlightenment by elevation to the lofty pinnacle of "true" clinical fact. Both negotiate acceptable fits for their own health-care belief systems to produce more optimal communication, compliance, and treatment outcomes (Good & Good, 1981; Hill, Fortenberry, & Stein, 1990; Katon & Kleinman, 1981; Kleinman, 1980; Pfeifferling, 1981; Stein, 1990).

Valle (1989) notes that when treating ethnic-minority elders, clinicians must make a correct assessment of the patient's location along an *acculturation continuum,* which is a means of marking one's degree of ethnic identification (Valle, 1989). On the acculturation continuum, the *traditional position* is characterized by a strong orientation toward cultural origins and homeland. A *bicultural position* is marked by patients' partial allegiance to their homeland culture and partial affinity with the current mainstream culture. An *assimilated position* is closely integrated with the mainstream culture. Of particular note are the bicultural and assimilated positions. These can be mistakenly ignored by clinicians because they do not appear "ethnic enough" to warrant special attention. In reality, such people have not lost their ethnic-minority heritage; they have simply added to it a great facility for using the cultural system of the majority population. Consider an example of a person who is a fourth-generation member of a family that emigrated to the United States from Spain and in which the youngest generation (ages 5 to 9) cannot speak Spanish but does participate with bilingual parents (who feel most comfortable using English) in Spanish holiday traditions, food preparation, religion, gender-role behavior, and so on. First names are English names with European surnames. Their political identification is the United States, yet their Spanish cultural roots are still alive and well.

Clinicians should recognize that ethnic minorities who are bicultural or assimilated may value what they remember as the intent, spirit, or benefit of their more traditional family values and life-styles. In fact, they may search for such "comforting presence in some surrogate form" (Valle, 1989, p. 129). For example, the value placed on personal, individualized interactions modeled by familial and small nonfamilial groupings is not often found in service bureaucracies. When the personal empathy and shared perceptions are found in support groups such as the ethnic-minority-specific support groups for Alzheimer's disease developed by this project, participants make use of the service and refer to the support group as a "little family."

Another major aspect of Valle's work underscores the importance of understanding intraethnic cultural variation. Valle (1989) writes,

> culture is not only expressed with considerable variation along a continuum, but also unevenly with indistinct domains of daily living where individuals and groups act out their lives. Behavioral and coping responses will situationally change as social environments change. One person's expression of ethnic culture may vary at home, the work place, or the broader community. (p. 131)

For example, so-called black English may be variably used—that is, at an ethnically mixed work setting it virtually vanishes, while at home it is the predominant mode of communication.

The stress of caregiving and its episodic crises does not cause caregivers to drop "ethnocultural veils" (Valle, 1989). On the contrary, ethnocultural response patterns have often served a positive and protective function in the life of the individuals and families involved (Simic, 1985). Relying on the family in time of need, with its familiar patterns unique to an ethnic-minority group, ethnicity becomes protective and sheltering. The episodic-crisis aspect of caregiving does not lessen the presence of differential, ethnocultural responses to dementia.

The Targeted Ethnographic Survey

In general, ethnography refers to a way of collecting information about aspects of sociocultural life. The ethnographer conducts fieldwork in the form of participant observation, interviewing, the mapping of the physical environment, collecting artifacts as tangible aspects of culture, and generally observing and absorbing a broad spectrum of life activities and their underlying philosophies. However, fieldwork is not a random inquiry. The fieldworker typically enters the field with specific domains of interest such as socialization, subsistence, or religion and predetermined concepts about how to inquire and make sense of the domains. Domains usually are perceived as interlinked systems. Ideally, the ethnographer will collect sufficiently in-depth data to understand the multiple systems and their interactions.

Targeted ethnography is a more selective approach. As the name suggests, one or more specific domains are selected for intensive data collection. The reality of multiple, interacting systems is not ignored, but data collection is focused on a subsample of domains. The purpose of targeted ethnography is to answer specific questions on selected topics in a time-efficient manner. Human society is so complex that no one could ever hope truly to have a complete and comprehensive understanding of its workings.

The targeted ethnographic survey process involves six main steps. Although the numeric listing of these six steps implies a unidirectional and sequential process of data collection, in practice things get mixed up. It is common for a few initial steps to take place in terms of identifying a given topic of study from the professional literature or observations made in the field. Then the researcher may make attempts to enter the field to interview people who are identified as holders of information or who will prove valuable to understanding a certain topic. A constant oscillation takes place between data collection in the field, its analysis, generation of new questions for clarification, and the collection of raw data in the field.

The targeted ethnographic survey usually begins with a community ethnographic profile based on existing data such as statistical abstracts and census information. Local newspaper records, the chamber of commerce, local medical associations, and ethnic-minority organizations are further valuable sources for gathering existing data. Community brochures or descriptive materials of any sort can provide an initial framework that reflects the way in which subjects organize themselves relative to the topic of study.

In our case, the target of ethnographic inquiry was a mix of topics: ethnic-minority status, aging, Alzheimer's disease, caregiver issues, and support-group development. To start, a list of ethnographic minority organizations was developed using telephone book headings appropriate to black, Hispanic, social, minority, and government agencies. We came to learn that many informal organizations in the ethnic-minority communities do not place themselves in the phone book.

Important information can be gathered from ethnic-minority media. Such a media roster can be started using the entertainment guide of majority population newspapers in which radio and television outlets are identified with their major programming content listed. Again, the phone book can be useful. Local newsstands can be examined for ethnic-minority print media, especially from newsstands located in ethnic-minority communities.

The project was based in a university gerontology center that had collaborated for years with other aging organizations in the community. Staff members of these organizations were contacted to assist the project with the identification of key community leaders. Contacts with chambers of commerce and other ethnic-minority agencies and ethnic-minority newspapers also had allowed for the identification of community leaders.

Once community leaders were identified, interviews were undertaken. All conversations were treated as data-collection opportunities. Formal interviews were composed of open-ended questions with repetitive follow-ups for clarification. The contents of these interviews were transformed into handwritten field notes, transcribed tape recordings, and interviewer notes made on tape immediately after interviews. Targeted ethnographic survey was crucial for staff members to become familiar with the community and life-styles of the ethnic-minority caregivers. Even for project staff members who were members of the ethnic-minority community, the targeted ethnographic survey brought conceptual clarity to the function and interrelationships of specific concerns within the ethnic-minority community relative to the project. For instance, in the Hispanic community, ethnic-minority organizations or "clubs" have existed for 100 years. Such clubs function as social and health-maintenance organizations. Their origin was based on the need of immigrants with similar language and cultural histories. The clubs were well known to the staff member who functioned as a liaison between the project and the Hispanic community. She was a native of this area, spoke Spanish, and was fully articulate in the majority population's culture and language. However, she reported that the project experience of discovering the strength of the social boundaries between the clubs both reinforced her implicit knowledge and added new insight to the importance, persistence, and separateness of the clubs.

A superficial trait listing of ethnocultural elements is insufficient for a realistic understanding of the life experience of the ethnic-minority caregiver. *Trait listing* is an inventory of sociocultural phenomena such as religious groupings, marriage customs, financial spending patterns, or any other identifiable behaviors or beliefs. Such inventories do not convey meanings, levels of importance, multiple functions, or other detailed aspects of the human condition that came into play in practice.

The ongoing nature of the targeted ethnographic survey continued to net data about the ethnic-minority community over the entire course of the project. The complexity of communities is such that no one in a brief time period can become completely knowledgeable about all aspects of social functioning. In fact, at the project's end, staff were still being surprised with new niches within the ethnic-minority communities that were unmentioned and unknown in the previous two years of the project. In one instance, an organization of African-American women was mentioned for the first time after the data collection stopped. A subject involved in the program for the previous 19 months had mentioned the name of the organization in an ordinary conversation. She stated that she had not thought of it until that moment, although the women's club could have been ideally suited to helping with data collection and intervention.

Because of the qualitative research design, flexibility and midcourse correction was possible. Rethinking and reanalyzing findings was particularly helpful in this project relative to determining an appropriate site for a support-group meeting location. The location of the site proved to be crucial. A literature review of community health interventions showed that in the African-American community, the Protestant churches could serve as a focus of community organization and offer support for the introduction of new services into the community (Carter, 1978, 1981; Chatters, Taylor, & Jackson, 1986; Levin, 1984; Neighbors, 1984; Tate, 1984). Such an idea is consistent with the notion of cultural relevance and cultural sensitivity. However, conditions prevented the African-American churches from functioning as project sites and sponsors. The African-American Protestant churches were overloaded with other basic survival issues such as dropouts, drugs, and teenage pregnancy. Although old age was considered important and the churches were enthusiastic about the project, they were unable themselves to add yet another need of this magnitude.

The original project design was to hold meetings at one African-American church that would be the common site for participation by members of other African-American churches in the Alzheimer's disease support-group meetings. The church's minister, a volunteer leader from the church, and a project staff member went to many other black churches to give educational and promotional presentation. This was designed to generate support for the project from members of other churches. However, when support groups were first offered at the original African-American church site, no one attended for three consecutive meetings.

In retrospect, we found that we were asking church members to violate "invisible" congregational loyalty boundaries. The allegiance to one's church and pastor is exceedingly strong, and to acknowledge the initiative and visibility accruing to the original church site and its leadership would by default cast a slight pallor on the nonoriginating church and its leadership. The effort at strong cultural relevance failed.

The successful location for support-group meetings in the African-American community was a culturally neutral site. A meeting room in a branch of a community public library was chosen and worked in attracting caregivers throughout the African-American community. The site was located for accessibility in the ethnic-minority community but had no attached factional, political, or social history.

In the Spanish-language community, the first meeting site was a hospital built by one Hispanic social and health-care organization. It had been part of the community for 90 years. Because of the lengthy immigration history of this city's Spanish-speaking population, several distinct social and medical clubs had developed. Attendance at one of these club sites and not others had a similar loyalty boundary effect. In fact, organizations of physicians within the community were distinctly aligned along lines of ethnic origins, such as northern Spain, southern Spain, and Cuba. Ultimately, the Spanish-language support group met in a private health-care clinic established in the 1920s in the Hispanic community. The founders of the clinic had sold it to its current Cuban owner, who attracted a predominantly Spanish-speaking patient population. Any vestiges of specific intraethnic origin disappeared, and the clinic site is now a familiar landmark within the Hispanic community.

The methodological lessons here for ethnic-minority qualitative research are (a) no single person in a multiethnic community knows every cultural niche or nuance, (b) existing data on ethnic-minority community organizations can be starting places for targeted ethnographic fieldwork, (c) vastly different cultures exist in the same community, (d) constant review of field notes will generate new insights and questions about ethnic-minority culture, and (e) the project plan should constantly change as new knowledge and understanding of ethnic-minority social systems emerge.

Fieldworker Status and Role Variations

People organize their lives into broad and fairly predictable patterns of behavior. Patterning is accomplished by the use of social rules (norms), expected behaviors (roles), and differences distinguishing individuals and groups (social boundaries). For example, an African-American woman may use generalized "civic" cultural norms (i.e., norms comfortable for most people) when at work in a mall shopping center or dressing up for her job as manager. When off work and shopping in the same mall, this same women may wear a casual shirt imprinted with "It's a Black Thing, You Wouldn't Understand," indicating a social boundary. In effect, she communicates, "There is a life experience in this community in which I am a part and non-African-Americans are not." Discovery and sensitivity to social boundaries is a talent of fieldworkers conducting qualitative research. Even the concept of ethnicity and race implies a certain set of cognitively held boundary markers.

Ethnic Disparity

Providing services to ethnic-minority elders has often assumed the necessity of matching the service provider's ethnicity with that of the receiver's to minimize disparity in the ethnic mix of service provision. However, this project showed no need for concern with ethnic matching. Two Alzheimer's disease support groups were formed in each population. One group was a Spanish-language group led by a native Spanish speaker. However, this person was not native to the area nor did she match the specific Hispanic background of members of the support group. Support-group members were predominantly of Cuban origin and secondarily of Puerto Rican origin. The support-group facilitator was a native Spanish speaker from Argentina and also very articulate in English. The African-American support group was formed by an Anglo male who had little difficulty in communicating with or developing rapport with the African-American support-group members.

Issues of language are often mentioned as barriers to service delivery, but in this project the Spanish-language speakers had been in this country for many years. English was a language with which they were familiar and in which they were highly fluent. Nonetheless, the support-group members chose to conduct their meetings in Spanish. At the beginning of the project, I was the only non-Spanish-speaking partici-pant. The group would hold discussions in English for my benefit only. I was urged to learn to speak Spanish and told that it was easy to do so. Moreover, it was said to be a much more beautiful sounding language than English. I took a conversational Spanish course and was able to boost my vocabulary and ability to use a few phrases. However, the major outcome of my effort was not fluent Spanish conversation but a recognition by the group that I valued this distinctive feature of its life experience enough to work at acquiring it.

In my work with the African-American group, the use of Anglo English rather than black English did not seem to be a point of concern. In listening to recorded conversations between African-American group members compared to conversations between myself, an Anglo, and another group member, no variances were detectable. However, it is not clear to me, as an Anglo-looking professional from the university, that there was no adjustment of language for my benefit. This was not enough time to observe and participate in all of the caregivers' speech environments. A definitive conclusion remains elusive.

Qualitative research among ethnic-minority elders requires close, sustained interaction and involvement in subjects' lives. One perspec-tive may be that the subjects and the qualitative researcher should be of the same ethnic-minority group so that an empathic connection can be made for real communication. This notion was proven wrong in this project. Acceptance of an Anglo researcher in the African-American community or an Argentine researcher among Cuban-Puerto Ricans is not based on race, but on respect and the perception of making a positive contribution to caregivers' lives. Personal involvement in peoples' lives is a hallmark of qualitative research.

Generational Disparity

Generations have cultural boundaries. Circumstances in which gen-erational cohorts are interacting constitute an analog to crosscultural groups attempting to interact with one another. The project facilitators in all cases were individuals ranging from 30 to 40 years of age.

However, most caregivers were 60 and older, so the issue of generational disparity emerged. To facilitate communication between the generations, principles of adult learning and cultural learning were used. Specifically, this meant that group members were not "taught to" but rather asked about their experiences and became co-solvers of their needs. The inability to experience being 88 years old themselves, for example, required that fieldworkers listen rather than instruct in order to understand old age, ethnic-minority status, and caregiving.

Conducting qualitative research among elders typically is done by people younger than their subjects. The personal involvement in the subject's lives demands not only respect for their subjects as people, but also the awareness that they are the teachers and the ethnographer is the student. The ethnic-minority elder has experienced realities that the qualitative researchers can understand only with the utmost effort. At best, the depth of cultural penetration is far from the bottom of the experiential pool. Even so, the effort to understand can help to bridge the gap between ethnic-minority elders and qualitative researchers.

Social Status Disparity

Status differences can be crucially important in rapport formation (Henderson, 1992). In one African-American support group, refreshments consumed an important part of each meeting. In contrast to the Spanish-speaking support group, the foods were much more basic and less lavishly presented. I learned firsthand that there can be social implications to the selections of foods brought for the refreshment portion of a support-group meeting. One evening I had brought a six-pack of Classic Coca Cola and a box of cookies. Another women had brought a six-pack of generic cola and home-baked cookies. During the meeting, she commented to me separately that I "naturally" had brought the name-brand items while she was forced by limited finances to select the least expensive items that would still serve as suitable refreshments.

Role Blurring

Role blurring became an issue during the delivery of this community-intervention project. Because qualitative research requires personal involvement in subjects' lives, the qualitative researcher also responds to the shifting needs of subjects as a broker of information or goods. In this project, for example, ethnic-minority elderly caregivers needed stress reduction and community-resource information to cope with the heavy demands of caregiving for Alzheimer's disease victims. The project implementors provided needed commodities, such as information on Alzheimer's disease, knowledge of community resources, empathy about caregiver burdens, as well as Alzheimer's disease support groups.

The complexity of ordinary life for caregivers is compounded by a progressively worsening disease in a loved one. The subjects of the research reached out and were sometimes desperate. Qualitative research also allows the researcher to reach out and play multiple, overlapping roles. The qualitative researcher can be simultaneously the objective analyst of individual behavior in the sociocultural context, a friend to subjects, and a broker of needed resources. He or she can learn about the culture at the same time. Conducting fieldwork requires multiple roles. Five specific roles were played by the project implementors in addition to being qualitative researchers (Gutierrez-Mayka & Henderson, 1993).

One was the role of *recruiter.* The qualitative research team had to identify ethnic-minority caregivers in the community, contact them, and encourage them to attend support-group meetings. Recruitment strategies included advertising the existence of the support group through the ethnic-minority media and waiting for caregivers to respond to these appeals, and identifying caregivers with the help of referrals and taking the initial step to get caregivers involved in the group.

Another role was that of *group facilitator.* Until an indigenous group facilitator was found, the groups' implementors had to be facilitators during the monthly meetings. The job entailed selecting topics for discussion, preparing a presentation on that topic using available literature or inviting a guest speaker to address the issue, mailing meeting reminders, calling caregivers for a final reminder just before the meeting, and organizing and directing the meeting's discussion.

The *trainer* role involved teaching the indigenous facilitator. Project researchers devised the basic training curriculum covering the following areas: principles of normal aging, fundamentals of Alzheimer's disease, alternative support-group models, and guidelines and techniques for facilitating group discussion. They trained facilitators accordingly.

The role of *adviser* developed as a result of a crucial element in the project: personalism. The advisory role involved acting as a liaison between the group and the potential pool of speakers, directing the group facilitator to the right contacts with social service agencies, and being available to the group to satisfy any requests they might have. The *social worker* role required a great deal of personal involvement. Through personal involvement, caregivers felt inclined to trust and confide in the implementor who took the time to listen to them. As a result, caregivers turned to the implementors with questions and problems they had about community resources and personal psychosocial issues.

The role of the social worker was the least expected. The researchers were prepared to act as trainers, advisers, facilitators, and recruiters, but the social worker role was assigned to us by the caregivers even though they knew we were not social workers by training. When we came into contact with caregivers in our recruitment efforts, they immediately began to share their problems with us and to ask for personal help, information, and referrals. Denying them help would have deterred caregivers and thwarted our efforts to attract them to a support group. We learned as much as possible about their concerns and acquainted ourselves with appropriate resources. We even turned to a skilled social worker as a consultant for answers we could not find on our own. On many occasions, we transferred calls from caregivers directly to the consultant. Our social worker role became one of the most significant in the project.

Benefits

In general, how did the project benefit from the use of qualitative methods? First, qualitative research was a means to get in-depth, empathic insight to phenomena for which the researchers had little personal experience. The immediate development of questionnaires for generating quantitative analysis would have been done in the absence of any understanding of what the significant questions were for the caregiver. Qualitative research assists in discovering the foundations of a group's actions. Qualitative research allows for the discovery of categories of action on which people situationally base their thinking, beliefs, and behaviors.

Second, qualitative research provides a broad context in which to understand ethnocultural behavior. Without context, isolated cultural traits are inert. A cultural trait becomes dynamic and meaningful when placed in real-life context.

Third, qualitative research detects and explains cultural elements that are subtle but significant. Perhaps the characteristic of subtlety itself may indicate that the observation has strong cultural significance. A behavior that is extremely subtle may be a clue that a sensitive element of culture brought to explicit awareness would introduce apparent incongruities with superficially held beliefs. For example, in physician culture no single physician would readily admit that he or she has performed an unnecessary hysterectomy. Yet epidemiologic surveys show great geographic variation in the number of hysterectomies performed. Apparently, some subtle but significant social, cultural, and professional forces are in effect.

Fourth, the element of dyadic communication in fieldwork and interviewing pulls the qualitative researcher into the lives of the researched. Interviews as conversations are not prescripted but contain many elements directly germane to the question posed. Also, many significant elements that are interspersed throughout the verbal discourse of the interviewee may help in understanding the broader context of earlier data collected. Over time, conducting ethnographic interviews places the qualitative researcher in circumstances in which he or she is around the subjects in diverse capacities, from acting as a social worker to overhearing phone calls to spouses, observing the activities of children, or attending to other matters seemingly unrelated to project goals. Such opportunities illuminate the life context in which project-specific questions are played out.

Fifth, qualitative research is sensitive to the situationally shifting cultural repertoire used by subjects as they negotiate their daily lives. In this project, sensitivity to changes along the acculturation continuum had to be noted. Otherwise, a static and stereotypical view of the ethnic-minority elder would have been obtained.

Sixth, qualitative research is inherently flexible and attuned to discovering details of subjects' ethnocultural realities. At the beginning of the project, I could not have predicted the importance of location for the support-group meetings. Nor could I have predicted the invisible boundaries between the African-American churches. Similarly, I could not have predicted that a culturally neutral site would be successful when the research bias is on cultural relevance.

Seventh and finally, the uninitiated should be forewarned that qualitative research can be frustrating. It allows the researcher to see the intricate details of cultural systems, all moving about at a rapid pace. This can mesmerize the researcher with a surfeit of information. Still, no other research method is as rewarding for discovering the complexities of culture, especially the sensitivities of ethnicity and race.

References

Carter, J. H. (1978). The black aged: A strategy for future mental health services. *Journal of American Geriatrics Society, 26,* 553-556.
Carter, J. H. (1981). Treating black patients: The risks of ignoring critical social issues. *Hospital and Community Psychiatry, 32,* 281-282.
Chatters, L., Taylor, R., & Jackson, J. (1986). Aged blacks' choices for an informal helper network. *Journal of Gerontology, 41,* 94-100.
Cox, C., & Monk, A. (1990). Minority caregivers of dementia victims: A comparison of black and Hispanic families. *Journal of Applied Gerontology, 9,* 340-354.
Garcia, J., Cuervo, C., Kosberg, J., & Henderson, J. N. (1989). *Perception of gender roles in older Hispanic women.* Paper presented at International Congress on Gerontology, Acapulco, Mexico.
Good, B. J., & Good, M-J. D. (1981). The meaning of symptoms: A cultural hermeneutic model for clinical practice. In L. Eisenberg & A. Kleinman (Eds.), *The relevance of social science for medicine* (pp. 165-196). Boston: Reidel.
Gutierrez-Mayka, M., & Henderson, J. N. (1993). Social work for non-social workers: An example of unplanned role negotiation in a community health intervention project. *Journal of Gerontological Social Work, 20,* 135-146.
Haug, J. (Ed.). (1981). *Elderly patients and their doctors.* New York: Springer.
Henderson, J. N. (1987). Mental disorders among the elderly: Dementia and its sociocultural correlates. In P. Silverman (Ed.), *The elderly as modern pioneers* (pp. 357-374). Bloomington: Indiana University Press.
Henderson, J. N. (1990). Alzheimer's disease in cultural context. In J. Sokolovsky (Ed.), *The cultural context of aging: worldwide perspectives* (pp. 315-330). New York: Bergin & Garvey.
Henderson, J. N. (1992). The power of support: Alzheimer's disease support groups for minority families. *Aging, 363-364,* 24-28.
Henderson, J. N., & Gutierrez-Mayka, M. (1992). Ethnocultural themes in caregiving to Alzheimer's disease patients in Hispanic families. *Clinical Gerontologist, 11,* 59-74.
Henderson, J. N., Gutierrez-Mayka, M., Garcia, J., & Boyd, S. (1993). A model for Alzheimer's disease support group development in African-American and Hispanic populations. *Gerontologist, 33,* 409-414.
Hill, R. F., Fortenberry, J. D. & Stein, H. F. (1990). Culture in clinical medicine. *Southern Medical Journal, 83,* 1071-1080.
Ho, M. K. (1987). *Family therapy with ethnic minorities.* Newbury Park, CA: Sage.
Katon, W., & Kleinman, A. (1981). Doctor-patient negotiation and other social science strategies in patient care. In L. Eisenberg & A. Kleinman (Eds.), *The relevance of social science for medicine* (pp. 253-279). Boston: D. Reidel.

50   Ethnic and Racial Issues

Kleinman, A. (1980). *Patients and healers in the context of culture*. Berkeley: University of California Press.
Kuhn, T. S. (1962). *The structure of scientific revolutions*. Chicago: University of Chicago Press.
Levin, J. S. (1984). The role of the black church in community medicine. *Journal of National Medical Association, 76*, 477-483.
Levine, E. S., & Padilla, A. M. (1980). *Crossing cultures in therapy: Pluralistic counseling for the Hispanic*. Belmont, CA: Brooks/Cole.
Maldonado, D. (1975). The Chicano elderly. *Social Work, 20*, 213-216.
Neighbors, H. (1984). Professional help use among black Americans: Implications for unmet need. *American Journal of Community Psychology, 12*, 551-566.
Pfeifferling, J. H. (1981). A cultural prescription for mediocentrism. In L. Eisenberg & A. Kleinman (Eds.), *The relevance of social science for medicine* (pp. 197-222). Boston: Reidel.
Simic, A. (1985). Ethnicity as a resource for the aged: An anthropological perspective. *Journal of Applied Gerontology, 4*, 65-71.
Stein, H. F. (1990). *American medicine as culture*. Boulder, CO: Westview.
Tate, N. (1984). The black aging experience. In R. L. McNeely & J. L. Cohen (Eds.), *Aging in minority groups* (pp. 95-107). Beverly Hills, CA: Sage.
Valle, R. (1989). Cultural and ethnic issues in Alzheimer's disease research. In E. Light & B. D. Lebowitz (Eds.), *Alzheimer's disease treatment and family stress: Directions for research* (pp. 122-154). Rockville, MD: National Institutes of Mental Health.
Wood, J. B., & Parham, I. A. (1990). Coping with perceived burden: Ethnic and cultural issues in Alzheimer's family caregiving. *Journal of Applied Gerontology, 9*, 325-339.

4

Problematizing Meaning

DALE J. JAFFE
ELEANOR M. MILLER

The purpose of this chapter is (a) to provide a general discussion of the problem of meaning in qualitative research and (b) to highlight two related issues—positionality and structural embeddedness. By *positionality,* we mean the relative status, status consciousness, identity, or world view of the researcher and the subject(s) of the research. By *structural embeddedness,* we mean the relationship between the phenomenon being studied and the broader social contexts of which the phenomenon is a part. Qualitative research on the experiences and social condition of frail elderly will be used to illustrate aspects of the problem of meaning and the importance of positionality and embeddedness for exploiting the unique character of qualitative method consistent with its philosophical underpinnings.

We are not suggesting that these issues are always prerequisite considerations in qualitative research. They must be considered if the researcher's goal is to examine the relationship between microlevel and macrolevel social processes.

We hope also to highlight the differences between qualitative and quantitative research by arguing that qualitative research that takes quantitative method as a model—and thereby ignores its own grounding—produces a perverse view of reality at the same time that it fails

AUTHORS' NOTE: The authors express their appreciation to Stacey Oliker, Karen Lyman, Eric Rambo, and the editors for their helpful comments in the preparation of this chapter.

51

both to meet positivist standards and use the unique strengths of qualitative method.

Meaning and Interpretation

The goal of qualitative research is to understand social life by taking into account meaning, the interpretive process of social actors, and the cultural, social, and situational contexts in which those processes occur (see Blumer, 1969). Qualitative research on aging begins just as quantitative research does: from a general concern with some aspect of aging or old age. One might be interested in the experiences of a particular group of old people, a specific problem in daily living that causes them pain, or an event that gives them joy. One may wish to investigate a process or sequence of events thought to characterize aging generally, or one might wish to sort out how the process or sequence varies crossculturally or by race, class, or gender. The qualitative researcher starts to differ as she attempts to enter in some way the world of the old people under investigation. She seeks to understand what the phenomenon or experience of interest means to the aged—that is, how they think about it, how they view their own and others' worlds, and what the consequences of the perspectives are for courses of action.

Attempts to capture the dynamics and outcomes of meaning and interpretation most often result in projects designed as in-depth interview studies. Some researchers in aging conduct participant observation or ethnographic studies, choosing to coexist in some fashion with elderly individuals in their natural settings. Typically, when researchers inquire about the meaning of something, whether it be an object, experience, relationship, or idea, they are asking about its personal and social significance. Of what significance is it for the group or individual? How is it used as a guide or justification for behavior or for thinking about something in a certain way? Answers to such questions help the qualitative researcher make sensible and comprehensible explanations and inferred reasons for social behavior of the group or persons under consideration. Meanings are then presented in a variety of ways: as broad themes that transcend time, place, and social context; as a set of concepts that capture some basic properties of how people think about something; or as situation-specific accounts for certain actions. A test of one's success is whether those being studied accept the researcher's account and whether it rings true to them both cognitively and emotionally. Qualitative researchers refer to this as the *member test of validity,* although so-called member validation has been the subject of debate in the field (see Bloor, 1983).

The Creation of Meaning

Central to the interpretive process of social actors is the creation of meaning. To create meaning is to make sense of something. It is to understand what one has come to know within the context of a particular moral universe. To say this is to stress Berger and Luckmann's (1966) observation that, on creation, meaning has a value attached to it. It is good or bad, or it may simply be valued because it is familiar. Humans constantly create meaning; it is part of being human. We construct and reconstruct our world and who we are in the process. As Simmel (see Levine, 1971) pointed out, in any particular instance the meaning we create is circumscribed by other meanings that we and other members of society already have created. The meanings we claim as our own are like cognitive and moral lenses: They present a framework that provides understandings for objects, acts, gestures, and words. Meaning creation is social. It emerges in and through social interaction (Blumer, 1969). It is accomplished by actors who create themselves and their social worlds as they create meaning. At the same time, actors are selves, having the unique ability to stand outside their world and perceive themselves and others in relation to it.

Positionality and Embeddedness

Personal positions with reference to cognitive and moral universes of meaning are also important. The world each of us sees is created from the social stuff that we all share, but it also varies because we are differently positioned or situated in reference to it. In other words, we may view the world of the aged through a lens that defines old age as a time of frailty and social irrelevance, but that lens is also colored by our own age, class background, gender, education, and even our own experience of aging. Our research experience encompasses not only having had the opportunity to know old people of various sorts but also our own feelings from the experience of aging, be it fear, compassion, disgust, or any other of a whole array of emotions. All this is what we mean by positionality, which creates meaning in its own right (Atkinson, 1990; Clifford & Marcus, 1986; Gubrium & Silverman, 1990).

Structural embeddedness is not unrelated to positionality, but it refers to a dimension that is underemphasized in some qualitative research (notable exceptions are Gubrium, 1988; Smith, 1987; Willis, 1977). Meaning construction and identity formation give the researcher and the researched shared and yet crucially different realities and are mediated by broader forces or social structures. For example, institutional caregiving not only is defined differently by different partners to care but also has its definitions affected by broader understandings or forces such that caregiving is profitable or that it is part of a corporate care structure. The structures have a permanence and reality that shape the creation of cultural and personal meanings. How the particular phenomenon being studied fits into the social structure of which it is part and how the phenomenon supports broader structures or resists the latter also are of great interest.

Qualitative method thus is grounded in a particular view of the world. It is a view that assumes the world is not something out there to be discovered but is, in fact, emergent. It is created and re-created by those sentient beings who people it. But also keep in mind that position and larger structures affect what emerges. Qualitative method is designed to reveal how this occurs and with what effect. Problems of meaning and meaning creation, in all the complexity suggested above, including considerations of positionality and structural embeddedness, are central to it.

Quantitative Assumption and Qualitative Method

Some qualitative research assumes that there is a social reality "out there" whose objective contours await discovery. It is assumed that the process of discovery is enhanced to the degree that spoken ideas are probed extensively, behavior is observed intensively, and both are measured precisely, often via counting techniques. To ensure objectivity, the researcher must be wary of "going native" or identifying too closely with the interests, thoughts, or feelings of those studied. Taken for granted is that the interpretive and meaning-creation process of the researcher in his or her own right can be rendered neutral through social and psychological distance. The aim is to combine qualitative methods with the positivist assumptions that undergird quantitative methods.

This melds logically inconsistent paradigms. It eviscerates the spirit of qualitative method. As feminist perspectives, cultural studies, and the fundamental insights of postmodernism in the humanities have crept into the social sciences, qualitative methodologists are reminded that the assumptions of their method mean that they not only discover meaning when they enter the worlds of others, but also bestow it. This is an unavoidable part of all human interactions, including those defined as research. Researchers are co-creators of meaning along with the subjects of their research. To attend to the conceptual and methodological implications of this premise is to problematize meaning. Because the notion of emergent, co-created meaning is methodologically baffling from a positivist framework, we devote the remainder of this chapter to a general discussion of the problematization of meaning in research generally and in aging research specifically.

A Structurally Sensitive Method

Neither the description of the organization of meaning nor an explanation of its source are straightforward matters. As we have stated already, meaning is mediated by several contexts and social lenses. The meaning or significance to an elderly individual of *caring,* for example, is shaped by cultural definitions, social norms, structural contingencies, and personal biographies, which are rendered understandable by unique configurations of membership in race, class, gender, ethnicity, and age groups (for example, see Abel, 1991). Because people do not experience these memberships or levels of cultural, social, or personal reality in isolation, people have difficulty attributing the way they think or why they act to a particular lens, membership, or level of reality. This is precisely the rationale for undertaking structurally sensitive qualitative research. A genuinely rich understanding of human behavior is achieved through a methodology that socially contextualizes action and thought.

As a social being, the researcher is no different. The researcher approaches the research question or topic, decisions about setting and subjects, and the data themselves as a member of a particular subculture and social group and with a unique psychosocial history. The researcher may be no more or no less conscious of the ways in which these factors shape her attempt to make sense of the phenomenon than her research subjects. The research act thus consists of *interacting* systems of meaning. Research results and knowledge are the products of the interaction.

Thus understanding the nature of the knowledge that researchers produce requires an examination of the researcher's social role as a research instrument and her interactions with the people she is studying.

Social science researchers—either wittingly through their explicit allegiance to positivist principles or unwittingly through the implicit expectations of others—occupy superordinate and socially distant positions vis-à-vis those whom they study. The researcher is the one who defines research questions, judges the appropriateness of methodologies, overlays the conceptual frameworks of relevant disciplines on the data, and attaches significance to subjects' words and acts. Who the researcher is and where she stands in relation to both the larger social structure and the researched is not usually at issue. But as we have argued, if knowledge is socially constructed, then the interaction that produces that knowledge is very much at issue. If qualitative researchers and those they study collaborate in the creation of meaning (Frank, 1980) and the researcher stands in a superordinate position in the process, then the outcome of the collaboration may reflect, be consistent with, and support the meanings and world view of the researcher.

Often the researcher is socially privileged vis-à-vis the researched, having more status, wealth, and power. Researchers are situated to see research problems in ways that leave this privilege undisturbed.

One oft-repeated argument holds that the slave, by necessity, must know more about her master, the world they share, and how it works than vice versa. The slave must have this knowledge because she must always be ready to duck. Masters resist this point of view because they feel as if they also are ducking all the time. The important point, however, is that the master's life rarely depends on how adroitly she manages to duck, whereas such skill is an absolute necessity for the slave. In a popular sociological essay, Goode (1982) relates the sociology of superordination to the relations between males and females. He argues that superordinates (males) are less motivated to see all there is to see of the world of the subordinates (women) than the other way around, because the lives of the subordinates are much more affected by superordinates than vice versa (Goode, 1982, p. 137).

Thus researchers who assume a superordinate position by virtue of their association with the authority of science and often by virtue of their demographic characteristics reduce their effectiveness as research instruments. Their superordinate position may blind them to important insights at the same time that it increases the power of their voice and perspective over that of the researched in the process of cocreating meaning. Although most qualitative researchers probably agree that they can never really walk in the shoes of those being studied, ignoring these fundamental issues of social structure and meaning creation make it difficult to even occupy shoes that walk next to those being studied.

An Alternative

How can a qualitative researcher create knowledge that is as true as possible to the view from below? We believe that a first step involves seriously transforming the objects of one's research into thinking and feeling subjects, conceptualizing those studied as key actors in the research process, and collaborating with them at every stage of the research process. Although this methodology does not always subordinate the researcher and her interests in every way and at every turn, it does draw attention to the implications of the social and political relations of research and helps shape a distribution of power that is more fluid and relatively narrow. Thus creating knowledge that is true to the view from below involves rearranging the structural relations of research.

Not only is it important for the object of the research to become the subject, the subject must become the object. This requires a continual state of introspection and self-knowledge on the part of the research team, particularly the member of team who is the traditional researcher or scientist. The focus of the introspection is on the cognitive lenses of the researcher and the ways in which those lenses influence the researcher's intellectual and emotional responses to the research experience. Because the creation of meaning and knowledge is a collaborative affair, attention to the internal cognitive and subjective life of the researcher is no less central to a fair rendering of the reality of objects than that of the subjects. Qualitative research that problematizes meaning thus requires a rearrangement of both the relations of research and the subjective orientation of researchers. The nature of this rearrangement is a movement from distance to closeness: closeness to those one wishes to understand and closeness to oneself as a research instrument.

Problematizing Meaning in Old Age Research

A certain restlessness has surfaced within the human sciences over the past few years. It has a great deal to do with the fact that most researchers do not problematize meaning in their work. Social scientific disciplines have been variously described as fragmented, without central paradigms, theoretically stale, increasingly disinterested in the relationship between theory and method, and not fulfilling the promises of either accurate prediction or the amelioration of the human condition. In social gerontology, a fine example of this sort of critique is offered by Tornstam (1992) at almost the same time as a key figure in the qualitative study of aging has pronounced that "qualitative research [has] come of age in gerontology" (Gubrium, 1992).

To accept that qualitative gerontology has come of age is not necessarily to agree that better research, better social science, or better knowledge in general is being created. Consider caregiving research, for example; it is arguably the single most popular area of contemporary gerontological inquiry, where both qualitative and quantitative researchers work. Major figures in the area have mused on paper about the value of existing work on caregiving and whether more caregiving research is needed (Chappell, 1991; George, 1990; Gwyther, 1992; Zarit, 1989). Drawing on our earlier discussion, we would argue that it is inattention to issues of meaning that accounts for the fact that a major research tradition, caregiving research, could arrive at the state we and others find it in today. Ironically, it is not about aging, old age, or old people at all, and its major theme, that which shapes public policy, is that the elderly are burdensome, draining problems with whom others must cope. Neither quantitative nor much qualitative work on caregiving problematizes meaning, which accounts for both the apparent staleness of the knowledge and its questionable utility in understanding and improving the experience of aging and old age.

How is this so? The quantitative researcher selects a large sample of potential caregiving respondents from community-wide surveys, agency records, or the like. A detailed questionnaire is prepared that includes dozens of closed questions about units of caregiving, the respondent's role within a larger caregiving network, and the impact of caregiving on aspects of the respondent's life such as family, work, and health status. Statistical analysis aims to establish typical patterns and relationships among variables. Senior authors of such studies rarely encounter in any personal way the subjects of their research, let alone the elderly for whom the respondents care. The qualitative researcher selects a much smaller convenience sample of potential interviewees. Rather than a questionnaire, she uses an interview guide that contains open-ended questions about many of the same broad topics that would be found in the closed questionnaire. Along with these questions, the interviewer makes extensive use of contemporaneous probes, or conversational questions that seek additional information about rationales, explanations, connections, and personal meaning or significance. Analytical induction (the process of moving back and forth between data and an emerging, tentative interpretation) helps the scientist produce a credible account of how caregivers see what they do and with what personal significance.

Although it is generally true that the quantitative approach obscures the contextual nature of both caregiving and research interactions, and the qualitative approach seeks to emphasize the re-creation of context in its narratives, both approaches to caregiving research can render their subjects' voices inaudible. In the vast majority of caregiving studies, the elderly voices are simply absent, the most extreme manifestation of distance between the researcher and the researched imaginable. The bestowal of meaning can occur in their absence and without their input, perspective, or notions of what is important to know and how best to know it. One cannot approach a subordinate status vis-à-vis the care receiver, and the result ensures that the researcher and caregiver maintain their authoritative voices in matters of care over the interests and voices of the aged. The bestowal of meaning occurs with little or no self-consciousness on the researcher's part—that is, no appreciation of the role of her own interpretive processes and cognitive lenses in collaborating with the caregiver to create the meaning of care.

This finds an even more extreme expression in the way social scientists have approached the study of Alzheimer's disease. We have many studies of services and their delivery systems as they relate to Alzheimer's disease, and we have many descriptions of various methods of testing memory, speech, and other cognitive processes. But the individual with the disease and his or her lived experience is conspicuously absent. This promotes a view of the person with Alzheimer's as a lifeless form with major cognitive and social deficits, the cause of overly stressed caregivers and strained service-delivery systems.

We assume that what is central to the Alzheimer's disease experience is either irrelevant or unimportant to scientific research or is something troublesome or problematic that requires control and management by others. As Lyman (1989) has pointed out, social scientific research on Alzheimer's disease has generally been framed by the biomedical model and reinforced by social service concepts that assume inexorable and irreversible decline through a series of stages characterized by clear symptomatology. A related assumption holds a unidirectional, causal link between organic phenomena in the brain and behavioral and cognitive processes. Social contextual factors are given short shrift, if they are considered at all. Although we cannot doubt that research of this sort has been influential in drawing national attention to Alzheimer's and mobilizing resources to support caregiving systems and individuals, the emphasis has been on shaping the social and physical environment of the person with Alzheimer's to promote safety and physical health and make her less a worry or burden.

With few exceptions, research on the disease has ignored the individual with Alzheimer's as a living, feeling human being. Rare is ethnographic work that seeks collaboration with those who have Alzheimer's. Even rarer is work that reveals the researcher's own ideas and fears about illness of this sort and how those ideas and fears find their way into each phase of the research process. As a result, our view of those who are afflicted is one in which their entire selves are defined by the disease. Researchers and practitioners refer to them as Alzheimer's *victims* rather than as people *with Alzheimer's*. The person becomes the disease, and it envelopes the self totally even when the disease actually is progressive.

As a society and as a community of scholars, we display more interest, concern, and empathy for the caregivers than for the people with the disease. We pay precious little attention to quality-of-life issues as defined by individuals who have the disease. It is considered a preposterous idea that caregiving actions and contexts could themselves conceivably shape the trajectory of the disease, a trajectory that most now see as strictly organically based, although a more complex relationship between social factors and disease is well accepted in medical sociology and in other areas of gerontology (Gubrium, 1987).

In ignoring the sufferer's lived experience, we forfeit a potentially exciting venue for learning more about the aging experience. Without problematizing meaning in Alzheimer's disease research through closeness to people with the disease and self-consciousness about our own roles in creating ideas about the disease, we generate little new grist for the theoretical mill. The field remains largely atheoretical, shaped by policy makers and aging network professionals whose interests are in behavioral management. In the process, we have ensured that little of our research will address in any significant fashion the questions and dilemmas surrounding what it means to grow old. By not problematizing meaning, researchers have little chance of either transforming the

Y

life circumstances of elderly people with Alzheimer's disease for the better or of making a significant theoretical contribution to the study of the disease experience.

From Conceptualizing to Doing

An extraordinary example of research that problematizes meaning—notably in relation to positionality and structural embeddedness—is presented in sociologist Timothy Diamond's *Making Gray Gold: Narratives of Nursing Home Care* (1992). This ethnography details the ways in which the care of frail elderly in nursing homes is transformed into "billable units" and profit. Diamond confronts the issue of positionality from the start. The idea for his study emerged from a chance meeting with two female African-American nursing assistants in a coffee shop across the street from the nursing home where the women worked. His initial questions about caregiving were suggested by early informal conversations with the women, and the conceptual and methodological design of his subsequent work was derived from his desire to experience situations just like those as related to him by the women.

So off he went to enroll in a program to get certified as a nursing assistant, to enable him to actually put himself in the nursing assistant's position. From there he interviewed for nursing home jobs, did the work of nursing assistant, rode the bus or walked through local neighborhoods and socialized with other aides, and chronicled his experience.

Although Diamond is in every frame he constructs, he is there as an equal participant, if not as subordinate to those he studied. One often has the sense in his account that Diamond is apprenticed to his informants. He is one member of a collectivity telling us a story, and while we learn about the everyday life of nursing homes as staff members and residents interact with him, his role as a researcher is submerged in the narrative. He participates in the world of his subjects as they participate in his.

Diamond is never the expert. He is candid about his presuppositions and oversimplified conceptions of nursing home life and sets about to show us how those ideas were challenged and altered. He is the learner, and we learn by his example. Diamond's self-consciousness is apparent and helpful in making sense of nursing home care at every turn. The attention and portrayal of his emotional responses to what he is doing as a participant are an important part of the narrative. Feelings such as exhaustion, fear, anger, disgust, and revulsion reveal to us important and human features of daily nursing home life. Diamond's awareness of his own race, gender, nationality, and employment status (he had only one job, while most of his peers had two) is not simply stated at the beginning of the book as an obligatory caveat but is an integral part of the narrative. He reveals much about the social relations of nursing home life by openly acknowledging the reactions of others to certain of his personal demographic characteristics and describing his sometimes embarrassing behavior toward others.

The world of nursing home caregiving is viewed as embedded within the wider political economy of corporate health care. Caregivers and care receivers instruct Diamond, and through him the reader is shown how caregiving becomes a commodity. For example, Diamond traces the transformation of a bowl of tomato soup from a tasteless substitute for the required allotment of vegetables into a unit of necessary sustenance that the nursing attendant, with the stroke of a pen, records as a billable amount of care. The way in which the meaning of something as seemingly insignificant as a bowl of soup is transformed into "gray gold," which obviously has a different meaning, and the role of the nursing attendant in the transformation becomes palpably apparent. One can only marvel at the absurdity of an administrator's directive to "go do some psychosocial stuff" when the aide's "real work" is completed before the end of a shift. Because "psychosocial stuff" is not easily transformable into a unit of care, it is viewed from above as irrelevant, invisible, and insignificant.

The nursing attendants' minimum-wage standard of living contrasts with the clear value of the humane relationships that they attempt to cultivate with those for whom they care. Minimum wages and the docility of vulnerable and fearful residents are conditions of corporate profit making, which Diamond reveals in human rather than statistical terms. Yet the transformation of gray into gold (changing acts of caring and kindness into dollars) depends on interpersonal shifts in meaning in the interactions of residents and aides. Establishing a link between this microlevel world of social interaction and the macrolevel of social, economic, and political structures is a rare accomplishment and is only possible because of Diamond's studied attention to structural embeddedness.

The theoretical insights Diamond produces are socially transformative. Diamond shows how the voices of both care receivers and their caregivers are muted, denied, and rendered invisible by a system of control that itself is shaped outside the realm of the activities within health care facilities. Diamond participates to raise previously submerged voices to an audible level. From the actual words of real caregivers and care receivers, Diamond proposes changes applicable to national health care and welfare reform, the training and collective organization of the health care labor force, and patients' rights and the ability of nursing home residents to help and care for one another.

Conclusion

Meaning and meaning creation are the stock-in-trade of qualitative research, but this often renders interests and power invisible. The reason for our emphasis on positionality and structural embeddedness is that these serve to highlight the complex forces that mediate the richness of a method. Because gerontology has been long dominated by the medical model and positivist research methodology, these issues have not received much attention even by those who consider themselves qualitative gerontologists. Increased attention to and debate about the issues cannot help but enliven research on aging and help us work toward improving the lives of the aged in the years to come.

References

Abel, E. K. (1991). *Who cares for the elderly?* Philadelphia: Temple University Press.

Atkinson, P. (1990). *The ethnographic imagination: Textual construction of reality.* London: Routledge.

Berger, P. L., & Luckmann, T. (1966). *The social construction of reality.* Garden City, NY: Doubleday.

Bloor, M. J. (1983). Notes on member validation. In R. Emerson (Ed.), *Contemporary field research* (pp. 156-172). Prospect Heights, IL: Waveland.

Blumer, H. (1969). *Symbolic interactionism: Perspective and method.* Englewood Cliffs: Prentice-Hall.

Chappell, N. L. (1991). Caregiving research and more caregiving research: What good is it? *Gerontologist, 31,* 567-569.

Clifford, J., & Marcus, G. E. (Eds.). (1986). *Writing culture: The poetics and politics of ethnography.* Berkeley: University of California Press.

Diamond, T. (1992). *Making gray gold: Narratives of nursing home care.* Chicago: University of Chicago Press.

64   Problematizing Meaning

Frank, G. (1980). Life histories in gerontology: The subjective side to aging. In C. Fry & J. Keith (Eds.), *New methods for old age research* (pp. 155-176). Chicago: Loyola University Press.

George, L. K. (1990). Caregiver stress studies—There really is more to learn. *Gerontologist, 30,* 580-581.

Goode, W. J. (1982). Why men resist. In B. Thorne & M. Yalom (Eds.), *Rethinking the family: Some feminist questions* (pp. 131-150). New York: Longman.

Gubrium, J. F. (1987). Structuring and destructuring the course of illness: the Alzheimer's disease experience. *Sociology of Health and Illness, 9,* 1-24.

Gubrium, J. F. (1988). *Analyzing field reality.* Newbury Park, CA: Sage.

Gubrium, J. F. (1992). Qualitative research comes of age in gerontology. *Gerontologist, 32,* 581-582.

Gubrium, J. F., & Silverman, D. (Eds.). (1990). *The politics of field research.* Newbury Park, CA: Sage.

Gwyther, L. P. (1992). Proliferation without pizzazz. *Gerontologist, 32,* 865-867.

Levine, D. N. (1971). *Georg Simmel: On individuality and social forms.* Chicago: University of Chicago Press.

Lyman, K. A. (1989). Bringing the social back in: A critique of the biomedicalization of dementia. *Gerontologist, 29,* 597-605.

Smith, D. E. (1987). *The everyday world as problematic: A feminist sociology.* Boston: Northeastern University Press.

Tornstam, L. (1992). The quo vadis of gerontology: On the scientific paradigm of gerontology. *Gerontologist, 32,* 318-326.

Willis, P. (1977). *Learning to labor.* New York: Columbia University Press.

Zarit, S. H. (1989). Do we need another "stress and caregiving" study? *Gerontologist, 29,* 147-148.

PART II

Planning

5

Proposal Writing

ROBERT L. RUBINSTEIN

This chapter addresses research-proposal writing as part of the overall use of qualitative methods in aging research. A consideration of proposal writing is integral to the research project. Little literature on qualitative research proposal writing is available, although proposal writing clearly is an important part of research (Coley & Scheinberg, 1990; Locke, Spirduso, & Silverman, 1987; Schumacher, 1992). Proposal writing appears to be the object of a good deal of folklore, informally learned and passed from researcher to researcher. This chapter will share insights about constructing qualitative proposals for research about old age and aging.

The first section of this chapter addresses how to justify the use of qualitative methods in a quantitatively oriented environment. The second section examines how to find an appropriate funding venue. A third and longer section deals with general features of good proposal writing, such as consistency, clarity, and simplicity. The fourth and final section discusses special problems in qualitative aging research, including the problem of qualitative sampling.

Justifying Qualitative Research

That we should have this book and this chapter within it signals a common perception of qualitative research: It is offbeat and neither the norm nor usual. This is especially the case in gerontological research in which project after project uses research techniques that incorporate standardized measures, survey-style samples, and statistically based data analyses. Even a cursory examination of recent conference programs and gerontology journals shows the dominance of such approaches. Unfortunately, the mainstream approach almost completely abjures meaning. The predominance of mainstream research gives the impression of insularity and ideological domination that rejects methodological criticism. Further, reviewers of proposals are often likely to be representatives of such mainstream approaches, both in federal funding agencies such as the National Institutes of Health (NIH) and the National Institutes of Mental Health as well as foundation-based agencies. Consequently, the research problems addressed by qualitative researchers may be marginal to the central methodological and topical areas of mainstream social gerontology. Examples are plentiful and include research on skid-row urban adaptation, childlessness, daily life in nursing homes, and cultural and critical analyses of aging, most of them undertaken by anthropologists and some sociologists.

Over the last decade, there has been an increasing acceptance of qualitative methods in old-age research. This is certainly good news. At the same time, however, the central issues that motivated the field of social gerontology a decade ago—for example, the social integration of the elderly—have been displaced by increasingly medicalized views of aging and by scholarly concern with such topics as depression and dementia. Ironically, the greater acceptance of qualitative techniques in social science is paralleled by the spread of the biomedical view in gerontology in which the social or meaning components are increasingly overshadowed by biomedical concerns. Although the area of medicine and aging has seen many fine qualitative research efforts, the acceptance of qualitative research by physician researchers, for example, has been slow.

Proposal writers may take one of three views of the centrality of qualitative methods. First, with a *qualitocentric* view of the research world, they can implicitly and explicitly voice their sense that qualitative methods are best for many research purposes. One might argue that these methods are more attuned to the lives of real people, exploring meaning and peoples' natural categories. A second view, a variation of the first, suggests the attitude "We have something you don't" with a goal of making quantitative researchers feel inadequate about their lack of qualitative research skills. A third view is the more modest smorgasbord approach that acknowledges the wide range of research perspectives from which we are able to select appropriate tools for specific research questions. In this view, qualitative and quantitative techniques complement one another in the overall research endeavor. This tactic would probably make a proposal most acceptable and fitting to a mainstream gerontological audience.

There are ways by which qualitative approaches can be arranged to fit with more mainstream approaches. First, qualitative old-age research fits around quantitative research issues and methods that are central to mainstream social gerontology and thus, in such a large scholarly space, have a distinctive place in conjunction with more formal quantitative studies. It would be useless for qualitative researchers to replicate yet another study of filial caregiving and employ already widely used measures in this area. Yet there exist both large niches—the question of what caregiving means to a caregiver, for example—as well as many small niches within the overall caregiving realm in which qualitative approaches would well fit. Examples of caregiving areas that are especially amenable to qualitative research include the meaning of caregiving, the effect of caregiving on generational self-concept or on family relations, the ways in which disability is locally defined, or the manner in which the self of the impaired person is preserved by family members, such as in the case of dementia.

Second, mainstream researchers often find it easy to see qualitative research as an enterprise that is best used before formal psychometric or survey procedures to identify salient aspects of the phenomena to be investigated. Gubrium (1992) however has argued against this justification.

Third, qualitative methods are the only ones suitable for the study of process and meaning. For example, if we wanted to follow a group of senior adults as they move through the health care system, informant-centered qualitative research would be ideal. Further, qualitative research is excellent for understanding the flavor or flow of experience, the perspective of both mainstreams and oddballs, and the multiple viewpoints involved in any social setting. Some researchers, especially those with an anthropological fieldwork background, may also feel it necessary to justify qualitative research strategies that are solely interview-based rather than community-based (as in traditional participant observation). An effective argument can be developed to demonstrate that person-oriented interviews are the final phase of a larger, multistage participant-observation procedure (Rubinstein, 1992).

Keith (1980) has outlined three stages in carrying out participant observation in old-age research. These stages move from the greatest personal outsidedness to the greatest insidedness. Stage 1, the initial period, is topically all-inclusive; the researcher asks as many questions of as many of her subjects as possible. Anthropological participant observation typically consists of residence in a community often for a year or more. Stage 2 consists of more focused, discriminating inquiry. At this point, the researcher has gained enough general background knowledge of a setting to enable her to investigate in detail specific areas of interest. Data collection becomes more specialized. In Stage 3, there occurs a further refinement of data collection and the posing and testing of hypotheses (for those who view research as a hypothesis-testing endeavor). Further, at this stage, there is increased personal attention to and work with key informants. This permits the researcher to gain the greatest degree of insight into informants' subjectivities and the inner workings and meanings of the culture.

Own-culture research strategies that feature series of one or more open-ended, nondirective, conversation interviews with subjects justifiably truncate the procedure, such that research begins late in Stage 2 or in Stage 3. Because much of the background cultural knowledge required to interpret a research topic in a familiar environment already has been gained, much of the background work of learning the culture is not necessary. The goal is to focus on a particular research topic in qualitative fashion and to elicit to whatever degree possible aspects of subjective experience under investigation. An example can be taken from research that was undertaken at the Philadelphia Geriatric Center of childlessness in later life. Because this was own-culture research, it was no longer necessary to ferret out general, widely held cultural and social meanings of parenthood or nonparenthood because these were shared among researchers and informants as members of the same culture. However, it was important to understand individual experiences and feelings through in-depth qualitative interviews that treated each respondent as a key informant.

Within the context of qualitative research, standardized inventories of various sorts may be included. This not only acts as a source of validation with the qualitative or narrative materials elicited but also enables the sample to be compared with other samples, to test hypotheses statistically, and to facilitate comparison with more mainstream social gerontology.

Finding a Funding Venue

Finding an appropriate funding source is an important part of proposal writing because, by and large, the funding source will dictate not only the topics and types of research permitted, but also the budget limitations and time frames. Two principal research venues are available: regular funding programs such as those sponsored by federal agencies and foundations, and special, one-time only sources known as *requests for proposals* (RFPs). Regular programs have set deadlines and descriptions that operate year-round, although program emphases may change. In general, both sorts will use a peer-review process—that is, the scientific merit of the proposal will be assessed by substantive and methodological experts in the area of the grant. It is this peer-review process to which qualitative researchers must accommodate themselves.

By and large, qualitative old-age researchers undertake smaller sorts of projects and, as a result, seek small-scale funding for their research, often within their university. Sources include faculty grant programs sponsored by college faculties, administrations, or smaller local foundations. However, many larger funding agencies, both government and private, do fund support research. Guidelines for what is funded by such agencies are often shaped by programmatic and political interests and qualitative techniques can be adapted to such interests. For example, many agencies sponsor research on the human effects of current social problems for which qualitative methods are ideally suited.

In locating a potential funding source, the investigator needs to do homework. The investigator can do a lot to help his or her cause. Besides understanding the guidelines for research by the prospective agency, the researcher can gain some sense of qualitative methods through formal or informal consultation with agency staff. A list of standing reviewers also can be obtained, as can a list of recently funded research projects. The review procedure can be ascertained and pertinent questions asked. How are "unusual" (i.e., qualitative) proposals handled? Are they farmed out to special reviewers who function to augment a standing review committee? Do agency staff members solicit the names of appropriate reviewers or categories of review expertise from investigators? If qualitative expertise is lacking in the peer-review process, is the investigator permitted to suggest names of potential reviewers? Answers to such questions should provide an indication of the agency's existing attitude to qualitative research methods. I have generally been pleasantly surprised by the degree to which many agencies have included a reviewer with qualitative expertise. Larger funding agencies that use a complex peer-review process do consider using appropriate qualitatively oriented reviewers.

It is possible to be funded by many federal and private research agencies when employing qualitative methods. To be sure, certain federal agencies do not seem to fund qualitative research while others do. How much of this is results from a lack of qualitative submissions is unclear. Rumor may come into play here—that is, a sense that one should not apply to certain agencies because, it is rumored, they do not review qualitative research proposals fairly or fund them at all. A concerted effort by qualitative researchers to locate and go after such agencies, especially those that incorrectly claim review neutrality and fairness, may prove useful. Qualitative proposal writers themselves need to assess fairly what makes a good proposal and a good description of problem and methods.

Proposal Writing

Proposal writing is a genre, a type of literary production following its own aesthetic rules. The best way to get familiar with this literary form is by reading and writing proposals. Writing, of course, needs reference to a successful or good model. Many proposal writers essentially serve an apprenticeship period with successful grant writers. Reading proposals is another matter. It would certainly be useful to have a book that consists of several successfully funded proposals along with reviewers' comments about them. Nothing like this apparently exists in aging. To be sure, proposals are collected informally.

A successful proposal has six important features: an authorial presence, vision, consistency, clarity, simplicity, and plausibility.

Authorial Presence

Authorial presence is the the voice the reader acknowledges when reading. In the best proposals, this voice is present throughout the text. The reader has the feeling of being confidently led by an investigator through a body of materials and being clearly presented the decisions and rationales that the investigator has made along the way. For example, if an investigator opts for one design over another, then he or she might usefully explain what was considered but not chosen. This reveals a person who has carefully thought this through. Part of authorial presence is leaving a paper trail of possible theory and design choices that have been considered and presenting a rationale for inclusion or exclusion.

Vision

Authorial presence is related to a firm sense of *vision*. A research proposal is an exercise in envisioning: This thought goes here, that part goes there, this is how they relate. Of course, a research proposal must incorporate a timeline, or the phases in which various parts of the proposed work are to be conducted. But as a genre the proposal also must demonstrate a sense of vision of the whole, especially an overall sense of direction: This is why we want to do the research, this is how we get into the setting, this is what we ask, this is how we ask it, this is what we do with the materials after we ask questions, and so on.

Vision also includes being able to delineate the nuts and bolts of the research process. Especially for qualitative research, it is not enough to state "participant observation will be employed" or "we will use qualitative, in-depth, ethnographically based interviews." These methods are described in other chapters in this book and in the references they cite. The investigator must be able to communicate what these methods will concretely consist of in the particular project, step-by-step and in detail, and then justify their selection. Certainly, an investigator can share with a review committee what open-ended questions will be asked, what is expected to occur in an interview setting, what prompting procedures will be used, the order in which questions will be asked, and so on. Even if these do not turn out to be precisely what happens when the research is undertaken, the reviewers need to see and understand what is expected.

Part of envisioning is deciding on a title for the project proposal. Investigators may be undecided about the specific aims of the research until the very end, when the project might finally coalesce and the title become clear. I see the title as more than just a name: It is an active symbol that condenses the project and "feels right." If an investigator cannot think of an adequate title, then perhaps the project is not yet ready for proposal.

Consistency

In my experience of reading proposals at various stages of completion, lack of *consistency* is a major source of negative evaluation. A consistent proposal is one in which all parts are accounted for, explained, tied together, and justified—that is, no loose ends. Everything must be introduced, described, accounted for, and rationalized. In many research proposals, something new suddenly appears halfway through the proposal. Because important elements have not been introduced earlier, the lack of effective anticipation and explanation renders the insertion less useful than it might be and confuses the reader. Furthermore, the lack of anticipation may signal a lack of vision by the investigator.

Clarity and Simplicity

Related to this is the need for a clear and straightforward presentation. Although grant application forms will often specify the categories and order of presentation, within this context, clear organization of a research project and clear descriptive writing go together. This does not mean that research in complex social settings should be oversimplified. In fact, qualitative research is the only approach that can adequately assess such complexities. However, clarity in describing procedures in such a research environment is necessary, especially if proposal reviewers are naive about what qualitative research can do. Simplicity also is a part of good design. Keeping study groups simple and manageable helps a reader view the research as plausible and doable. Clarity also relates to the specification of goals. It is useful to state one general goal, such as, "The general aim of the proposed research is to explore the relationship of X to Y." Particular or specific goals that operationalize and specify the general aim also should be listed and described.

Plausibility

Proposals often suffer because they are implausible and the research just cannot be done in the manner designated. Examples are unrealistic assumptions about the amount of tape transcription time needed, the amount of audiotape really necessary, and overambitious samples. Those who have little knowledge or experience may appropriately question such assumptions.

Implausibility is in part a product of failing to take oneself seriously as a researcher. There is often a sense among qualitative researchers that proposing qualitative methods for certain funding venues is an innately hopeless task. One thinks, "The reviewers just won't get it. Unless I get a large enough sample or use fancy statistics, they'll never fund it." In general, however, reviewers take their tasks quite seriously, act professionally, and try to understand projects on their own terms, sometimes more so than the investigators themselves.

Another plausibility factor is pilot work and professional credentials. Completed, significant, and well-described pilot projects that feed directly into the proposed research underscore a project's plausibility. Similarly, publications based on related research endeavors assure reviewers that the proposed work is likely to achieve concrete results. Newer qualitative researchers may wish to seek help from more experienced investigators, adding them to a project part-time or as project consultants.

It is often a good idea to write proposals with others as a reality check on what is being proposed. A big advantage in working with others is that it helps to determine whether something is sensible, simple, and clear. One might find it useful to read aloud the draft of a research proposal to see just how easily general listeners can follow.

Although a daunting task, writing a proposal in isolation does permit the development of a distinctive authorial voice and sense of ownership. In cooperative writing with several investigators, a single senior writer supplying a unified authorial voice may be necessary for the sake of coherence and consistency. It helps to demonstrate that someone is responsible for the gamut of details.

Special Problems in Qualitative Proposal Writing

Writing qualitative research proposals poses several special problems. Among these are the extent that one need explain qualitative methods, the question of hypothesis specification, the problem of translating critical concepts into research language, and sampling issues.

How Much Must Qualitative Methods Be Explained?

The extent that one needs to explain qualitative research methods is a function of the funding organization, who the reviewers are, and the limitations placed by the agency on proposal form and length. For example, concerning this last issue, when there were no page limits for NIH proposals, I invariably included a long, complex discussion of the rationale and purpose of qualitative methods within the proposal proper. My proposals ran to 75 single-spaced pages or more. With the adoption of page limitations by federal agencies, I have cut such explanations in the main body of the proposal to rather brief statements such as "It is now generally recognized that qualitative methods are useful in gerontology for X, Y, and Z reasons." I note the epistemological flavor of qualitative research but relate the theory and details to one or two proposal appendixes. Reviewers may or may not choose to read such appendixes.

Some argue that discussions of the philosophy of qualitative research need no longer be spelled out in research proposals. Experienced multidisciplinary research committees generally are thought to be knowledgable enough, because they are by now familiar with qualitative research. This is an overly optimistic assessment. First, reviewers change. Once they are well educated in the peer-review process, they circulate off review committees, and new unseasoned members come on board. Second, the reality is that qualitative methods are still seen by many as somewhat exotic and quixotic and thus need all of the legitimation they can get. Where proposal formats do not invite extended explanation (for example, foundation grants with strict page limits and no permitted appendices), it is useful to take a few lines or paragraphs to give a philosophical overview of the methods and provide a related justification for their selection, along with appropriate references. Warranting qualitative research unfortunately is still necessary.

The Question of Hypothesis Specification

Proposal applications generally request the specification of research goals or aims; the description of or background to a problem, which will generally contain a literature review; a discussion of any pilot research leading to the proposal; and a designation of research methods, which includes a description of what the data will consist of, how they are to be collected, and how they will be analyzed. Some applications may require the inclusion of a detailed timeline, which is a good idea in any case.

Certain application formats mandate the inclusion of hypotheses. This can pose a difficulty for qualitative research because much qualitative research is descriptive, thematically analytical, or hypothesis-generating. Various strategies can be used to deal with this difference. An investigator may deliberately choose not to have one or more hypotheses and instead elaborate a descriptive and qualitative-analytic strategy, explaining and defending the decision in the proposal. One may adopt *qualitative hypotheses* or *qualitative expectations* to indicate what data analysis should yield and the analytic mechanisms that will be used to find the data. Or one may actually adopt several formal hypotheses, based entirely on qualitative modes of data analysis, and describe appropriate qualitative ways of testing them. Although the term *hypothesis* is not generally associated with qualitative research, thinking in terms of the sorts of issues and generalities that will come up and how these will be demonstrated is nonetheless useful in conceptualizing it.

Further, the investigator must plan carefully for the types of data required; the means of collecting, storing, and transcribing it; the method of managing data; and the way to analyze them. It is important not to present a boilerplate or generic data plan, but to instead show evidence of thought about and adaptation to the proposed research situation. For example, one may profitably include as appendixes the list of open-ended questions one proposes to use, as well as any related standardized items. It should be realized that what an investigator proposes to use in research and is funded for often ends up somewhat different from what is ultimately used.

Translating Critical Concerns Into
Standard Research Language

Standard social science research techniques commonly fail to empower informants and often represent class, ethnic, and gender-biased "ways of knowing." Many researchers see qualitative research as one means of countering such biases and empowering the other. Whatever private thoughts on such matters proposal reviewers may have, the values shared publicly by them appear to conform to the mainstream social science perspective in which research and scientific concepts are assumed to be privileged and separate from the world of, say, political discourse.

Investigators who use or think in terms of concepts derived from recent advances in critical social science need to pay special attention to both the packaging and scientific design aspects of their research. Strident, unexplicated, and politically frank research proposals have little chance of being funded, unless they yoke their social concerns to a scientific design that passes the muster of sober and systematic presentation. Another risk is involved in introducing political content: Some who review grants may simply personally disagree with it. If an investigator is willing to try to formulate issues in the language and concepts of the larger mainstream scientific community and to the extent that this community now tolerates or invites qualitative research, such a proposal can be evaluated on its scientific merit.

Some design strategies suggest themselves here. For example, if one has interest in a group of elders who are disadvantaged in some way or who have a socially stigmatized identity, then investigation may be appropriately scientized by the inclusion of a more normative qualitative-comparison group. Although the investigator may have a primary critical interest in only one of the groups, the comparison will add standard scientific balance to the design. In addition, there is little doubt that this will in fact enable the investigator to add an important degree of general insight to the understanding of the focal group.

Problems or understandings deriving from critical social science can be strategically rephrased so that overt political content is muted. For example, a concern with a political economy that engenders poverty and alienation can be reframed in the context of scientific questions concerning what people who inhabit particular social circumstances experience. This is a less strident phrasing that is contained in a humanitarian rather than a political vocabulary. Such rephrasing can be further scientized by attending to factual and statistical detail of the problem. The presentation of facts and statistics about any social problem in obsessive and even numbing detail is an acceptable and indeed desirable feature of proposal writing.

Further, justification of the use of qualitative methods in research proposal writing is amply and properly provided by appeals to our continuing need to understand and represent the subjective dimension of social problems, by the need for elders to share their experiences in their own voices and from their own perspectives. For example, in all of the mainstream research to date on filial caregiving to impaired elders, virtually no studies have considered the elders' views of being cared for.

Sampling Issues

A perennial issue in writing qualitative research proposals for main-stream reviewers is sampling and sample size. This "problem" exists for community- or organization-centered participant observation as well as informant-oriented, interview-based research. The issue is particularly knotty in that it may be especially difficult to "read" the views of a mixed-discipline review committee concerning what is an adequate or appropriate sample. In quantitative research there has been increasing concern with power analysis, especially in the context of modeling and other sophisticated statistical techniques, the question being, Are there enough subjects to empower one's variables?

What seems most difficult to explain to a review committee is that in much qualitative research, we do not really know beforehand how many informants will be needed to learn about a particular subject matter, and yet we do know when enough is enough. Those who review qualitative proposals may not appreciate the lack of specification. It may be difficult for them to accept what appear to be the capricious or subjective components of this process.

Qualitative researchers tend to think in terms of certain areas as either still productive or "mined out." Perhaps the best technical explanation of this has been offered by Bertaux and Bertaux-Wiame (1981; see also Glaser & Strauss, 1967), who describe the notions of *pattern saturation* or *theoretical saturation* in qualitative research: Inquiry stops when patterns become repetitive and materials are thematically saturated.

My own habit in specifying sampling strategies in qualitative proposals has been to describe in general the differences between quantitative and qualitative methodologies. Here is an explanation of sampling size from a qualitative research proposal I recently wrote:

Sample size. It is important to note that the approach taken here is one of ethnographic or qualitative sampling. As such, it differs in several ways from more standard types of sample. Foremost, the unit under study is personal meaning and experience. As such, instead of a relatively short, standardized interview with a larger number of subjects chosen to fit requirements of statistical procedures, ethnographic sampling usually relies on a smaller number of informants chosen to inform in detail about personal meaning and experience. Unlike standard sampling in which size is driven by the desired strength of significances or the number of variables in a model, ethnographic sampling is driven by the desire *to learn* in detail and in depth about the *experiences of individuals.* Such sampling has been called purposive, strategic, judgment sampling, or experiential or theoretical sampling.

In sum, we have no hard and fast rules about numbers because, in fact, an adequate sample size in qualitative research is linked to the unfolding conceptual consistency of the data and thematic pattern saturation. Qualitative research in old age and aging has used experiential cell sample sizes of from 10 to 100, with clustering around 50. Several writers (Bernard, 1988; Honigmann, 1970; Johnson, 1990; Pelto & Pelto, 1979; Strauss, 1987, 1990; Warwick & Lininger, 1975) have described various types of sampling procedure only generally described here.

Conclusion

The gradual acceptance of qualitative methods is based both on the proven ability of this approach to provide insight for a wide variety of human circumstances and on the increased sophistication and ability of these methods to connect with, augment, and provide findings independent of other research perspectives. In research on old age, aging, and later life, the opportunities for using qualitative techniques are many. These range from investigations of the setting and communities in which elders reside to the multifaceted institutions, such as health care settings, that affect them, and to such critical and nuanced entities as personal meaning, identity, and self-conception. Although the use of qualitative methods in old-age research initially represented a marginal perspective, these topics clearly are central to understanding aging as a cultural, social, experienced, and biological phenomenon. As qualitative aging research itself comes of age, investigators increasingly seek support in diverse ways. The preparation of informed, convincing, and well-planned research proposals is an important part of the growing enterprise.

References

Bernard, H. R. (1988). *Research methods in cultural anthropology.* Newbury Park, CA: Sage.

Bertaux, D., & Bertaux-Wiame, I. (1981). Life stories in the bakers' trade. In D. Bertaux (Ed.), *Biography and society: The life history approach in the social sciences* (pp. 169-189). Beverly Hills, CA: Sage.

Coley, S. M., & Scheinberg, C. A. (1990). *Proposal writing.* Newbury Park, CA: Sage.

Glaser, B., & Strauss, A. (1967). *The discovery of grounded theory.* Hawthorne, NY: Aldine.

Gubrium, J. F. (1992). Qualitative research comes of age in gerontology. *Gerontologist, 32,* 581-582.

Honigmann, J. (1970). Sampling in ethnographic fieldwork. In R. Naroll & R. Cohen (Eds.), *Handbook of method in cultural anthropology* (pp. 147-160). New York: Columbia University Press.

Johnson, J. (1990). *Selecting ethnographic informants.* Newbury Park, CA: Sage.

Keith, J. (1980). Participant observation. In C. Fry & J. Keith (Eds.), *New methods for old age research* (pp. 8-26). Chicago: Loyola University Press.

Locke, L. F., Spirduso, W., & Silverman, S. (1987). *Proposals that work: A guide for planning dissertations and grant proposals.* Newbury Park, CA: Sage.

Pelto, P., & Pelto, G. (1979). *Anthropological research.* New York: Cambridge University Press.

Rubinstein, R. (1992). Anthropological methods in gerontological research: Entering the world of meaning. *Journal of Aging Studies, 6,* 57-66.

Schumacher, D. (1992). *Get funded! A practical guide for scholars seeking research support from business.* Newbury Park, CA: Sage.

Strauss, A. (1987). *Qualitative analysis for the social sciences.* New York: Cambridge University Press.

Strauss, A. (1990). *Basics of qualitative research.* Newbury Park, CA: Sage.

Warwick, D., & Lininger, C. (1975). *The sample survey: Theory and practice.* New York: McGraw-Hill.

6

Managing Large Projects

LINDA S. MITTENESS
JUDITH C. BARKER

Qualitative research is sometimes thought to be synonymous with small-scale studies done by individual fieldworkers. From the earliest days of anthropological ethnographic work and the Chicago School of Sociology, path-breaking qualitative research has been done in relatively small-scale studies, with one fieldworker working in one circumscribed setting. Of course, there have always been the exceptions—from Redfield's (1941) work in the Yucatan, the Whitings' Six Cultures studies (Minturn & Lambert, 1964; Whiting & Whiting, 1975), the Sterling County Project in maritime Canada (Hughes, Tremblay, Rappaport, & Leighton, 1960; Leighton, Harding, Macklin, Macmillan, & Leighton, 1963; Leighton, 1959), through many of the long-term projects discussed by Foster, Scudder, Colson, and Kemper (1979), to Project AGE (Ikels, Keith, & Fry, 1988).

In today's research climate, where multidisciplinary collaboration and funding patterns encourage larger studies, the lone researcher is no longer so dominant. Although individual and small-scale research continue to be important, it is the rare researcher who is not at some time confronted with the need to participate in a large research project. Large-scale projects need specific skills that are crucial for successful qualitative research.

Qualitative research comes in many varieties. Studies may be based on ethnographic research, participant observation, structured observations, in-depth interviews, life histories, collection of archival records

82

or historical data, or some combination of these. Any of these methods may be used in either small-scale or large-scale projects. The theoretical, epistemological, or methodological paradigm underlying the study has a considerable effect on its scale.

Much qualitative research, especially that based in the grounded theory tradition (Glaser & Strauss, 1967; Strauss & Corbin, 1990), depends on emergent design procedures (Sandelowski, Davis, & Harris, 1989). Studies based on such epistemological and methodological models are unlikely to reach large scale.

In contrast, hypothesis-testing or comparative studies are more likely to be large projects. Whether the study focuses on comparing subgroups within a single population (e.g., men versus women) or on distinct communities (e.g., Project AGE; see Ikels et al., 1988), the comparative task itself creates a project of large scale.

Much of what we write in this chapter is as pertinent to research design and grant writing as it is to management. As other authors in this book and elsewhere (Bernard, 1988; Goetz & LeCompte, 1984; Marshall & Rossman, 1989) have elaborated on the design and grant aspects, we concentrate on management issues. Our advice is geared toward practical "nuts and bolts" issues. First, we examine what is meant by the term *large project* and ask, "Why do a large project?" Elements that increase the scale of a project are discussed next, followed by a section that examines three key points in successfully managing large projects: phasing the steps of the research, training and coordinating staff efforts, and ensuring the quality of data. We end by exploring when work with older populations creates specific management issues, what these are, and how they can be handled.

Examples come from one of our own studies, namely, an investigation of the management of chronic illness by community-living older people, with a special interest in the impact of urinary incontinence on daily life (Barker & Mitteness, 1988, 1990; Mitteness 1987a, 1987b, 1990a, 1990b; Mitteness & Wood, 1986). The semilongitudinal research design of the study involved accessing a sample of frail elderly people through a home health care agency. An initial (Time 1) extended, in-depth interview and completion of structured instruments to assess physical and cognitive functioning was followed by monthly telephone contacts. Six months after recruitment into the study, participants were again contacted in person at home for a follow-up (Time 2) intensive interview and completion of the same structured instruments. The sample was stratified by continence status and gender; a total of 211 older people participated.

For a while, we thought we had 212 respondents—until double-checking revealed one person was too young and had to be dropped from the sample. We could have lived with her inclusion if she had been 64 (because the minimum age was set at 65), but she was much younger (in her late 50s). This is just one of the myriad "goofs" possible in any project. Fortunately, with good management, most such errors can be detected and fixed before they ruin the investigation.

Large Projects: Why Do Them?

One of the most important questions to be asked at the research design phase of any study is, "Why on earth do a large project if a small project will meet my needs?" From our experience, the size of a research project must be carefully tailored to the research question. This may seem obvious, but many studies are damaged by a large-scale approach when a simple small-scale study was needed, just as some small studies try to answer questions that demand large-scale research. Time and money are wasted in doing something big when something small would suffice. Large-scale research certainly has no a priori virtue.

As with quantitative research designs, the bigger the project gets, the greater the management complexities. So, why do a large qualitative project? What can it do that a smaller one cannot? Choosing a large project is best when:

- one is interested in hypothesis testing and explanation and not just in exploratory research or hypothesis generation (with careful design, qualitative research is as rigorous and explanatory as survey research),
- random sampling or sample stratification are needed (e.g., such as for comparing two or more groups or stratifying by gender or age),
- investigating the range of variation within sampling cells (small samples in qualitative work are often reductionist in their search for shared universal and modal meanings rather than diversity or the range of meanings present),
- one is concerned with the effects of location or recruitment of participants on results (e.g., clinic versus community versus institutional populations), and
- there is a longitudinal design (and thus a concern with sample attrition).

Managing large projects is especially likely to become an issue for gerontological researchers because of three major defining characteristics of the subject matter: (a) the specific methodological dilemmas raised by asking age-related questions and the necessity of dealing with chronology, (b) the increasing centrality of gender and ethnicity as organizing constructs in contemporary gerontological models, and (c) the truism that the clearest understanding about aging is that as it increases, diversity among people increases.

Each factor leads researchers toward large-scale research. The inherent methodological difficulties of studying time-related phenomena have been discussed by many authors (e.g., Schaie, 1986). Essentially, to assert that some phenomenon is related to age, more than one age group must be studied. To make assertions about change over time, longitudinal studies are imperative and cross-sectional studies are wholly inadequate. Comparative studies (e.g., of gender or ethnicity-related issues) demand appropriate samples, usually leading to large sample sizes. Finally, any study needs to capture the full range of the phenomenon of interest. Because diversity among older people is so extensive, large samples are necessary for adequate analysis, whether we are speaking of statistical power or theoretical saturation. In each case, whether comparing age groups, studying change over time, or working with diverse groups of people, issues of scale quickly present project management problems that must be addressed.

Elements of Scale

A variety of elements of scale each require their own management talent. Large projects have at least one of the following characteristics:

- many research participants;
- more than one type of respondent;
- complex recruitment procedures;
- multiple investigators;
- many research aims, instruments, or disciplinary perspectives;
- more than one research site; and
- long duration with repeated contacts with participants.

Studies that share many of these characteristics are both large and complex (and may be classified as nightmares!).

Participants

The simplest approach to identifying large studies is to focus on the number of research participants: Large projects have more participants than do small studies. Any dividing point between large and small is an arbitrary figure, but qualitative research studies with 100 or more research participants share structural complexities that qualify them for the label of large projects. Complex recruitment procedures, and repeated contacts with participants, further complicate the size issue.

Although sample size is an important indicator, it is only one relatively simple aspect of scale. In research with sick or frail populations, scale is often magnified during the data-collection phases, because people are too ill or too tired to participate in the study, or their participation is intermittent because of energy or health limitations. Thus, a sample of 50 frail participants will be a larger project than a sample of 50 healthy participants. This needs to be considered when planning the time frame and work schedule. In our study, for example, 12% of the 211 subjects had to be visited on three or more separate occasions to complete what was labeled in the research design as the *initial* visit or the Time 1 interview. In fact, only just more than half (54%) of our sample of frail elderly people was able to complete the Time 1 interview in a single visit.

A corollary to this point about the effect of frailty is that decisions must be made before beginning the project about what are essential rather than what are merely desirable (albeit highly desirable) pieces of information. To exclude frail or sick informants with minimal energy from a study examining the impact of sickness is to bias it unduly; to subject them to exhausting interaction is unethical. The investigator must cope with varying information from some respondents. It is far better to have key data from all respondents, along with more detailed or contextualized information from a smaller number of subjects (that nevertheless still represents a good proportion of the sample, say, 75% or more), than to skew the sample. At Time 1, 94% of our respondents provided us with complete essential information (which we designated to be health beliefs and behaviors with respect to urinary conditions). Complete interviews (which included far more extensive sociodemographic, medical, and functional information) came from only 85% of the sample.

Investigating the perspectives of different classes of people within a single study make it larger in scale than works that concentrate on one group of respondents. The same is true for studies that use multiple methods or instruments. In our study, we interviewed older people, their physicians, and their caregivers (when present). In addition to semi-structured interviews with lots of open-ended questions and probes, we also gathered data through the use of checklists, standardized instruments, and structured observations. Coordinating and integrating the data from all of these sources is difficult, challenging, interesting, and frustrating. Torturous though the process is, the understanding that we now have is more complex and intricate than if we had limited ourselves to fewer classes of respondents and fewer methods of data collection.

Researchers

Large projects may use more than one fieldworker, requiring a team approach to data collection and analysis. Often these teams are multi-disciplinary, requiring special communication and negotiation skills. Early, detailed, and extensive discussion about differing theoretical underpinnings and assumptions, hypotheses, aims, methods, standards of evidence, and analytic procedures will go a long way toward circumventing problems. It is far better to prevent trouble by initially ironing out potential difficulties than to run into insoluble problems when it is often far too late to resolve them—that is, after the data have been collected.

The special difficulty of multiple investigators in qualitative research is that, until recently, data-collection and data-analysis procedures have not been carefully codified for qualitative research, with the arts of interviewing, observation, and especially analysis being individually based. Even in large-scale qualitative projects, the researcher is a key instrument that is a defining aspect of the fundamental outcomes of the study. When working with a group of investigators, a variety of special strategies must be used to make things work well. We discuss some of these strategies later.

Design Issues

Comparative studies that focus on two or more research sites are large-scale projects with a variety of special problems. These problems are especially magnified when the sites are culturally different or geographically separate from one another, particularly if geographic distance is compounded by the crossing of national borders. Thus a study comparing two nursing homes in the same state is complex, although probably much less complex than a study of nursing homes in two or more different societies. The crosscultural study has a long tradition in anthropology, and these studies should be consulted for insights into the complexities of large-scale crosscultural work. Ikels et al. (1988), in particular, have already generously shared the trials and tribulations of Project AGE, a large crosscultural project in gerontology in which different teams of researchers worked with diverse groups, such as Bushmen in the Kalahari desert, villagers in France, and suburban dwellers in the United States.

Sometimes studies may have only one investigator and a relatively small number of research participants—and still are highly complex for other reasons. Common causes of complexity are using a multiplicity of instruments or approaches to data collection, having to integrate quantitative and qualitative data, and the use of longitudinal designs.

As with any other research, when time is introduced as one of the analytic dimensions of the research questions, the scale of the project is markedly increased. Not only does the project have a long duration, with a need to schedule and coordinate the collection of successive waves of data, but also sample attrition becomes a prominent management issue, especially when researching with a sick or frail population. Approximately one third (36%) of our informants did not provide us with Time 2 data. Of the 65 people who completed Time 1 but not Time 2, 49% died in the intervening 6-month period, 8% were institutionalized, 11% could no longer pass the cognitive tests necessary for informed consent, 22% withdrew because they felt too ill to continue, and 11% were lost to follow-up because telephones were cut off or mail was returned.

Successful Management of Large Projects

The past decade has brought a tremendous improvement in the quantity and quality of literature on qualitative research (Bernard, 1988; Goetz & LeCompte, 1984; Lincoln & Guba, 1985; Miles & Huberman, 1984; Strauss, 1987). Some of this literature addresses project management as well as data collection and data analysis (e.g., Werner & Schoepfle, 1987), but most published work operates at one level of abstraction higher than we aim in this discussion. In a small project, the details of project management do not threaten to swamp a project in quite the same way as is possible in large projects. Therefore we think it necessary to speak at a very mundane, nuts-and-bolts level about procedures that keep a project afloat.

We have learned most of these things by doing them wrong at least once. The school of hard knocks is still open, and we have been attending for a long time now. Our students and research associates will recognize in this discussion a variety of things that we have done wrong in the past and some, hopefully few, that we have never successfully mastered and so chronically mangle.

Phasing Research Steps

Research studies usually are described as proceeding in the order of design and instrumentation, sampling, data collection, coding, and analysis. This sequence is not nearly so clear-cut in qualitative research, especially when emergent designs are involved. This murkiness creates special management requirements.

In qualitative research, one constructs feedback loops so that early analyses can change the focus of attention in later data collection and so forth. This is an advantage as it allows for fine tuning of instruments, for honing in from initial (more exploratory) ideas and interviews to later (more structured and hypothesis-testing) ideas and interviews. Most important of all, it allows for the *ethnographic veto* of some instruments, some designs, or types of analysis.

Negotiation of Entrée

One early (and ongoing) phase in any research project consists of the negotiation of entrée to the field and access to relevant data, establishing procedures to protect confidentiality, and the general interface of the research project and the community in which the research project takes place. Many researchers find that negotiation of entrée is something to be done repeatedly during a project. Large projects, especially those of some duration, probably will find their negotiating partners change time and again. In our work using the home health care agency, we ended up with two years of data collection. During that period, the administrator who was responsible for our access to the organization, changed four times. Each time, access was renegotiated, with each change resulting in less commitment on the part of the agency to the project. The initial vision of the project held by the director with whom we first negotiated was invisible to the administrators of the agency at the end of the project. By that time, not one administrative staff member that had been employed at the agency when we first arrived was still working at the agency. This amount of staff turnover is not uncommon in health care settings (or in many other research settings) and can have devastating effects on research projects.

One special aspect of relationship with gatekeepers relevant to large studies is the size of the research staff. It is important to make sure that both formal and informal gatekeepers (from the chief administrator to the file clerk) know that more than one person will be doing the research. Although research team members may understand the necessity for multiple fieldworkers, people in the field site may not share that understanding, unless it is explicitly discussed. It is much better to say, "There will be six of us doing this fieldwork, although there will never be more than two of us here on any one day" than to have the administrator call the principal investigator and say, "Just how many people are working with you? I don't want so many different faces here."

Do not assume that the person with authority to grant access to an institution or population will have informed other people what you are doing. At the beginning of the project, be prepared to reiterate in detail to everybody when you first encounter them what the purpose of the study is and the procedures being undertaken. This can be wearisome, but is absolutely essential to generating the goodwill and cooperation necessary to get the job done. The public relations problems of large studies are well discussed by Pelto (1970).

Integrating Data Sets

Most large projects face the difficulty of integrating data from several data sets into a single analysis or a sequence of analyses. This is common in all qualitative research when one brings to an analysis data from archives and documents, interviews, structured observations, and daily field notes. In large projects, the difficulty is compounded by scale and by the involvement of multiple researchers or sites.

The management task begins at the research-design phase, when sketches of the interrelations among data from diverse sources need to be developed. These sketches then become early drafts of analysis codebooks, which guide the construction of interviews and other data-entry procedures and later drive the analysis forward. For example, the proximity of a person's bedroom to bathroom (from observations on the physical environment of their home)—for example, up a flight of stairs—and their accounts of urinary behavior (from a structured interview protocol about actual behaviors)—for example, needing to micturate three times at night—and mobility impairment (from a standardized measure of functional ability)—for example, needing to use a walker to ambulate—gave us specific insights.

It is tempting to respond to the multiple data-set issue by analyzing each data set entirely separately. This has its usefulness, as each data set (interviews with particular classes of people, types of field notes, archival data, etc.) has its own integrity. However, until data sets are put together, the full richness of a large project is invisible.

Codebook Construction

The codebook for a large project becomes a multilayered "map" of the data and of the work done in analysis. The construction of a codebook not only documents the coding criteria for particular topical or thematic codes, but also documents the sequence of analysis decisions. This, of course, begins when the project is in the design phase and continues through data collection and analysis. All members of the research staff participate in codebook construction through the documentation of their data-collection and data-analysis difficulties.

For example, we were interested in how people whose urination was no longer under voluntary control managed their bladder functions. Based on information from the first respondents, we developed a code for various urine-collecting strategies. Called "Appliance," this code was subdivided by type of device and degree of personal control over it:

1. in-dwelling catheter
2. external catheter
3. intermittent self-catheterization
4. diapers

We thought that covered the range. Six months into the study, however, we encountered yet another way to have no voluntary control over urination: Informant number 51 was on dialysis because of chronic renal failure, and like all such people she simply did not urinate. So we had to redefine "urination not under voluntary control" and add another subdivision to the Appliance code:

5. dialysis

Interviewers and fieldworkers are more successful and happier when they participate in analysis. The quality of the data collected is also improved. However, the complexity of codebook construction and data analysis sometimes lead to the need for staff changes if the skills of the interviewer, observer, or fieldworker are not up to the analytic tasks. In the ideal world, every interviewer would have or could be trained in analysis skills. Few of us live in an ideal world, so we do change staff as necessary. This fragmentation of tasks makes continuity and staff commitment of concern.

Mixing Qualitative and Quantitative Data

One complexity of large projects is that we are often drawn into mixing qualitative and quantitative analyses. The complexities of such mixed approaches deserve a chapter of their own; we will not dwell on them here. Other authors have addressed this issue (Brewer & Hunter, 1989; Connidis, 1981, 1983; Marshall, 1981; Pillemer, 1988). For now, however, the analyst needs to be able to move between types of data sets with ease. A major help in such movement is the existence of an overarching data-analysis codebook that explains the origin, coding, and analytic level of every data set used in the study. It is also very important to have, if at all possible, a project manager who is present throughout the entire project.

It is a great temptation to introduce structured, normative instruments into the data-collection procedures of large projects. The reasons for this are complex. These projects tend to be multidisciplinary and need to speak to a variety of audiences. The information from such instruments provides a rich backdrop against which to display ethnographic findings. Such instruments provide a sense of coherence and structure to a project that can easily feel as if it is teetering on the brink of total disorganization. So structured instruments can have many rewards, but be mindful that they also create a need for yet another level of management.

The researcher will find many instances where the data obtained from the structured instruments differ from those obtained by observation or intensive interview. Do not automatically assign higher "truth value" to one data-gathering mode or another. For instance, we found that in completing a self-report functional-status measure, an informant indicated that he does his own shopping independently. Yet reliable observations and interview data make it clear that he regularly had someone else do his shopping. Fundamental decisions need to be made about the reliability of data and the resolution of such conflicts. Sometimes keeping the scale response is appropriate, and sometimes keeping the observational response is appropriate: The decision depends on what is being attempted and what fundamental questions are being addressed.

Training and Coordination of Staff Efforts

Most large projects require the dedicated work of more than one researcher, whether a team of fieldworkers or a large staff of people with differing research tasks. The use of a team approach demands heightened attention to training, documentation, communication, and ownership or authorship.

A key aspect in training staff members is to involve them early and often in discussions about the project and about their specific tasks: Why are we doing X activity? What does it contribute? Where does it fit with what else is being done? How will it help us achieve our analytic goals? What are my specific tasks? How can I best accomplish them? Seek staff input so that procedures make sense to them. Check their work regularly for conformance with the project's guidelines.

In a team project, research goals, research design, and analysis strategies cannot remain implicit: They must be known to all and be well documented. Communication and documentation of changes and coordination of research phases is an absolute must, because they affect directly the feedback loops, the ethnographic veto, and shifts from exploration to hypothesis testing. Such changes in focus or direction must be documented. A written summary of research goals is of immense value throughout a project.

One key to the success of a team project is communication. Regular meetings are vital for sharing ideas, data, and frustrations. Staff meetings have several functions; these should not be confused with one another and yet they should all receive attention. These functions include:

- keeping all research staff members focused on the same research goals, which ensures common definitions and approaches and reinforces previous training and decisions (e.g., making sure that all interviewers know which is essential rather than desirable information);

- passing essential information between staff members (e.g., a change in an interview protocol or recruitment procedure);
- bringing analysis to the fore (e.g., by constantly focusing on why and how certain data or events address, clarify, expand, or complicate specific research questions);
- preventing "instrument" decay (e.g., by incorporating the insights of individual members into the analysis and encouraging staff members to be reflective and reflexive); and
- making coding and analysis decisions that are comprehensible to the entire group (e.g., reducing errors in coding because everyone understands the basis for a coding decision).

For the individual researcher, much analysis takes place in the interstices of writing and reviewing field notes, coding, and introspective thinking while driving, eating, or trying to sleep. As the research team increases the number of people involved, these periods of thinking about analysis and doing analysis need to be communicated and coordinated among several people.

Specialization by team members in various phases of research can be a strength, but this means extra effort must go into training and coordination. Specialization can be achieved in several ways: by timing data collection, timing data analysis, topical foci, and site.

Ownership and Authorship Issues

Julius Roth (1966) identified several problems with "hired hand" research—that is, research done using multiple fieldworkers (often, graduate students) who are not particularly invested in the research outcomes. Large projects follow a variety of models of relationship among researchers, from strictly hierarchical models, where the principal investigator is the only person with an investment in the project, to fully collaborative research, where all participants share equally in decision making, work, and responsibility. Most projects lie somewhere between these two extremes. In our experience, the more fully involved the individual researchers, the more productive the project. Of course, some research assistants are temporary participants in a project, with no real interest in the outcomes or in any payback to themselves other than a paycheck. Most qualitative research staff members, however, are highly skilled professionals who need to feel some sense of ownership of the work they are doing. Most important, it must be perfectly clear when someone joins a project whether his or her participation will be at the mundane or the fully involved level. This must be discussed clearly at the beginning, or bad feelings and poor work relationships will inevitably ensue.

Our policy is to explain to research staff members that a research project has X number of components and that authorship in papers is shared to the extent that people participate in multiple components. Generally, we feel if someone has contributed three types of work (e.g., interviewing, coding, and analysis; or, design, analysis, and writing), then he or she is eligible to be a coauthor. Further, we generally offer new research staff members the option to develop some part of the project as their own individual work responsibility—that is, to choose a domain of special interest and, under our guidance, to develop its analysis and write-up. This is the *niche* concept that Foster et al. (1979, p. 339) refer to when discussing long-term field research in anthropology.

Ownership of work or products and ownership of data are quite distinct. A person who leaves a team at the end of a particular project can legitimately expect to be an author on work arising from the project. But this does not confer rights to take copies of data on departure. Ownership of data must be negotiated carefully and separately from the issue of ownership of work or products.

When peers engage in collaborative research, these issues of ownership and participation become even more acutely important than when dealing with graduate student assistants or professional research staff members. Ownership of data, authorship, and degree of participation in the various phases of the research must be discussed explicitly. Innumerable projects have been ruined or have been miserable experiences because the participants did not agree in advance about such issues. We routinely create letters of agreement between ourselves and potential collaborators to force us to discuss these issues and to keep a record of our decisions. Such agreements often need to be renegotiated as circumstances of the project and people's lives change. These agreements have forestalled significant distress on more than one occasion.

Ensuring Data Quality

Coordinating, storing, and integrating data is a major management task. We have found that this is best undertaken by an individual who is not actively involved in the nitty gritty of data collection (such as actually conducting interviews) but who is able to keep the broad picture in mind—that is, someone who is literally able to oversee the project. Our central controller, for example, designed forms and flow sheets to record progress in completing the various phases of the research with diverse types of respondents or sources of information; meticulously recorded the recruitment process so we knew who was eligible to participate, who refused, and who did not reply; scheduled contacts, including telephone calls and Time 2 follow-up visits; logged the completion of protocols and reasons for failure to maintain contact or secure all information; coordinated staff efforts to collect data from various respondents (e.g., physicians, caregivers, and family); organized the timely review of archival records; and devised storage and retrieval systems and tracked the passage of data (interview protocols, tapes, and transcripts) between interviewers, transcribers, coders, and analysts.

This seems unimportant: perhaps just time-wasting, unnecessary "housekeeping." Ignore such mundane chores at your peril. These tasks are central to successful management. If you do not take deliberate charge in this fashion, you run the risk of losing control, of not knowing who has done what, with whom, and when; what data exist, where they are, what state of analysis they are in, who is working on them, or what remains to be done.

Management of Large Quantities of Data

By their very nature, large projects generate lots of data. Combined with the fact that qualitative data tend to be bulky and lengthy, this leads to the cardinal rule of project management: Every piece of paper (or its electronic equivalent) must have written on it the project or subproject title (or both), the researcher's name or initials, a description of the analysis or idea, and a date. For the single investigator, the name may be optional. This rigid rule applies to data coding, notes about staff meetings, field notes, and random scribbles that are created in the heat of the creative process. Every research assistant we have ever worked with has first thought this silly, but everyone eventually learns the hard way that what is written on a piece of paper loses meaning unless one knows when it was written, by whom, and for what purpose. Frequently, it is impossible to reconstruct the sequence of coding decisions that have led to a particular conclusion unless this documentation is available.

Other researchers (e.g., Foster et al., 1979) also have strongly emphasized this need to document, standardize, collate, and organize notes,
codes, analyses, and theoretical ideas so that when one returns to data
after an absence (of any duration from months to decades) the process
by which the study was performed is transparent and comprehensible.

Computers and Database Management

The sheer volume of data created in large projects calls for more specialized management tools. Computerized database-management systems are absolutely vital to today's large-scale qualitative research
project. They are used for a variety of tasks, ranging from keeping
track of multiple research sites and data-collection tasks in those sites,
through producing reminders for scheduling participant interviews in
a longitudinal study, to managing field notes and other diverse pieces
of data.

The choices available fall into a variety of classes:

- flat-file database managers (where the program operates only within a
  single file),
- relational database-management systems (where the program can operate
  across several or many individual files—that is, can relate files to another),
- text-database managers,
- qualitative analysis-assistance programs,
- indexing programs, and
- word-processing programs.

In choosing programs, we find that two general rules are helpful.
First, because one of the most onerous aspects of qualitative research is
writing field notes, the computer program for managing them should be
as transparent as possible, requiring so little from the fieldworker that
all she or he has to do is the intense cognitive work of preparing the
notes without worrying about formatting or meeting other computer
program conventions. Second, use the simplest computer programs
possible. If a program is so complex to use that the learning curve is
lengthy, then only one research team member probably will learn the
program. If a significant portion of the data or the analysis is accessible
only through that computer program, then research comes to a halt if
the knowledgeable team member is absent. One major problem with
relational database systems is the difficulty in learning to use them. It

is infuriating to have one's data in a database system and not be able to get at them because you have not spent six months learning the program. Similarly, with word-processing programs, do not buy a desk-top-publishing program if you just want to produce text. This "simple is best" rule is especially important when you are working with a large research team. The time required to train new staff members on three or four complex computer systems is time taken away from research.

Computers are useful, but obsessing about which tools to use is effective only for avoiding work. We have known people to spend months debating about which software package to choose and only minutes actually planning a research design or an analysis. Basically, almost any software package will work if you learn the program well enough to take advantage of its features. To know if the package has the capabilities and features you need, you first have to spend time planning, going right down to the nitty gritty, a detailed analysis plan and management procedures. Once you have a detailed picture of what you are going to do, choosing between software packages becomes a matter of the best match among plans, program capabilities, economics, and personal preferences.

We have known researchers who swear by specific database programs, others who will only use tools specifically designed for qualitative text manipulation, and still others who cannot seem to see beyond a word-processing package. Some people do very well simply with a word-processing program and or a qualitative analysis-assistance program. It largely depends on the style of research and the management demands of specific study designs. We use a word-processing program, a flat-file database manager, a statistical package, and a text-based qualitative assistance program, and we are experimenting with an indexing program.

Comparability of Data

When a research project is the product of multiple researchers or a single researcher working in multiple sites, then comparability of data across researcher and site becomes a major concern. Whether doing ethnographic observation or highly structured interviews, training researchers to see and record in the same way is a vital step in the research process. When research sites are culturally different from one another, as in crosscultural studies, the problems caused by the competing demands of comparable data and within-site integrity of the data are significant. Ikels et al. (1988) have done an exemplary job of addressing this issue for gerontological research, based on their experience with Project AGE. Foster et al. (1979) also have discussed these issues in relation to a variety of long-term anthropological field research projects.

Time as a Troublemaker

The duration of large projects, if extended, causes two problems for the researcher. The first is a real risk of historical changes in the phenomenon under study. If these changes are situated outside of the sphere of investigation, they are likely to be invisible to the research team. In our research on the management of urinary incontinence by elderly people, a series of studies that spanned eight years of data collection, two major historical changes had a direct impact. Fortunately, both changes were situated within the sphere of our study, so we could see their effects.

In the middle of the first year of study, after half of our initial sample had been interviewed, companies producing adult diapers suddenly began advertising on television and selling their products in grocery stores. This was providential for us, because we could observe the response of our older informants and could investigate various aspects of the issue as part of our study. The second historical change came when diagnosis-related groups (DRGs) were introduced as Medicare reimbursement guidelines just as we were beginning the project using home health care clients. We were lucky that this happened early in the study because these regulations had a profound impact on the health status of the clientele of home health care agencies. If it had happened in the middle of the study, we would have had a nice "natural experiment" on our hands, but we also would have found that people in the first part of the sample were quite different in certain key health indicators than later study participants.

Historical changes that are out of one's control but in one's awareness have analytic value. Historical changes that are invisible are deadly. For example, studies of classroom interactions often use intensive observations and qualitative analysis methods (Miles & Huberman, 1984). If a long-term investigation is planned, then historical changes in divorce rates of young parents or state funding for public schools, both of which can be expected to have major impact on children's well-being and behavior, can have fatal effects on the quality of a study by confounding changes because of age, educational interventions, or other variables of interest with these secular trends that are powerful but perhaps invisible to the investigator. The second time-related concern is with a problem we may call (in concert with our quantitative colleagues) *instrument decay*. The qualitative researcher's instrument is his or her own self. More research skills are wrapped up in the person of the interviewer and in feedback loops so vital in qualitative research than in data derived from questionnaires or survey materials. Thus over time the researcher will inevitably change and begin acting in the research setting in a way different from her or his initial stance. This is natural and to be expected, and if the researcher is reflective enough, the change can itself be a research tool.

Being reflective enough is no easy task, even for experienced researchers. Furthermore, when more than one investigator is working on a project, this evolving experience and stance is magnified into multiple changing positions. As previously mentioned, coordination and communication of reflection on how the research team is changing is a complex but vital management issue.

Problems With Writing

The use of research teams rather than the lone investigator has one particular risk for large projects. Some way must be found to keep the research team together through the writing phases of the study. In many studies, the money runs out before the books and articles are written. In studies where all data are clearly and simply quantified, this is not an analytically fatal problem, because the remnants of the research team can analyze data and write up the results in physically separate places. The introduction of electronic communications systems, including electronic mail (E-mail) and facsimile devices (e.g., fax machines), has greatly enhanced this capacity. But in qualitative research, where data collection, analysis, and write-up are intertwined in a different way, the loss of the research team before the writing is finished has a dampening effect on the quality and quantity of the output because the researchers are the major study instruments. The magnitude of this loss can be minimized through strategies to enhance documentation of research procedures, coding decisions, and so forth, but manuscripts written or at least reviewed by all members of the research team are inevitably going to be richer and of higher quality than those written by one person who did not do every piece of the report's research and analysis.

Large Projects in Gerontological Research

Are there special problems in managing large research projects involving older populations? Yes, but many such problems stem as much or more from the normative pressures of the gerontological enterprise than from intrinsic attributes of older people themselves.

Management concerns generated by working with older populations are manyfold. First, more than in younger populations (where proportionately less research attention is devoted to health-related issues), in older populations the reasons for refusal to participate in a study are often of central interest in the research (e.g., a person feels too tired or weak or does not have resources). This makes recruitment of subjects and comparison of refusers with participants and with those lost to contact crucial aspects that need careful monitoring. Second, access to community-living samples of older people can be difficult. Often there is no easy route. Work settings, voluntary organizations, clinics, and so forth do not allow access to a sample of *all* elderly people. Thus it is very easy to bias samples toward the healthy *or* the sick. Unless it is pertinent to the research questions under investigation, such bias must be rigorously guarded against. Third, sometimes there is pressure to use particular instruments that are common in the literature but which are highly reactive and thus interfere with data collection and quality. These instruments also are sometimes insufficiently established as valid or reliable for specific older subpopulations (e.g., using the CESD for measuring depression, particularly among lower-class, nonwhite, or non-English-speaking older people). Finally, by virtue of age alone, and usually without a shred of theoretical or practical justification, there is pressure to get data on particular topics even if they are irrelevant to the study's focus or research questions (e.g., testing cognitive status in a study of economic-investment strategies in people aged 65 or more who are running their own small businesses).

Interviewing

Sometimes older informants are not used to being interviewed and so must be taught how to let an interviewer guide the research conversations that make up the major data-gathering techniques of qualitative research. This is usually not a difficult task, however.

When dealing with a frail or sick population, project time management is different than with a healthy population. Interviews may take a little longer to accomplish because of respondents' limited energy. There is a shorter window of opportunity for scheduling interviews. For example, we could only interview between approximately 10:30 a.m. and 3:30 p.m. It takes that long in the morning for people to get through their routines and into free time; by midafternoon, they are tiring or are preparing for evening meals and bed.

As Pelham and Clark (1986) demonstrate, an interviewer has to be willing to adopt many roles when studying older people: from being a friendly visitor or good neighbor; through acting as confidante, information and referral resource, and advocate; to being a formal researcher. Flexibility and empathy are vital to establishing rapport and to obtaining good quality data. Empathy involves chatting about local issues or family news, consuming specially made cookies, drinking innumerable cups of tea or coffee, mailing letters, graciously rescheduling forgotten appointments, tolerating querulous and sundry complaints, and patiently sorting through digressions and side comments to get to the nub of the story. All of these are time-consuming activities that wreak havoc with neat management schedules, and yet they are absolutely vital to establishing rapport. Once good rapport is established, then large projects run smoothly and are enjoyable for all, subjects and researchers alike.

Advocate Role

The role of advocate for the older person is a tricky one, because it can involve serious ethical dilemmas. What if a researcher receives an account that makes her or him suspect the informant is being abused or neglected, is actively suicidal, or is in dire straits of some nature? What does the researcher do? What responsibility does she or he have? Under what circumstances, and to whom, are these suspicions reported?

These are difficult issues. They are not just idle and speculative comments: They reflect actual dilemmas that we encountered. The first step we took was extensive discussion of the case by all team members to clarify what was actually known, what was merely suspected, and what the possible outcomes would be if no action were taken by us. This was accompanied by some unobtrusive checking of the informant's account with the staffs of agencies providing services or with family members, as appropriate. In two cases, the informants' claims could not be substantiated, so we took no further action. In one case, however, we informed a mental health agency. It turned out that, unknown to us, some years earlier the informant had had extensive contact with that agency for a similar reason. Because of our action, the agency was able again to offer timely intervention.

Conclusion

The management of large projects is not merely an administrative task but is integral to all phases of research design, data collection, and analysis. Although the actual procedures used by researchers or research teams will differ, the ultimate goal is the clear articulation and documentation of the research process. Once this has been achieved, the likelihood of timely productivity of a project is greatly enhanced.

References

Barker, J. C., & Mitteness, L. S. (1988). Nocturia in the elderly. *Gerontologist, 28,* 99-104.

Barker, J. C., & Mitteness, L. S. (1990). Invisible caregivers in the spotlight: Non-kin caregivers of frail older adults. In J. F. Gubrium & A. Sankar (Eds.), *The home care experience: Ethnography and policy* (pp. 101-127). Newbury Park, CA: Sage.

Bernard, H. R. (1988). *Research methods in cultural anthropology.* Newbury Park, CA: Sage.

Brewer, J., & Hunter, A. (1989). *Multimethod research: A synthesis of styles.* Newbury Park, CA: Sage.

Connidis, I. (1981). The stigmatizing effects of a problem orientation to aging research. *Canadian Journal of Social Work Education, 7*(2), 9-19.

Connidis, I. (1983). Integrating qualitative and quantitative methods in survey research on aging: An assessment. *Qualitative Sociology, 6*(4), 334-352.

Foster, G. M., Scudder, T., Colson, E., & Kemper, R. V. (Eds.). (1979). *Long-term field research in social anthropology.* New York: Academic Press.

Glaser, B., & Strauss, A. L. (1967). *The discovery of grounded theory.* Chicago: Aldine.

Goetz, J. P., & LeCompte, M. D. (1984). *Ethnography and qualitative design in educational research.* New York: Academic Press.

Hughes, C. C., Tremblay, M. A., Rappaport, R. N., & Leighton, A. L. (1960). *People of cove and woodlot.* New York: Basic Books.

Ikels, C., Keith, J., & Fry, C. L. (1988). The use of qualitative methodologies in large-scale cross-cultural research. In S. Reinharz & G. D. Rowles (Ed.), *Qualitative gerontology* (pp. 274-298). New York: Springer.

Leighton, A. L. (1959). *My name is Legion.* New York: Basic Books.

Leighton, D., Harding, J. S., Macklin, D. B., Macmillan, L. M., & Leighton, A. L. (1963). *The character of danger.* New York: Basic Books.

Lincoln, Y. S., & Guba, E. G. (1985). *Naturalistic inquiry.* Beverly Hills, CA: Sage.

Marshall, C., & Rossman, G. B. (1989). *Designing qualitative research.* Newbury Park, CA: Sage.

Marshall, V. (1981). Participant observation in a multiple-methods study of a retirement community: A research narrative. *Mid-American Review of Sociology, 11*, 29-44.

Miles, M. B., & Huberman, A. M. (1984). *Qualitative data analysis: A sourcebook of new methods.* Beverly Hills, CA: Sage.

Minturn, L., & Lambert, W. (1964). *Mothers of six cultures.* New York: John Wiley.

Mitteness, L. S. (1987a). The management of urinary incontinence by community-living elderly. *Gerontologist, 27*, 185-193.

Mitteness, L. S. (1987b). So what do you expect when you're 85? Urinary incontinence in late life. In J. A. Roth & P. Conrad (Eds.), *The experience and management of chronic illness: Research in the sociology of health care* (Vol 6., pp. 177-219). Greenwich, CT: JAI.

Mitteness, L. S. (1990a). Knowledge and beliefs about urinary incontinence in adulthood and old age. *Journal of the American Geriatrics Society, 38*, 374-378.

Mitteness, L. S. (1990b). Consequential myths about urinary incontinence. *The Southwestern: The Journal of Aging for the Southwest, 6*(2), 19-30.

Mitteness, L. S., & Wood, S. J. (1986). Social workers' responses to incontinence, confusion and mobility impairments in frail elderly clients. *Journal of Gerontological Social Work, 9*(3), 63-78.

Pelham, A. O., & Clark, W. F. (1986). Interviewing challenges of the California senior survey. In A. O. Pelham & W. F. Clark (Eds.), *Managing home care for the elderly: Lessons from community-based agencies* (pp. 117-139). New York: Springer.

Pelto, P. J. (1970). *Anthropological research: The structure of inquiry.* New York: Harper & Row.

Pillemer, K. (1988). Combining qualitative and quantitative data in the study of elder abuse. In S. Reinharz & G. D. Rowles (Eds.), *Qualitative gerontology* (pp. 256-273). New York: Springer.

Redfield, R. (1941). *Folk cultures of the Yucatan.* Chicago: University of Chicago Press.

Roth, J. A. (1966). Hired hand research. *American Sociologist, 1*(4), 190-196.

Sandelowski, M., Davis, M. H., & Harris, B. G. (1989). Artful design: Writing the proposal for research in the naturalist paradigm. *Research in Nursing and Health, 12*(2), 77-84.

Schaie, K. W. (1986). Beyond calendar definitions of age, time, and cohort: The general developmental model revisited. *Developmental Review, 6*, 252-277.

Strauss, A. L. (1987). *Qualitative analysis for social scientists.* Cambridge, UK: Cambridge University Press.

Strauss, A. L., & Corbin, J. (1990). *Basics of qualitative research: Grounded theory procedures and techniques.* Newbury Park, CA: Sage.

Werner, O., & Schoepfle, G. M. (1987). *Systematic fieldwork* (Vols. 1, 2). Newbury Park, CA: Sage.

Whiting, B., & Whiting, J. W. (1975). *Children of six cultures.* Cambridge, MA: Harvard University Press.

7

Consequences for Research Procedure

JENNIE KEITH

Qualitative approaches have a suffusing effect on research design similar to the *complete immersion* involvement they require from their practitioners. This chapter describes the consequences for research procedure that follow from a choice of qualitative methods for collecting data.

The research conditions that most clearly call for qualitative methods are: a limited amount of previous research to guide a new study, an emphasis on meaning and the perspective of participants in the context to be studied, a need for understanding of a social setting as a whole, and the impossibility of using quantitative strategies. Current research in aging and old age frequently fits at least one of these criteria and often more than one (Keith, 1980, 1982).

Many experiences of persons who are old now are unprecedented in the history of our species socially or physiologically. Exploratory research is thus often necessary before more focused study can begin, for example, on the experiences of the "old old" or of elderly who attend college, enter retirement residences, join mobile-home clubs, or follow fitness regimens. Most lacking in research on old age and aging are the points of view of the diverse individuals who are aging or old. Misleading generalizations about old people or old age derive directly from this lack of information about meaning. For research related to service delivery or policy analysis, data about the assumptions, values, and wishes of intended recipients are essential. The impossibility of more quantitative approaches may result from illiteracy, inexperience with the testing techniques encountered in school, or risk of biasing results by cultural assumptions built into highly structured instruments. These constraints may be encountered in work with contemporary cohorts of old persons in industrial societies as well as in many less technologically developed areas of the world.

Consequences of qualitative data collection for research design span the entire process from application for funding to the interpretation and presentation of data.

Proposals for Funding

Authors of research proposals that include qualitative methods have a heavier burden of description and explanation than those whose proposals rely on methods more widely used across the social and natural sciences (see Chapter 4). Exploratory research offers a special challenge because it is by definition impossible to include any but the broadest questions and nothing close to hypotheses or operationalized measures for concepts that are yet to be discovered. The key to successful presentation of qualitative methods is to deliver a detailed program of research goals and, for each goal, the associated activities and type of resulting data, divided into chronological stages and exemplified with specific reference to other work by the author or in the literature. *Participant observation* or *guided conversation* do not conjure up familiar images of a fieldworkers' words, actions, and recording techniques for many of the professional gerontologists who are likely to review a request for funding. Proposals must take this into account and make as explicit as possible what the qualitative researcher will be doing, and to what end, in each stage of the project, as well as the logical connections between these stages.

Structure and Timing

These connections among the various goals and activities of a research effort are not likely to be solely linear when qualitative methods of data collection are included. The qualitatively oriented research process as a whole is less a linear sequence than a holistic activity in which different aspects of inquiry are more and less intense but always interrelated. Collection and interpretation of information, for example, does not occur in linear sequence as it might when data are elicited through a survey administered by one set of workers and then transferred to another group for electronic storage and yet another for statistical analysis. In a project that collects qualitative data such as life stories, for example, neither the process nor the personnel is likely to be as temporally segmented and specialized.

Interviewers more typically engage simultaneously in data collection and interpretation (Luborsky, 1987; Luborsky & Rubinstein, 1987). As interviews are completed, they are transcribed and discussed by the interviewers in search of themes in meetings interspersed with the ongoing schedule of interviews. There are several reasons for this timing. First, qualitative data are often collected through more than one session with a given respondent, and it is often important to follow up in subsequent sessions on information either present or absent in an earlier interview. In the relatively unstructured interview format used to elicit qualitative information, for instance, it is difficult to be sure whether a specific topic or theme has been omitted because it has low salience for the respondent or because the flow of the session led elsewhere. Thus it is important to read and discuss an interview at the point in the project when it is still possible to explore the missing theme in another session. Second, in some projects using qualitative data collection, the decision about adequate number of cases is made based on evidence of *saturation,* which occurs when additional cases no longer introduce new themes.

The holistic structure and timing of research involving qualitative data have implications of their own for research design and its presentation. This research is typically very time-consuming, especially if this is viewed as a ratio of research time to number of subjects. It is important to include in a research design adequate time for the management of lengthy texts and the many hours of discussion required for a team of researchers to make the collective judgments throughout the intertwined processes of data collection and interpretation. Continuity of the research team over the history of an entire research project also has great importance because of the shared learning process that must take place as meanings are gradually discovered in a corpus of qualitative information (see Chapter 9). It is important to point out these issues in justifying a budget for qualitative research.

Technology

Great advances have been made in computer-assisted techniques for managing texts. This means that computer equipment and software have an important role in contemporary qualitative studies. Specialized software for the manipulation and analysis of texts is a major tool for the interpretation of data collected in interviews or as notes on observations. Texts can be searched for frequency of themes and reordered in various ways depending on the specific research question. A relational database is an essential tool if qualitative data are to be translated into numeric codes or linked with quantitative information such as scores on psychological tests or economic or demographic data. The database must be able to store in its fields substantial text as well as numbers. The relational feature is important because bulky text files can be created separately for strictly textual interpretation and then temporarily joined ("related") to files with numeric information such as ages, incomes, or survey responses. During various stages of analysis it is invaluable to be able to view subsets of texts that should display different characteristics, according to a research hypothesis. For example, in the Project AGE research, we expected to find variation across our sites in both the content and the degree of difference between men's and women's views of reasons for well-being as expressed at various stages of life. It was important for us to be able to examine texts that described reasons for well-being separately by gender and by age. Computer equipment must also have storage space and speed to support these procedures. For many qualitative research projects, equipment should include portable computers with hard drives for fieldworkers, desktop computers with hard drives for the research office, tape recorders for interviewers, transcribing machines (with foot controls and headphones) for the office, and software for word processing, text management, and the creation of a relational database (Bernard, 1988).

Personal Demands

The individuals who collect qualitative data also must prepare for demands of initiating, maintaining, and withdrawing from the human relationships that are key in the methodologies they use (Shaffir & Stebbins, 1991). Although the relationships are of different scope and duration, both in-depth interviewing and participant observation depend on establishing rapport between researcher and respondent. These demands must be taken into account in the training and debriefing of researchers. In projects involving particularly painful topics such as bereavement or disabling disease, some research teams have included professional counseling for interviewers and observers, usually at the point when they must exit from a relationship developed during the research.

Qualitative Data in Comparative Research

Strategies for both the collection and interpretation of qualitative data are now available in various sources (Bernard, 1988; Keith, 1980). However, little critical attention has been directed to the implications of qualitative data for comparative research. Comparative research that includes qualitative data is a pressing need in gerontology. Without it the danger is very great that generalizations about human aging will be skewed—if not by the lack of information about diverse cultural contexts, then by the collection and interpretation of that information through quantitative strategies that distort it. The following sections present implications of qualitative data for comparative research, with examples from Project AGE, a recently completed comparative study of aging in Africa, Ireland, the United States, and Hong Kong (Draper & Keith, 1992; Ikels et al., 1992; Keith, Fry, & Ikels, 1990).

Two characteristics of research involving qualitative data create distinctive challenges for comparative research design. First, qualitative data are often collected to present the perspective of the individual or group being studied. The standardization of definitions and measures usually seen as prerequisite to systematic comparison thus may be in direct opposition to the goals of eliciting qualitative data. Second, the reliance on immersion in a text or field site as a basis for judgments about meanings to be coded from qualitative texts is not compatible with the usual "intercoder reliability" evaluation used to legitimate comparative analysis.

The special challenges of using qualitative data in comparative analysis can be summed up as the attempt to balance the cultural validity of the data on the one hand and the reliability of the comparison on the other. These map closely onto the balance of qualitative (focus for evaluation of validity) and quantitative (focus for evaluation of reliability) data in a research design. This is not simply a balance in amounts of either type of data that are collected or displayed and interpreted.

Rather, the more difficult and more critical balance in views of qualitative and quantitative data is in terms of their relative influence on evaluation of data quality. Another way to say this is that in research that is both cultural and comparative, the key questions about data quality have to do not only with the quality of each type of data, but also, and most important, with the balance of validity for the cultural data and reliability for the comparison.

Balance is the important word here, as distinct from sequence or choice. Frequently the issue of balance is not adequately addressed because the relationship between qualitative and quantitative data is defined as linear or sequential. Because the collection of these two kinds of data occurs at two separate stages of the research, it may be assumed that issues of data quality also can be addressed separately and the issue of the balance between validity and reliability is consequently bypassed.

Quantitative crosscultural comparisons using large data files (hologeistic research) are good examples of the sequential relationship: Validity of the cultural information consulted is assessed at the beginning of the project in terms of the quality of the original fieldwork and used as a basis for inclusion or exclusion from the sample of societies. Then attention shifts to the comparative effort, and the reliability of coding judgments becomes the major concern. (See Glascock, 1982, for an example of this approach in gerontology.) Within such sequences the emphasis on one goal or the other is sometimes so great that the relationship nearly becomes "either-or." The original comparative study of well-being by Hadley Cantril (1965) comes close to exemplifying an either-or choice between the demands of collecting valid cultural information and the demands of carrying out a reliable comparison. In the Cantril study the coding and comparison of survey responses are the main foci of evaluation of data quality. Another example that approximates either-or choice is the Six Cultures project (Whiting, Child, & Lambert, 1966; Whiting, Whiting, & Longabaugh, 1975), in which the focus is on reporting extensive ethnographic information about each cultural context in separate chapters or monographs.

Relationship of Qualitative to Quantitative Data

If we begin with the familiar temporal or sequential basis of linking qualitative and quantitative data, then certain logically possible relationships appear in both the collection and interpretation of data.

One possible relationship is the use of quantitative data for selection of appropriate units (social or spatial) in which the qualitative work will take place. In Project AGE we used census materials—which were available in the United States, Hong Kong, and Ireland, and were collected by us for the Herero and !Kung in the Kalahari—as the basis for selecting samples of people to be interviewed. In the two U.S. towns, our emphasis on qualitative data led us to use a cluster sampling technique, because the units chosen (residential blocks) provided areas in which fieldworkers could collect information through observation and informal encounters in addition to carrying out formal, individual interviews. Simple random sample of the entire town would have produced an adequate set of individuals but not the social context within which the fieldworker could make connections between the individual responses. For example, when respondents described old persons they saw or helped, the fieldworker was likely to have complementary information from and about the old person who was typically a neighbor on the same block, as well as to have seen the persons described on the sidewalk or in their yards. Inventories of types of organizations in the seven sites were the basis for the choice of settings for participant observation. This reliance on a quantitative basis for selecting units of qualitative data is similar to hologeistic work, although the timing is reversed. In the field study, the qualitative data are collected after the sample is defined. When ethnographic archives such as the Human Relations Area Files (HRAF) are used, the sampling is done long after the fieldwork has been completed and reported in the books and articles from which the files are constructed.

A second possible relationship is the use of qualitative data for the design of appropriate quantitative instruments. In Project AGE the requirements of functionality in our different sites were discovered through observation and *guided conversation* interviews. We defined functionality on the conceptual level as the capabilities needed to participate as a full adult member of a specific group or community. As for all of the concepts in our research questions, we agreed on a common conceptual definition of functionality, with the understanding that specific measures of function would need to be appropriate to each research site. In other words, the capacities required to be viewed as a functional member of one community were not necessarily the same as those required in another. Discovery of the measures or indicators for functionality that were appropriate to each site was a major goal of the first stages of research. Recorded in field journals, for example, were references to people who were no longer able to participate fully or self-references by older people about the declines that would force them to leave a community or to live in less-independent circumstances. In an Irish village, being able to carry in fuel from the pile of turf outside was one indication of functionality. In a U.S. suburb, being able to drive a car was one appropriate measure, being able to manage money was another. Neither measure was salient in Africa, where ability to walk long distances, ride on a donkey, or draw and carry water from a well were requirements of everyday life. In Hong Kong, where technological change has been extremely rapid, literacy was an important indicator of ability to be a full social participant. Once salient abilities were identified in each location, data collection shifted to a quantitative strategy as respondents were asked to rank themselves on items describing physical capacities as well as the abilities appropriate to their site.

Such qualitative to quantitative sequences appear in other comparative research, although sometimes the sequence is stretched over a longer period of time than in our work. The *field manual* approach used by the team in the Harvard study of adolescence (which was modeled on the Six Cultures study of early childhood), for example, uses cultural knowledge that researchers already have about the sites as a basis for designing a field guide for collecting information on specific topics in the new, comparative study (Davis & Davis, 1989).

In our case, each fieldworker, although familiar with the site, left discovery of specific measures such as the functionality rating items for the beginning months of fieldwork. In terms of the qualitative-quantitative relationship, however, we discovered that ethnographic information should exert its influence at an even earlier point in the development of measures. Knowledge of sociolinguistic norms, for example, should guide the choice of the proper genre of an eliciting device. This became most important for us in the attempt to collect information from !Kung using an interview format with its customary features of sequenced questions posed by the researcher to an individual respondent. !Kung felt that the interviewer's following up each response with another question was impolite and challenging. More accustomed to verbal communication in which individuals take turns presenting fairly lengthy monologues to a group of others, the !Kung experienced the interrogatory dialogue format of our interviews as a series of rude or suspicious interruptions.

A third relationship between qualitative and quantitative data is the transformation of qualitative information into quantitative units for statistical analysis. In Project AGE, the texts recorded in response to interview questions (for example, about sources of well-being or characteristics of older persons doing well or poorly) were assigned numeric codes to represent various themes, such as "material resources," "need for care," or "dependence." This process is conceptually similar to the extraction of numeric data from existing ethnographic records catalogued in archives such as the HRAF.

These first three relationships are all familiar in crosscultural comparative research. Other relationships that appeared in our work are a bit less familiar and begin to highlight differences between live and archival use of cultural information.

A fourth relationship is the use of quantitative data as a guide for displaying and interpreting qualitative material, for example, to define the age categories used in a comparison of text materials such as life stories. In Project AGE, participants in each site were asked to categorize by life-stage descriptions of imaginary individuals described in terms of attributes such as parental status, occupation, and living arrangements (Fry, 1988, 1990; Ikels, Keith, & Fry, 1988). Once they had defined life stages, respondents were asked a series of questions about each stage, beginning with what they called it and ending with a request for the age range it spanned. It was then possible for us to analyze the labels and the age ranges together to calculate the average age for entry into and exit from stages labeled in various ways. This procedure provided a site-specific basis for the choice of age boundaries, ensuring that comparisons between "old" persons in Africa, Ireland, Hong Kong, and the United States were grounded in culturally valid definitions of age.

A fifth relationship occurs when qualitative information serves as the key for deciphering the meanings of quantitative data. An important tool for our measurement of well-being was a Cantril self-anchoring ladder (Cantril, 1965). Respondents are asked to place themselves on a rung of a ladder (six rungs in our version) whose bottom and top rungs represent the worst and best lives they would define for themselves. Although this tool produces convenient quantitative data, the cultural knowledge we acquired through more qualitative strategies was essential to interpretation of the resulting rung placements in meaningful ways. For example, in Hong Kong, a source of cultural "interference" with a face value interpretation of the ladder scores was the Confucian value of the mean (Chinese scores clustered in a middle range). In the North American middle-class community, cultural emphasis on progress and achievement led younger people to reserve higher scores for later in their lives, as they expected to improve their circumstances. In Africa, the belief that the rich should share their resources discouraged Herero elders (who were often village leaders and the owners of the largest herds) from giving positive evaluations of their own well-being. In these cases, access to the live ethnographer who can interpret the influence of a cultural context on responses to rating scales is essential.

Access to the ethnographer is also necessary in a sixth relationship, which occurs in the transformation of quantitative data back to qualitative. An example of this transformation is the use of the *patterns* in numeric scores or coded themes as new, nonnumerical data for interpretation (e.g., multidimensional scaling portrayals; dendrograms of card-sort results; principal-component graphs of functionality by site, gender, and age; and gender and age patterns in well-being scores within each site). Here again, the ethnographer is needed to do the interpretation.

Reliability and Validity in the Comparison of Qualitative Data

Reflecting on these six different ways of linking qualitative and quantitative data, the Project AGE team realized that we had shifted away from a strictly sequential relationship. More significant, we also realized that as the temporal pattern of relating the two kinds of data shifted, we could no longer rely on the corresponding familiar sequences of validity and reliability—that is, validity (culture) at the beginning followed by the focus on reliability (comparison). The major danger of the sequential model is that the validity issue is considered resolved, and standards of reliability alone become dominant as coding and comparison proceeds. When qualitative data are centrally involved, validity needs to be considered and reconsidered throughout the process. Reliability of comparison depends on code definition at many levels, and these definitional decisions cannot be evaluated without reference back to cultural validity.

The Project AGE team was able to develop more complicated relationships between the two kinds of data because we were using live rather than archival sources of cultural information. What we realized in the process was how close we had come, perhaps under the influence of the hologeistic and sequential model, to losing much of the value of having collected primary data in the first place. Adherence to standards of evaluating reliability derived from the archival strategies would have lost us much of what we gained by going to the field. Of course, the related pitfall would be to lose any basis for maintaining the quality of comparisons. The question faced by researchers who wish to rely on qualitative data in comparative analysis is, How do we demonstrate standards if they cannot be evaluated with intercoder reliabilities?

Two concepts are key to the maintenance of rigor in these circumstances. One is a notion of *data quality control* that resonates back to an original definition by Raoul Naroll (1962). In his formulation, designed for assessment of data quality in comparative research using data archives such as the HRAF, the fundamental basis for evaluating any decision about ethnographic data is the quality of the fieldwork that produced it, which is evaluated by the fieldworker's training, time in the field, and language expertise, among other elements. The second key concept is our shorthand for the role of fieldworkers in the interweaving of cultural and comparative standards, which we call *secondary ethnography*. This is somewhat like the debriefing process described by Bohannan (1981) or the return to field notes requested by Cowgill and Holmes for their book *Aging and Modernization* (1972) (also see Cowgill, 1974). However, the differences are important. *Debriefing* refers to interviews of individuals who are not trained ethnographers but who participate in settings of interest to the researcher who debriefs them as soon as possible about their observations. In the analytic stages of Project AGE, by contrast, team members (all professional anthropologists) were interviewing one another. Cowgill and Holmes presented a set of questions to professional ethnographers, but they had been away from their field sites for a long time and had already "cooked" their observations into various kinds of reports. Our fieldworkers were consulting fresher and more recently obtained data.

Secondary Ethnography

In Project AGE, these secondary ethnographic strategies emerged gradually. However, it has been important for us to make explicit the choice points and bases of choices as we present our data. We also think it may be useful to others to have this outline, especially because this type of data quality control has specific implications for research design that in turn must be justified for both consumers of data and funding agencies.

Secondary ethnography is our name for the return to the field data each fieldworker had to make many times during the comparative, interpretive part of our work. Every team member at times has played the role of coordinator for specific articles and chapters, as well as of responder to requests for data, analyses, and interpretation from others. In different phases of the research, each fieldworker has had to act as a *culture broker* in several senses. One has been to redefine what appeared to be "noise" in our comparative scheme as important information about their sites.

In Clifden, our research location in western Ireland, and among the !Kung, the sorting task with which we asked people to categorize life stages appeared not to work. The comments people made to the field-workers during frustrating efforts to use the technique sounded like noise rather than data. It took ethnographic knowledge of these two settings, combined with visits and queries by other team members, to understand finally that the static was the message. The fact that people did not sort items into piles representing life stages did not indicate simply that sorting and categorizing were unfamiliar or not salient, but that life stages were unfamiliar and nonsalient. From the point of view of our research, this was hardly noise in the system: It was central information.

A second sense in which Project AGE fieldworkers acted as culture brokers for the rest of the team was to validate, or speak for, absence of data or negative cases. For example, when the naive reader and two of us from other sites read through the responses about well-being from Chinese respondents in Hong Kong, we saw texts that seemed to us to refer to the theme of dependence and independence: "I am not rich. I have to depend on the children." Similar statements were coded as references to the dependence and independence theme in the data from both African groups and in the two U.S. communities, where they appeared with moderate (United States) to high (Africa) frequency. However, such statements were never identified as references to dependence and independence by the coders of Hong Kong texts. Was this absence of dependence and independence codes an error in coding? Was the disagreement about coding of the Hong Kong data an indication of low intercoder reliability among readers of the texts? Using her ethnographic knowledge of Chinese lives in Hong Kong, the AGE researcher who led the study there was able to persuade the other AGE ethnographers that in the context of Chinese culture in Hong Kong these statements did not highlight dependence or independence but rather the stress of material circumstances. For the team to have outvoted the ethnographer with low intercoder reliability or for the ethnographer to have trained the others to the point where we could read the texts with the same cultural expertise as she would have undermined the rationale of having an experienced and trained ethnographer for each site to begin with. The presence of the live ethnographer resolves one of the most intractable problems of secondary data analysis: that is, how to interpret the absence of reference to the item or theme of interest.

A third sense in which qualitative information may be needed for appropriate interpretation of numeric data is to validate *categories* of comparison: for example, the age boundaries used in construction of tables. For a project on age, the definition of age itself was central. For every display of information, such as levels or sources of well-being, we needed to set age boundaries for comparison. Built into each numerical display and analysis is culturally specific information about age boundaries in each site. When well-being sources for old and young are compared across our sites, we are comparing old and young as perceived within each group.

A fourth sense in which qualitative data guide quantitative analysis is the validation of *data reduction*—for example, coding and clustering for comparison. As textual records of cultural information were transformed into numerical codes and these were clustered into broader dimensions for comparison, the fieldworker as culture broker had to be vigilant that important cultural meanings were not lost or imposed. Each decision was negotiated with every ethnographer, and a great deal of cultural knowledge was articulated and made usefully explicit in these discussions. To explain to the rest of the team, for instance, why the potent and polysemantic term *active* used to describe an older person in a U.S. suburb is not adequately captured by a theme of physical status requires explication of a good deal of ethnographic information about upper-middle-class U.S. culture.

Working through this negotiated process reveals how intertwined are the cultural and the comparative information, the standards for validity and reliability. The process of comparison when qualitative data are involved is more like the double helix than the linear sequence. The reduction of qualitative data for comparison is only possible with vigilant validation by the fieldworkers as culture brokers. On the other hand, negotiation of the comparisons elicits a great deal of additional cultural information. There are three practical implications of data quality control and secondary ethnography as strategies for comparison of qualitative data:

1. Participation by all members of the team must be simultaneous. Project planning, fieldwork, and analysis must take place at the same time for all members. The greatest obstacle for Project AGE was the division (required by the funding agency) of fieldwork into two phases.
2. Techniques of data management must facilitate the combination of qualitative and quantitative information. A relational database capable of storing substantial texts, as well as numeric information, is necessary.
3. Visits to all locations must be made by at least the coordinators—and preferably by all field researchers. This is a tremendous aid to the process of negotiated interpretation, which involves cultural information from all research locations.

Conclusion

Qualitative data collection has implications for every other aspect of the research design. Given the many questions about aging and old age that can only be answered with qualitative information, a critical approach to gerontological methods must include both evaluation of the circumstances that require qualitative data collection and the consequences for the entire research design of using qualitative strategies.

Particular attention to the implications of qualitative data for comparative research designs is essential to the very enterprise of gerontology. Comparative research is the first safeguard against conflating the attributes of human aging with the attributes of aging in the modern, industrial societies in which the research questions and techniques of gerontology are most often created. The inclusion of qualitative data in comparative research is the second safeguard. Without the use of qualitative strategies to reveal culturally shaped meanings of aging experiences and of age itself, any comparison can include diverse groups in only biased and superficial ways. In addition, for comparison to reach valid results, the demands of qualitative data must be allowed to influence procedures and standards for reliable comparison. Qualitative researchers in gerontology should be leaders in creating research about aging that is both reliable and culturally valid, and both rigorous and humane.

References

Bernard, R. (1988). *Research methods in cultural anthropology.* Newbury Park, CA: Sage.
Bohannan, P. J. (1981). The unseen community: The natural history of a research project. In D. A. Messerschmidt (Ed.), *Anthropologists at home: Towards an anthropology of issues in America* (pp. 29-45). New York: Cambridge University Press.
Cantril, H. (1965). *The pattern of human concerns.* New Brunswick, NJ: Rutgers University Press.
Cowgill, D. O. (1974). Aging and modernization: A revision of the theory. In J. Gubrium (Ed.), *Communities and environment policy* (pp. 123-146). Springfield, IL: Charles C Thomas.
Cowgill, D. O., & Holmes, L. (1972). *Aging and modernization.* New York: Appleton-Century-Crofts.
Davis, S., & Davis, D. (1989). *Adolescence in a Moroccan town.* New Brunswick, NJ: Rutgers University Press.
Draper, P., & Keith, J. (1992). Cultural contexts of care: Caregiving for the elderly in Africa and the U.S. *Journal of Aging Studies, 6,* 113-134.
Fry, C. L. (1988). Theories of age and culture. In J. E. Birren & V. L. Bengtson (Eds.), *Emergent theories of aging.* New York: Springer.
Fry, C. L. (1990). The life course in context: Implications of research. In R. Rubinstein (Ed.), *Anthropology and aging* (pp. 129-152). Boston: Kluwer.
Glascock, A. (1982). Decrepitude and death-hastening: The nature of old age in Third World societies. In J. Sokolovsky (Ed.), *Aging and the aged in the Third World. Part I: Studies in Third World societies.* Publication No. 22 (Dec.), 43-66.
Ikels, C., Keith, J., & Fry, C. L. (1988). The use of qualitative methodologies in large-scale cross-cultural research. In S. Reinharz & G. Rowles (Eds.), *Qualitative gerontology* (pp. 257-264). New York: Springer.
Ikels, C., Keith, J., Fry, C. L., Dickerson-Putman, J., Draper, P., Glascock, A., & Harpending, H. (1992). Perceptions of the adult life course: A cross-cultural analysis. *Aging and Society, 12,* 49-84.
Keith, J. (1980). Participant observation. In C. Fry & J. Keith (Eds.), *New methods for old age research* (pp. 8-26). Chicago: Loyola University Center for Urban Policy.
Keith, J. (1982). *Old people as people.* Boston: Little, Brown.
Keith, J., Fry, C. L., & Ikels, C. (1990). Communities as context for successful aging. In J. Sokolovsky (Ed.), *The cultural contexts of aging* (pp. 245-261). Westport, CT: Greenwood.
Luborsky, M. (1987). Analysis of multiple life history narratives. *Ethos, 15,* 366-381.
Luborsky, M., & Rubinstein, R. (1987). Ethnicity and lifestyles: Self-concepts and situational contexts. In D. Gelfand & C. Barresi (Eds.), *Ethnic dimensions of aging* (pp. 35-50). New York: Springer.
Naroll, R. (1962). *Data quality control.* New York: Free Press.
Shaffir, W. B., & Stebbins, R. A. (Eds.). (1991). *Experiencing fieldwork.* Newbury Park, CA: Sage.
Whiting, J. W. M., Child, I. L., Lambert, W. W. (1966). *Field guide for a study of socialization.* New York: John Wiley.
Whiting, B. W., Whiting, J. W. M., & Longabaugh, R. (1975). *Children of six cultures: A psycho-cultural analysis.* Cambridge, MA: Harvard University Press.

PART III

Data Collection

8

In-Depth Interviewing

SHARON R. KAUFMAN

In-depth interviewing is a data-gathering technique used in qualitative research when the goal is to collect detailed, richly textured, person-centered information from one or more individuals. It is used when the researcher wants to investigate what is meaningful to the individual (Rubinstein, 1988). In in-depth interviews, the investigator initiates a dialogue with a real person and engages the interviewee as human being, not as study subject. This approach differs significantly from that used in surveys, preworded or structured questionnaires, and other fact-finding data-gathering tools. Thus conceived, in-depth interviewing carries special expectations and responsibilities.

This chapter considers the two demands of in-depth interviewing: intellectual and interpersonal. It is organized around the steps and stages of the interview process, from formulating the interview guide to completing the interviews and thinking about them for analysis.

Research Questions and the Interview Guide

The interview guide is designed to explore and answer questions pertinent to the research topic, problem, or goal. Before creating the interview guide, the investigator must formulate the research questions of the project and identify the study population best suited for providing answers to those questions. The research questions identify and specify the phenomenon to be studied (Strauss & Corbin, 1990). They delimit the study, clarifying for the investigator the subtopics to be included and omitted from the investigation. It is extremely important that the investigator have a clear idea of the research questions before embarking on the construction of both the interview guide and interviewing itself. Articulating and then keeping in mind the research questions focuses the research conceptually. Once the investigator defines and then internalizes the research questions, there is less likelihood of straying from the conceptual problem while designing the guide or conducting the interviews.

An example of research questions and interview guide are provided from the author's ongoing research.[1] The overall research goal is to examine the experience and meanings of health transitions and decreased independence among people older than 80. Research questions are formulated to explore that broad topic: For example, how do old people describe health transitions they face in late life? What are their definitions of independence in light of their health status? What does dependence mean to them? How do those definitions change as their health status changes? What are people's expectations about bodily and functional changes? How, if at all, does the self-concept change in relation to declining health in late life?

Interview questions derive directly from the research questions of the study and attempt to elicit answers to them. In in-depth interviews, conceptual and substantive topics that the investigator wants to explore are recast into open-ended questions designed to invite talk about the topic as conceived by the informant. Questions are structured into a guide. The interview guide is only that. The investigator refers to it to make sure all topics are covered during the interview sessions. The exact wording of specific questions, the order in which they are asked, and probes for greater detail are unique to each interview and depend on the investigator's relationship with that informant and the nature of informant responses during that particular session.

Specific interview questions from the study on health transitions include the following open-ended questions: What is the nature of your health problem(s)? How did it (they) come about? Could you describe for me a typical day now? How does it differ from your usual routine before the health problem? What types of community services and help from family and friends do you rely on now? How is that different from before? Do you feel differently about yourself since this problem began? In what ways? Could you talk about what independence means to you now? How have your health problems affected your independence?

The open-ended approach is fundamentally different from research using closed questions or those that appear in preworded questionnaires. The latter guide the study subject to a particular kind of answer, closing off the possibility of broad-ranging responses that cover topics of concern to both interviewer and interviewee. Closed questions also can be answered frequently by yes or no responses that discourage the interviewee from elaborating further on a subject and from discussing its personal meanings (e.g., Did you have a heart attack or stroke? When? Are you able to cook now? To get out of the house?). Preworded questionnaires force study participants to structure their responses according to the researcher's priorities and notions of the answer's parameters.

In contrast, open-ended questions elicit subjective, idiosyncratic responses from each interviewee, and the interviewer must be prepared for highly variable answers. Specific queries are not answered in an objective sense, and informants' answers to the same question may not contain similar material. Instead, content and boundaries of the research problem are identified and defined by informants themselves; they are allowed to describe the research topic in their own ways. Specific interview questions should be designed with this goal in mind. By asking open-ended questions, the investigator learns not only what is pertinent to the individual about those topics, but also something about the identity of that individual and how he or she defines and constructs the self in relation to the subject matter at hand.

The investigator must make a conscious effort to design interview questions that elicit empirical discussion of the research topic. When interview questions are thoughtfully conceived to address substantive and conceptual research questions, qualitative research is extremely powerful. For then the data speak the experience of the informant about a particular topic, and the investigator has a conceptual guide in the form of the research questions by which to organize and analyze these experiential data.

The various sociodemographic and functional characteristics of the study population must be kept in mind while questions are being created. For example, how much formal education will informants have had? Will they be of the same cultural background as the interviewer? Will English be their native language? How much cognitive impairment will they have? Will they have vision or hearing problems? In addition, great care should be taken in the wording of interview questions so that people of various cultural and educational backgrounds can understand

and respond to them comfortably, if not easily. One of the strengths of in-depth interviewing is that generally people enjoy talking about themselves and their lives; they want to communicate. If questions are posed carefully, then informants will thoughtfully respond.

The Interview Guide: Building and Maintaining a Relationship

In in-depth interviewing, social interaction between the interviewer and the interviewee is part of the interview itself and generates both tone and content of data collected (Watson & Watson-Franke, 1985). Thus a formal and distant, or open and friendly, or wary and tentative relationship will be reflected in the type of subject matter covered, the degree of detail invoked, and the emotional tone of informants' responses to questions. If the interviews are part of a larger study involving participant observation, informant and interviewer may know one another, slightly or well, before the formal interviews begin. Whether known to one another or not, both interviewer and interviewee will carry preconceptions of one another to the encounter as well as expectations about what an interview is, how one should behave, and how much personal information can be safely disclosed. Such preconceptions of the other and of the relationship color both the way questions are posed and responses are framed.

One image many younger people hold of the elderly is that they tire easily or more easily than a younger investigator. In 15 years of interviewing all kinds of old people, young old, old old, extremely frail, functionally limited, and those bound to wheelchairs, their own homes, or nursing homes, I have rarely found this to be the case! It is important to be as conscious as possible of our preconceptions and, particularly, our stereotypes of older people as we prepare for and enter the interview setting. Stereotypes are part of our preunderstanding of a person, and they influence the formulation of our questions, our style of presentation (i.e., speaking loudly to people who look frail), and our attitudes toward an older person's capabilities to respond to the interview process. It behooves all researchers in the aging field to be as aware as possible of the notions we bring to the field. Regardless of our intentions to remain neutral researchers, our stereotypes and other presuppositions become part of our representations of elderly individuals and the aging process and part of the "knowledge" we produce about them. As social scientists conducting gerontological research, we must acknowledge that our attitudes and interaction styles, as well as our research, contribute to social and cultural constructions of aging.

The Nature of Collaboration

In-depth interviews are drawn from multiple methodological sources, a fact that contributes both to the potential depth and richness of data they can generate and the complexity and variability of the interviewer-interviewee relationship. They combine aspects of (a) the ethnographic interview, in which social and cultural features of a topic are explored vis-à-vis the informant's life (Spradley, 1979); (b) the biographical interview, through which a narrative of a person's identity and life course are constructed (Levinson, 1978); and (c) the therapeutic interview, in which people express their problems and concerns in an attempt to come to terms with them. In-depth interviews also are similar to (d) conversations with friends or acquaintances: They are informal in style and engaging emotionally (Kaufman, 1986; Rubinstein, 1988). Most topics that researchers want to investigate with elderly informants are about long-term, emotionally charged processes: health, illness, bereavement, family, coping with loss and change, social relationships, living situations, privacy, loneliness, and so on. When asking about deeply personal and subjective topics, the interviewer is in fact inviting the person to recall, reveal, and construct aspects of the personal life and to make that discussion coherent and meaningful (Kaufman, 1986).

The content of the in-depth interview will reveal the informant's experience and point of view, but researchers must be cautioned that an interviewee's responses to questions are only partial revelations, shaped and made meaningful because of the interview dialogue. First of all, the researcher influences the content of the experiential data in many ways. Questions are posed for the interviewer's purposes, not the purposes of the informants. Thus informants are not carrying on a conversation in a conceptual vacuum. They are responding to the frameworks of understanding (such as feminist, Marxist, or psychoanalytical) used by the interviewer. Those frameworks emerge in the actual content of specific questions (As a woman, how would you describe . . . ?) as well as in the interview context created by the researcher when explaining to informants why he or she is there and what he or she is trying to learn.

Equally important, informants are responding to the interviewer as a person—of a certain age and gender, known or unknown, with a unique appearance and communication style. All those personal features of the interviewer will influence the manner in which interviewees respond to questions, choose from a storehouse of memories, and decide which aspects of their identities and lives to present. In summary, it is the combination of personal characteristics and expectations of the interviewer, the attitudes toward aging he or she indicates, and the conceptual grounding of the questions themselves that influence the topics informants choose to express and expand on as well as the topics they omit from discussion entirely.

Second, interviewees may have an agenda of their own as they respond to questions. They may consciously choose to portray themselves in a specific way and as certain kinds of people (hero, victim, main protagonist) regardless of the questions posed (Behar, 1990). Very elderly informants sometimes choose to discuss material that shows them to be invulnerable, able to survive alone despite great frailty and disability. Some wish to represent themselves as content with their housing, families, or health care, even when those aspects of their lives are inadequate, impoverished, or painful. Fears of unwanted intervention coupled with long-held values of autonomy and self-reliance will influence informants' narrative constructions and the images they wish to present to the interviewer and to the world (Rubinstein, Kilbride, & Nagy, 1992). Informants come to the interview with feelings about what can and should be revealed to express a certain self while satisfying the interviewer. At the same time, they also have feelings about what must be withheld to preserve a sense of dignity, self-esteem, and emotional privacy.

Thus the in-depth interview is somewhat of a paradox. Data are not simply collected. Rather, they are created only through the collaboration between researcher and informant. Data emerge in the process of dialogue, negotiation, and understanding. Both coproducers will come to that dialogue with attitudes, values, personal agendas, and conceptual frameworks that find their way into the content of the interview as it unfolds over time.

Because in-depth interviews combine aspects of the four methodological sources described above, they can illustrate an informant's multiple voices and roles and may reveal different kinds of information at once. An example from the author's field notes very briefly illustrates the sorts of dimensions this type of interview generates. The following is an excerpt from an interview with an 89-year-old woman crippled by severe osteoarthritis after a series of falls. At the time of the interview, she lived in the skilled nursing facility of a life-care community residence, bound to a wheelchair.

SK: Could you start off by telling me how and when your health changed?

Informant: It was June of last year. I'm a bird watcher. I live independently here and have my own apartment. I do my own cooking, cleaning, everything. I was taking a bird walk as I do almost every morning before breakfast at 6 a.m. I had my binoculars, of course, and a friend told me there were some special birds. I knew better than to walk underneath a eucalyptus tree to go looking for the birds. It's dangerous. They drop their nuts; they're like jagged marbles. I thought, "I mustn't do that," but then I thought, "Oh well, I'll do it." I fell and broke my hip and collarbone. I couldn't get up, and I was alone there for awhile. That was the beginning of the complete change in my whole life. I've always been very active and independent and drove a car. I did all my house cleaning and cooking and had lots of company and entertained sometimes. And a big bunch of family and friends. I loved it. It was a good life. But the whole thing changed, and that is when you lose being your own self, your own independent self. And you have to learn to accept it, and that's the thing I'm trying hard to do. Last fall they did an X-ray. The bones are fragile and that's it. I'm trying to do my best. I have no complaints. I have fine care. . . .

SK: Could you talk about what independence means to you?

Informant: It means the world to me. It's impossible to be independent now. Because they call me the worry wart. That's one of the difficulties for me because I was so used to planning my life. I find it not easy to accept that whatever comes and whoever takes care of me—that's it. And not to worry. I'm a worrier because of planning. It's difficult to adjust to getting what you need, like being taken to the bathroom on time, so that you won't make mistakes. It's very hard, not worrying too much about it. That's all I can say to you. It's all very personal to talk to you about, but I guess I can. I feel a loss a great deal.

From only a short excerpt, one gets a sense of this woman's biography and narrative construction: making plans for herself, being with people, bird watching. People and nature are her priorities; she enjoys being active. The value of independence weaves through the entire interview; it both helps to situate her culturally (white, American, middle-class) and illustrates a continuous sense of self—in spite of her recent severe physical limitations. She uses that value to introduce herself to me in the beginning of the excerpt: "I live independently here and have my own apartment. . . ." Her use of the present tense to describe herself is deliberate. She returns to the past tense to talk about the events that led to her change in health status. The therapeutic nature of our conversation and my role as confidant emerge later in the excerpt when she states, "It's all very personal to talk to you about, but I guess I can."

Because of the personal nature of in-depth interviews, an interviewee's expression of his or her thoughts needs to be acknowledged by empathetic listening, respectful and tactful probes, and appropriate responses. In such an engaged encounter, the in-depth interviewer automatically takes on a variety of roles, as the above excerpt suggests, including confidant, friend, counselor, and pupil in the case of a younger researcher with an older informant. Different roles will predominate at different moments, depending on social and biographical characteristics of the informant that emerge in the interview, degree of distance or intimacy between interviewer and interviewee, topics under discussion, needs of the informant, and the particular nature of that investigator-informant relationship.

Rapport and Trust

Because the in-depth interviewer wants full, honest, and thoughtful answers to the questions he or she poses, rapport and trust are essential features of the interviewer-interviewee relationship. There is simply no substitute for building a trusting relationship before plunging into difficult questions about existential matters. Although building trust takes time, it is well worth it. The time spent in chatting about general matters, explaining why these interviews are so important, and discussing how the interviews fit into a larger study pays off with thoughtful responses to questions. People want to contribute to some larger good, and they usually welcome the opportunity to participate in research. In the end, the data are as rich as the informant-interviewer encounter. Investigators are always constrained by time; it is therefore important to build into an interview schedule enough time (perhaps half or all of the first interview session) for simply getting to know and feel at ease with the informant. The building of trust and ease is critical to the content of the interview, regardless of how many hours or sessions an interview takes.

Reciprocity is an important ingredient in building trust. Informants will sometimes ask the interviewer as many questions about him- or herself as are asked in the research. The interviewer should expect such questions and be prepared to answer them as openly and honestly as is comfortable. Other kinds of reciprocity will depend on the depth of the relationship with the informant and how much time is spent together. Older people without transportation appreciate occasional help from someone with a car in going to the grocery store or post office. Those with functional limitations who live alone appreciate such small things as getting something down from a high shelf, bringing in the mail, or running an errand.

Rapport building includes the discussion of confidentiality. Whether or not the investigator has institutional informed consent forms (required by a committee on human research or institutional review board) for the informant to sign, some discussion of the privileged nature of the interview should precede the actual collection of data. Some informants are not concerned about issues of anonymity and disclosure; others are extremely concerned about privacy, publicity, and confidentiality. Regardless of the particular stance, all informants appreciate knowing that their words, in spoken, recorded, and written form, are considered confidential by the investigator. They also appreciate knowing the uses to which the data will be put once the interviews are completed. Discussion of confidentiality with informants to build trust is a separate issue from the ethics of confidentiality in qualitative research. That latter topic is discussed in other chapters of this volume.

In-depth interviewing may be part of a larger project involving participant observation and other forms of fieldwork, or it may constitute the sole method of data collection for a particular study. Depending on the type of investigation, informants may be interviewed at one time only for an hour or more, at several times over the course of a year, or dozens of times over a period of months or years. Expectations about informant participation need to be discussed at some point during the first interview session. Sometimes it seems best to let the informant or prospective informant know what you are up to well in advance: For example, "I am conducting a study of health transitions in late life. I would like to come and talk with you three or four times over the next year about what your life is like with this health problem. Would that be okay with you?"

In other kinds of studies, especially the collection of life histories, it may be best to have one or two initial interviews to get to know the person broadly and to assess whether that particular informant seems appropriate for participation in a long-term project. In such a case, the interviewer might say, "I am interested in talking with you a bit about your life; could we set up an appointment?" If the session goes well, the interviewer could state, "I have enjoyed talking with you tremendously. I am embarking on a large project and wonder if you would be willing to meet with me regularly over a period of X months to talk with me further." On the other hand, if at the end of one or two sessions the investigator feels the informant is not appropriate for further in-depth interviews, the informant can be thanked for his or her time, and no long-term commitment has been made.

Especially in long-term studies, the investigator must periodically remind the informant that the project will end and that the interviews will come to a conclusion by a certain date. Informing study participants of the close of a project makes it easier to extract oneself from the field, an otherwise often difficult task, especially when informants become friends or when it becomes clear that the interview is serving a thera-peutic purpose as it frequently does for informants. Discussing the termination of interviews in the context of moving on to the next phase of the project—writing about what you have learned from your sessions together for books, monographs, articles, and lectures—lets informants know that they are not being dropped and forgotten and that the findings gleaned from their words are important enough to be disseminated to a wider public.

Pacing and Preparation

The pacing and spacing of in-depth interviews is an important con-sideration for the optimal unfolding of the research project. When more than one interview with an informant will be conducted, enough time should be allowed between one interview and the next for field notes to be typed, audiotapes to be transcribed, data to be thoughtfully read, and follow-up questions to be formulated. This part of the research process should not be jeopardized.

Preparation between interviews accomplishes three goals. First, it disciplines the investigator to think about the data in relation to the research questions. The research questions can be fine-tuned and modified, depending on what the data are about, and the interview questions can be modified or redirected to address the emerging research problem. Qualitative research is a dynamic, unfolding process. Thinking about the data as they are being collected, and even analyzing the data while interviews are still in process, allows for constant feedback among the data, interview questions, and research goals. Theoretical constructs stay grounded in the data, and emerging data force a reconsideration of the conceptual problems. The project stays on track and evolves conceptually (Strauss & Corbin, 1990). When returning to the informant for the next session, the investigator can state, "I have been thinking a lot about what you talked about last week (month), and I would like to ask you more about that." Or, "Today I would like to start with a new topic." Careful preparation before each interview keeps both the informant and interviewer from straying from the research agenda.

Second, transcribing and reading field notes regularly forces investigators to stay current with rapidly accumulating data and prevents them from feeling constantly behind or overwhelmed. Third, preparation between interviews becomes evident to an informant. "I have been listening to (reading over) your words since the last time we met and I would like to ask you more about X," shows that the interviewer takes informants' participation seriously and considers their words beyond the interview setting itself. Rapport and trust continue to be built, resulting in the ongoing collection of rich and useful data.

Listening

Listening actively and thoughtfully is very important. Once an open-ended question has been asked (e.g., "Can you tell me how your health problem came about?"), the investigator must allow the interviewee to answer the question as he or she wishes. Content and length of answers to open-ended questions cannot always be predetermined. Answers may range from one simple phrase (e.g., "with my fall in 1990") to a richly descriptive narrative discussion (e.g., of a variety of illnesses and their possible causes, or the role of family, or the desire to leave the nursing home and live independently) that takes many minutes. However long or short, detailed or sparse the response, the interviewer must honor it as the answer to the question and as a meaningful statement from the informant. Sparse answers can be easily followed by open-ended probes from the interviewer; for example, "And then what happened?" or "Could you tell me more about that?"

Often informants will intersperse direct answers to questions with talk of their pressing concerns or with talk about topics seemingly unrelated to the research. This is natural, especially in long-term studies when rapport and trust have been established and the interviewer becomes a friend and confidant. Empathetic listening, even if the investigator does not consider some discussions relevant to the research problem, is appropriate and important for two reasons. First, as a reciprocal gesture, interviewers owe their informants the courtesy of listening to their concerns, especially when informants have spent a lot of time articulating subjects deemed important to the interviewer. The role of the empathetic stranger or listener—someone outside the intimate, complex, and emotional circle of family, neighborhood, and caregivers—cannot be overestimated. People are frequently comfortable sharing their problems with a neutral, concerned person; that is why in-depth interviews often serve a therapeutic purpose.

Second, it is the interviewer's question that prompted the informant's response, even if that response seems off-track to the interviewer. When the informant concludes his or her commentary, the interviewer can rephrase the question more precisely in the attempt to bring the informant back to the investigator's conception of the topic; for example, "Now that you've told me about your husband's troubles, I'd like to know what happened to you after your fall and hip fracture. What were the next several weeks (months) like for you? What happened during that time?" The interviewer's awareness of reasons for digression from the topic coupled with his or her ability to bring the informant's talk back to the research agenda both go a long way toward preventing frustration with a particular informant and emotional burnout with a project that seems to have gotten out of hand.

Interviewee-initiated topics that at first seem irrelevant to the research endeavor may be cause later for expanding the nature of the research questions themselves. Thinking about informants' "unrelated" comments serves to keep the investigator grounded in the primacy of the data. When several informants bring up similar "irrelevant" topics in their answers to particular questions for instance, the interviewer has a clue that the topic is not unimportant. Then it is time to rethink the research questions, as well as rethink one's own preconceptions about the limits on the kind of material one wants to collect. Perhaps an informant-initiated topic simply had not occurred to the interviewer before fieldwork had begun and now needs to be incorporated into the research problem.

Perhaps the investigator needs to carefully consider the phenomenology of the interview. A goal of phenomenological studies in the social sciences is to describe and clarify fundamental aspects of human experience (Frank, 1986): Phenomenology attends to the reality of experience. The term *phenomenological* has been used increasingly in the social sciences to refer to perspectives that focus on the native's point of view and on meaning, subjectivity, or consciousness—perspectives that account for the phenomenon under investigation as irreducible and autonomous in its own right. If an interview is perceived as a text that reflects the experience of the informant, then a follow-up round of questions can be constructed to probe issues raised by the informant that are relevant to the research topic.

In that way the interviewer acknowledges the voice of the informant in both the expansion and refinement of the research topic or problem and in the construction of the data. Such deliberate collaboration between informant and researcher is one of the strong and exciting features of in-depth interviewing: It is a technique that has the flexibility to consider and use the insights and discoveries offered by interviewees. Information gathered through such collaboration has a great deal of impact as both real and meaningful when presented later in written forms.

Thinking About the Data

When going over field notes and tape transcripts weeks, months, or even years after interviews have been completed, some data usually are categorized as good and important and other data as not useful. Although this winnowing process is natural and appropriate in the attempt to code interviews, conduct analyses, and make sense of the material, remember that the "irrelevant" remarks have been categorized that way because the researcher brings his or her own preunderstandings and conceptual frameworks of what constitutes important and irrelevant to bear on the data. Informants' words themselves are neither useful nor useless. They represent part of the subjective understanding of the topics discussed. They are examples of the informant's life world—that is, the self-evident and taken-for-granted experience of the individual, grounded in both the cultural and natural environments (Natanson, 1973).

A thoughtful investigator will always be struggling to represent the competing voices of the project: investigator's analytic categories (the *etic* approach in traditional anthropology) as well as informant's subjective account (the *emic* approach). Depending on the audience and dissemination goal, some analyses will emphasize explication of substantive and conceptual categories as conceived by the investigator before and during the study. For some other analytic purposes it may be appropriate to step back and look at the transcribed interview or set of interviews as a text, a subjective document worthy of attention and study in its own right. The development of both analytic voices is important for qualitative social science. In-depth interviewing provides a well-suited method for both kinds of interpretive endeavors.

Note

1. The author thanks Jay Gubrium and Andrea Sankar for their help in refining this chapter, which was written while the author was funded by National Institute on Aging research award No. AG09176, "From Independence to Dependence Among the Oldest Old." Gay Becker, Ph.D., was principal investigator; Sharon R. Kaufman, Ph.D., was co-principal investigator.

References

Behar, R. (1990). Rage and redemption: Reading the life story of a Mexican marketing woman. *Feminist Studies, 16,* 223-258.
Frank, G. (1986). On embodiment: A case study of congenital limb deficiency in American culture. *Culture, Medicine and Psychiatry, 10,* 189-219.
Kaufman, S. R. (1986). *The ageless self: Sources of meaning in late life.* Madison: University of Wisconsin Press.
Levinson, D. J. (1978). *The seasons of a man's life.* New York: Knopf.
Natanson, M. (1973). Introduction: Phenomenology and the social sciences. In M. Natanson (Ed.), *Phenomenology and the social sciences* (Vol. 1, pp. 3-44). Evanston, IL: Northwestern University Press.
Rubinstein, R. L. (1988). Stories told: In-depth interviewing and the structure of its insights. In S. Reinharz & G. D. Rowles (Eds.), *Qualitative gerontology* (pp. 128-146). New York: Springer.
Rubinstein, R. L., Kilbride, J. C., & Nagy, S. (1992). *Elders living alone: Frailty and the perception of choice.* New York: Aldine.
Spradley, J. P. (1979). *Participant observation.* New York: Holt, Rinehart & Winston.
Strauss, A., & Corbin, J. (1990). *Basics of qualitative research.* Newbury Park, CA: Sage.
Watson, L. C., & Watson-Franke, M. (1985). *Interpreting life histories.* New Brunswick, NJ: Rutgers University Press.

9

Life Stories

J. BRANDON WALLACE

Social scientists have found survey and experimental methods, with their precoded categories, inadequate in addressing the lived world, revealing little of how ordinary people experience everyday life. Increasingly, researchers have come to rely on methodologies that focus on personal meaning. These so-called biographical methods (Denzin, 1978) allow researchers to examine how experience is assigned meaning; they include the analysis of biographies and autobiographies (Kohli, 1981, 1986; Matthews, 1986), oral narratives or life stories (Bertaux, 1981; Bruner, 1987; Cohler, 1982; Kaufman, 1986; Wallace, 1990, 1992a), personal documents such as diaries and letters (Plummer, 1983), and the development of life histories, case histories, and case studies (Bertaux, 1981; Denzin, 1970; Plummer, 1983).

This chapter focuses on one type of biographical research: the collection and analysis of life stories in the study of aging and the life course. Life stories are narrative accounts of a person's life, in part or as a whole, delivered orally by the person him- or herself (Bertaux, 1981). Although other forms of biographical research have their strengths, life stories allow researchers to study how people ascribe meaning to and communicate about life experiences within the framework of the present (Bertaux, 1981; Cohler, 1982; Kohli, 1981, 1986); this makes life stories important methodological tools for studying the lived experience of aging. We begin with a framework for conceptualizing the use of life stories as a research tool. This is followed by a discussion of basic methodological issues that must be addressed in life story research. The chapter concludes with a brief discussion of a current project that uses life stories to analyze how family members narratively frame the experience of placing an aging member in a nursing home.

The Nature and Use of Life Stories

Scholars disagree about what exactly life stories are and how they can be used (Bertaux, 1981; Bertaux & Kohli, 1984; Cohler, 1982; Kaufman, 1986; Kohli, 1981, 1986; Matthews, 1986; Plummer, 1983, 1990; Sarbin, 1986; Spence, 1982; Wallace, 1990, 1992a, 1992b). Central is the question of the relationship between life stories and the lives they are claimed to describe.

Some researchers view life stories as a means of discovering the objective facts of an individual's life. Life experiences are seen as real, objective occurrences that can be described and combined to formulate a life history (Denzin, 1970). Through the use of life stories and other types of biographical data such as conversations with friends and relatives, personal documents (diaries, letters, etc.), and official records (medical, school, and police), a factual account of what really happened in an individual's life is produced. For these scholars, life stories, when checked against and verified by other data sources, are invaluable tools for gaining access to subjects' real lives (Denzin, 1970; Plummer, 1983).

Another view is offered by those who stress the subjective nature of life stories. Not seeking an objective remembrance of the past, these scholars point out that life stories are subjective interpretations and evaluations. Instead of emphasizing what life narrative accounts reveal about the "facts" of a subject's life, they focus on what such accounts say about "perceptions, values, definitions of situations, personal goals, and the like" (Bertaux & Kohli, 1984, p. 219). Subjective perceptions, meanings, and understandings become the central focus. From this perspective, life stories are ideal for studying how life is seen and experienced by individual life narrators.

A third set of scholars emphasizes that life stories are social constructions that are created and sustained through social interaction. Stories are social products emerging out of and shaped by the context in which they are produced. Life stories do not represent the solitary voice of a single subject reflecting on his or her life experiences; they are joint products created as two or more social actors engage in developing a situationally and culturally meaningful account of the subject's life

(Gubrium, Holstein, & Buckholdt, 1994; Plummer, 1990). Wallace (1990, 1992a, 1992b) emphasizes the role that interviewers and others in the "audience" play in initiating and shaping the telling of life stories (also see Mishler, 1986). Gubrium (1992) demonstrates how others may "speak in behalf of" the narrative subject and documents the different versions of stories that come from various perspectives (Gubrium, 1991). Luborsky (1990, forthcoming) stresses how lives and life stories are edited, organized, and presented according to situational, professional, and cultural norms. For these scholars, life is socially constructed, made real and meaningful in the telling and presenting of life stories (Bruner, 1987).

Not focusing on lives per se, some researchers use life stories to address "patterns of historically given sociostructural relations" (Bertaux & Kohli, 1984, p. 219). By collecting life stories from several individuals that address, in one form or another, the same set of social relationships in historical context, information about the relationships can be obtained. For example, Bertaux and Bertaux-Wiame (1981) use the life stories of French bakers to study the structure and organization of the French baking industry. Bruner (1987) describes how the life stories of different members of the same family reveal certain common organizing principles and themes that are indicative of their shared cultural milieu and the "meshing" of their respective lives within the family. Although most advocates of this usage emphasize the *historically given* (i.e., objective or factual) nature of the social phenomena being addressed, others highlight subjective perceptions of historical realities (Bertaux & Kohli, 1984; Bruner, 1987; Kohli, 1981, 1986).

Table 9.1 presents a summary of these usages. The columns represent views of the epistemological relationship between life stories and social reality. The rows represent differences in substantive focus, whether the life of the subject or some other social phenomenon is the topic of study. Note that these are ideal types (Weber, 1949); it would not be unusual for a single study to incorporate aspects of two or more kinds of analysis. Nevertheless, the typology does provide a view of the current diversity in the area.

Doing Life Story Research

Substantive and epistemological differences in life story research make defining a standard methodology difficult (Bertaux & Kohli,

Table 9.1 The Conception and Use of Life Stories

Substantive Focus	Life Stories' Relation to Reality		
	Objective Data	Subjective Data	Social Construction
Individual's Life	Tools for collecting "facts" about individual lives	Provide access to subjective perceptions of life experiences	Social constructions of life
External Social Phenomena	Tools for collecting cultural and historical facts	Subjective perceptions of social and historical events	Social constructions of the shared past

1984) because the relevant methodological issues differ from study to study. Yet, bearing in mind these differences, we still can provide general guidelines for doing life story research.

Clarifying the Epistemological Stance

Researchers using life story methods must be clear about their epistemological position. For example, if the objective of the researcher is to produce a factual account of what family life was like in London during World War II and life stories are seen as tools for obtaining such data, then the methodological issues of sampling, representativeness, and generalizability as well as questions of validity, reliability, accuracy, and truthfulness are central. In contrast, in a study of how the experience of retirement is defined and redefined in the course of telling life stories, where stories are seen as a means by which narrators construct and make retirement meaningful, then questions of the representativeness of samples or the truthfulness of accounts are insignificant. The researcher's epistemological stance shapes the relevant methodological issues.

Sampling

Having clarified the epistemological stance, the question becomes, Whose life stories will be collected? Sampling in life story research depends on several considerations. For example, are empirical generalizations being sought or is the goal the production of a substantive understanding that ideally has broader theoretical implications? Commenting on the number of life stories collected in previous studies, Bertaux and Kohli (1984, p. 218), state:

> Some research projects are based on several hundred, others rely on a single one, and the majority fall somewhere in between. The number depends on whether empirically grounded generalizations are sought or whether one is using a case study approach, where only generalizations based on theoretical plausibility, not statistical induction, are possible. Quite obviously, problems of sampling, analysis, and publication present themselves differently, depending on one's position along this continuum.

If, as in a study of family life in London during World War II, the goal is to make some general statement about what all or most families experienced, then researchers must assess how representative their samples of life stories are. Can it be argued that the 20, 50, or 100 life stories in a sample will accurately portray family life in general during the time period? If empirical generalization is the goal, then the general rules and procedures for generating representative samples should be followed or, at a minimum, an effort should be made to match the characteristics of the sample with those of the larger population. On the other hand, if the goal is to document how and if people use the concept of family to frame accounts of their experiences during the war, because other organizing frameworks such as work and career may have been disrupted, a few cases might provide tremendous insight. Concerns about the size and representativeness of samples would not be pertinent. This does not mean that sampling is not an issue in the latter approach. Researchers still must decide whose particular stories to collect and analyze. According to Plummer (1983):

> The issue of traditional sampling strategies is . . . not usually at stake; . . . the problem becomes this: who from the teeming millions of world population is to be selected for such intensive study and sociological immortality? The great person, the common person, the marginal person? The volunteer, the selected, the coerced? (p. 87)

Convenience and Chance

Subjects of life story research admittedly are often chosen because of convenience or by chance. If one is interested in studying, say, the personal meaning of home ownership, then anyone who has ever owned a home is a legitimate subject. Historically, subjects for life story research have been obtained through chance encounters, word-of-mouth referrals, and the solicitation of volunteers (Plummer, 1983). One of the appeals of this type of research is the ease by which informants acquainted with the subject matter can be found.

Substantive Acquaintance

Participants in a project must be able to meaningfully address the phenomenon being studied. Acquaintance with the matter under consideration is essential. For example, a researcher who is interested in how longevity is experienced and made meaningful probably will not interview 50-year-olds. Similarly, a scholar focusing on perceptions of the McCarthy era would not be likely to interview recent immigrants to the United States.

Narrative Ability

Practical concerns also play an important part in choosing subjects for life story research. Participants not only should be acquainted with the subject matter but also be willing and able to tell their stories. Subjects must be physically and mentally capable of communicating their experiences and have the time and inclination to do so. This is particularly pertinent to gerontologists, who frequently find themselves studying individuals suffering from physical or mental limitations or both. For instance, a researcher interested in the narrative structure of life in a nursing home must be certain that participants possess both the physical and mental stamina to communicate their experiences. Stamina is especially important, because life stories typically require comparatively lengthy responses.

Availability

Subjects also must be available if life stories are to be collected. If the subjects live too far away, require special permission to be seen, or present scheduling problems, then getting their life stories may be difficult (see Climo, 1992). If a study requires subjects 100 years and older, the researcher must be able to locate and identify individuals who meet the age criteria, whether it be through service agencies, churches, word of mouth, or other avenues. Remember that if subjects cannot be identified and contacted, then they cannot be asked to tell their stories, no matter how good those stories might be (Plummer, 1983).

Theoretical Concerns

Mainly, sampling should be guided by one's theoretical concerns. To illustrate, assume that a researcher is studying the schemes or frameworks used by older adults to organize their life stories. While interviewing an African-American woman, the researcher notices that the organization of the woman's story differs radically from the accounts given by European-Americans who were previously interviewed. The researcher begins to speculate that there are subcultural differences in the way life stories are organized. To explore the possibility, the researcher decides to interview additional subjects—males and females from both ethnic and racial categories. This kind of *purposive* or theoretical sampling (Glaser & Strauss, 1967) allows developing hypotheses to be explored, ultimately providing a more complete understanding of the phenomenon under study.

When Is Enough Enough?

As with survey research in general, several factors determine the size of the sample in life story research. Sampling ceases when time, money, and patience have been exhausted or when no more subjects with knowledge or experience of the phenomenon being studied are available. Ideally, sampling and data collection continue until an empirically grounded theoretical understanding of the subject matter has been formed. Glaser and Strauss (1967) suggest that sampling proceed until the collection and analysis of new cases adds little additional insight to the phenomenon under study. When such *saturation* occurs, further sampling is unnecessary.

Extraordinary Subjects

Researchers using life stories have a tendency to focus on the lives of "extraordinary" individuals. Bertaux and Kohli (1984) and Plummer (1983) have pointed out that U.S. scholars in particular have emphasized the lives of so-called deviants, marginals, or great persons; with few exceptions, they have neglected ordinary people (Denzin, 1984). Accordingly, a note of caution: Gerontologists using life story methods should not focus exclusively on such extraordinary elderly as centenarians and nursing home residents. They should endeavor to include ordinary elders with "normal" aging experiences. Needless to say, efforts to include all kinds of people—African-Americans, Hispanics, males, females, rich and poor—should be encouraged, especially when aging as such is the purview of research. A strategy of diversity not only would allow minorities and others to "have their say," but also would provide a more complete picture of the experience of aging. (See Luborsky, forthcoming, for a critique of narration as a form of "empowerment.")

Interviewing

Once it has been decided whose life stories will be collected, attention turns to actual collection. As oral narrative accounts, life stories are most frequently collected through interviews. The basic principles and issues of life story interviewing are similar to those of qualitative interviewing in general and have been discussed at length elsewhere (Denzin, 1970; Lofland, 1971; Mishler, 1986; Plummer, 1983). Rather than focus on such basics as developing an interview guide, demeanor and personal style, establishing rapport, and how to probe for additional data, this section will emphasize those aspects of interviewing that are especially relevant to life story research.

Interview Format

Because the goal of life story research is a narrative account produced by the subject, life story interviews are usually unstructured, although considerable variation is seen in the actual "unstructured" nature of the interviews. As a way of framing respondents' narratives, some researchers ask subjects a series of specific questions such as:

- When and where were you born?
- What was it like growing up then and there?
- How many brothers and sisters did you have?
- Did you get along with your brothers and sisters?

The researcher may seek to direct the story to ensure that the specific information being sought is conveyed. The questions asked may have been predetermined as a part of developing a structured interview guide or they may emerge during the interview in a more conversational manner.

Other researchers place greater restrictions on the involvement of the interviewer in the production of stories. Few questions are asked, and comments are kept to a minimum. The central and sometimes only question is a version of the request "Tell me your life story." The respondent is free to decide what details will be included in the story, how they will be connected, and perhaps even how long the story will be. (See Bruner, 1986, for a directive that limits the length of the life story.) The interviewer adopts the role of the interested and yet uninvolved other. Although follow-up or topical questions may be interspersed, the aim is to allow subjects to construct their stories in their own ways.

In general, the interview format chosen depends on the substantive interests and theoretical concerns of the researcher. For example, a researcher interested in gathering data on a particular substantive topic—say, sibling relationships across the life course—is likely to encourage respondents to structure their life stories around such relations, asking specific questions about the subjects' family lives as the interviews unfold. However, a researcher interested in how the immediate context of inquiry itself affects the telling of life experiences is likely to encourage subjects to tell their stories with as little substantive involvement from the researcher as possible.

The interview format also is shaped by the scope of the story. The complete life story covers the subject's whole life from birth to the present, touching on different aspects of the subject's experiences. The partial life story focuses on a segment of the respondent's life—say, childhood—and seeks an in-depth understanding of that particular time period. The topical life story addresses particular facets of the respondents' lives, such as family experiences, while deemphasizing others (e.g., education and career), and it may provide either a complete or partial account (see Denzin, 1978; Plummer, 1983). Again, the choice here depends on the researcher's substantive and theoretical aims.

Multiple and Group Interviews

Researchers seeking extensive and detailed accounts of subjects' lives may find a single interview inadequate. Collecting life story data over a series of interviews is not uncommon. The series of interviews may be structured topically, chronologically, or as continuations of earlier sessions. If conditions permit, interviews may extend over long time periods (McCrachen, 1988). Although the decision to use multiple interviews may be based on practical considerations, theoretical and substantive concerns also must be addressed (see Plummer, 1983).

Occasionally, life story researchers interview more than one person at a time, with each participant addressing the same topic. For example, a researcher might interview a husband and wife together in an effort to understand how they mutually construct a story—say, addressing the impact of the husband's retirement on domestic life. Whether group interviews are appropriate depends largely on the researcher's substantive and theoretical aims. For example, group interviews would be inappropriate for obtaining individual subjective perceptions but could prove informative in an investigation of the social construction of past experiences.

The Social Nature of Interviews

Remember, interviewing is a social process (Mishler, 1986). Even when social construction is not the focus of the study, interviewers should recognize that life stories are produced in and through social interaction. They are affected by the meanings that subjects ascribe to the interview and interviewer and by the interviewer's involvement in the storytelling process. Further, because narration is shaped by cultural expectations, diverse backgrounds based on gender, race, or ethnicity may lead to different narratives.

Recording, Data Analysis, and Reporting

Because most life stories are collected in the context of an interview where the relevant data are the subject's spoken words, they are typically tape recorded. Tape recording has several advantages over note-taking, not the least of which is greater accuracy and speed. In addition, the interviewer is freed to think about what is being said and to focus on the substance, not the flow of the narrative. Of course, tape recording presents its own practical questions. Where should the recorder be located to get the best sound? Should it be placed in obvious sight or hidden so it will not be noticed? Should batteries that might run down be used or an adapter that requires locating an electrical outlet? What should be done about subjects who do not like being tape recorded? Recorded interviews also must be transcribed, a tedious and time-consuming task (Denzin, 1970; Glaser & Strauss, 1967; Lofland, 1971; Plummer, 1983).

Coding life story data is similar to coding other types of qualitative data. Researchers interested in what life stories say about objective experiences will develop categories, typologies, and other coding schemes that reflect this aim. At the other end of the spectrum, those who are interested in the social construction of the life story will build their analyses around the process of story production. The coded data then are used to organize conceptual and theoretical understandings of the phenomenon under study (Glaser & Strauss, 1967; Lofland, 1971).

The matter of reporting life story data presents two important issues. First is the issue of editing. How and how much will the life story be edited? Will repetitive or contradictory material be left out? Should every "you know," "and uh," and "um" be retained or can they be left out if they add no substance to the presentation? Should the researcher correct poor grammar to make the prose more understandable? Will all of the life story be reported or only those portions that address issues of theoretical interest?

Second is the issue of interpretation. How much interpretation will be included in the report? Should the researcher interpret and explain the respondent's life story or let it stand on its own? Should the researcher's insights be mixed and intermingled with those of the respondent? How are they to be distinguished? As a general rule of thumb, the more subjective the goal of the researcher, the less intrusive the research should be at all points of the research process, from the interview to the final report.

An Example

The usefulness of life stories in aging research can be illustrated through a brief example, providing a concrete demonstration of design and implementation. The impetus for the research comes from a survey of the literature on institutionalization in old age. Much of the literature aims to define predictors of nursing home placement. A spectrum of variables has been considered: age, sex, race, income, availability of caregivers and community social support programs, degree and type of impairment, and limitations in activities of daily living (ADLs). In a review of this literature, Wingard, Jones, and Kaplan (1987) found that several variables—age, sex, availability of a caregiver, and functional status—were positively and repeatedly associated with nursing home use. Shapiro and Tate (1988) noted that age, the absence of a spouse, recent hospitalization, limitations in ADLs, mental deficits, and living in retirement housing increase the probability of institutionalization, individually and cumulatively.

Studies of the families' role in placing aging members in long-term care institutions also aim to uncover predictors of the family's decision to seek nursing home placement. Identified predictors include increases in the physical, emotional, and financial burdens of caregivers; the illness or death of a caregiver; and dramatic or gradual declines in the health of the care recipient (Colerick & George, 1986; Morycz, 1985; Poulshock & Diemling, 1984; Smallegan, 1985; Soldo & Manton 1985; Teresi, Toner, Bennet, & Wilder, 1980). There is general agreement that most families provide a tremendous amount of care, seeking nursing home placement only as a last resort (Brody, 1978; Knight, 1985). Although the literature provides general information about who among the aged are likely to be institutionalized, little insight is offered into the experience of decision making. The subjective perceptions, reasoning, and understandings of the aged and their families are largely ignored.

The Study

A study using life stories to investigate how families make the institutionalization of an aging member meaningful began in January 1992. Family members of recently institutionalized elderly were located by contacting the administrators of five nursing homes; after the project was explained, the administrators were asked to assist in recruiting study subjects. All five administrators agreed to help, assigning their social service directors the task of identifying and making initial contact with family members of residents admitted to their facility within the past six months. Thus far, 20 family members have agreed to participate in the study and have been interviewed. Fourteen of the interviews are transcribed and provide the data for the present discussion.

Respondents

Family members were interviewed in their homes or at the nursing facility in which their relative resided. Of the 14 completed interviews, 12 were female and 2 male. Two were the wives of the institutionalized elders, eight were daughters, one was a granddaughter, and one had both a mother and a sister in a nursing home. Of the two males interviewed, one was a son and the other a son-in-law. The son-in-law was the husband of one of the females interviewed. They were interviewed together. Respondents' ages ranged from 35 to 85 years, and all but four were between the ages of 45 and 65. The debilitating conditions of the institutionalized family members included cancer, stroke, hip fracture, arthritis, and Alzheimer's disease, with the last predominant.

The Interview

Interviewing began with a series of background questions that were presented in an informal, conversational style. The questions asked about age, educational attainment, employment history, religious participation, household composition, and the health status of both the respondent and the institutionalized elder. Each respondent then was told,

> What I would like for you to do now is tell me how your [institutionalized family member] came to be placed in the nursing home. You can begin wherever you would like and include or leave out whatever you choose. I'm just interested in finding out a little about your family's experience.

The request was phrased openly to allow respondents to organize their stories as they wished, applying their own time frames and including the details they deemed relevant. By limiting the involvement of the interviewer, we hoped that the accounts would reflect the respondents' own sense of the boundaries and substance of the institutionalization decision.

Once respondents finished their stories, the interviewer asked a variety of questions based on notes taken during the storytelling, including requests for clarification or further elaboration of some detail or incident mentioned. The interviews took from 30 to 90 minutes to complete. Each interview was tape recorded and transcribed.

Preliminary Findings

One focus of the data analysis is the narrative boundaries and topics of the stories. Relevant questions include where the stories begin, where they end, and what events or experiences are included as relevant. Preliminary analysis suggests that understanding the reasoning involved in institutionalizing an elderly family member requires an appreciation of both the history and progress of the aged family member's illness and the family dynamics that develop as members seek to respond to the illness.

Respondents often went back several years to begin their accounts. Indeed, the husband (H) and wife (W) who were interviewed together felt it necessary to return to 1954 to describe the onset of their thoughts about the wife's mother's institutionalization, as the interviewer (I) discovers in the following excerpt from their story. As multirespondent stories often do, their account takes the shape of a conversation.

W: Well, she . . . she was in two major wrecks.

H: Car wrecks.

W: Yeah, car wrecks, where she was really broken up, just all the bones and. . . .

H: It's a wonder she lived through either one of them.

W: Yeah . . . and uh . . . that left her not in good health. I mean, she had a lot of problems.

I: Okay. When was that?

W: Do you remember the years?

H: Oh, the one was 1954. I go by the car they had. And the other one wasn't too awful far away from that, when she was in that second wreck. Might've been '56, '57, '58, somewhere along in that. They were two bad wrecks, not too many years apart.

Although other respondents do not go back quite as many years, not uncommonly accounts might begin 5, 10, and even 15 years before the aging family member is placed in the nursing home.

There appear to be two common points of departure in the accounts. First, many respondents begin their stories by telling about when they first noticed the signs of their family member's illness. The typical story starts when it is first suspected that something is wrong. As the following excerpt from another story shows, the account of a husband's eventual institutionalization begins when others notice that he occasionally loses his way while driving to his son's home.

The first thing that we noticed about his forgetfulness was that he didn't know the way from here over to across town to the Will's. He could handle an automobile better than you, me, or anybody else in town. [Pause] And he didn't forget how to drive, but he didn't know the way, which street to turn off to get where he wanted to go. That was the first thing we noticed. Then he just kept getting worse and getting worse and getting worse and getting worse.

Not all symptoms develop gradually. One respondent recalls much less subtle signs of her husband's illness: "At first, I guess it was back May of last year, he started . . . he had a stroke at work. He wasn't supposed to work that day, but he went on to work because he had a customer coming in. And he passed out there."

A second point of departure is a significant life event that is believed to either signal or precipitate the symptoms of the illness. Two sisters interviewed together (S1 and S2) preface their account of their grandmother's illness by pinpointing two events that may have contributed to the onset of her symptoms. Notice that there is some disagreement as to when the sisters "really" began to notice changes in their grandmother.

S1: I think when that last sister [the respondents' great aunt] died is when we were beginning to be more aware, or we really took it seriously . . .

S2: Uh huh.

S1: . . . that Granny was beginning to. . . .

S2: We knew she was being affected from the time our mother got sick.

S1: Yeah, but. . . .

S2: But we really didn't notice the . . . how much until the sister died.

S1: Aunt Jane died before Momma got sick.

S2: No, because didn't we have to tell Momma and uh. . . . [Pause] I was thinking she died after Momma got sick, but maybe she did [die before].

S1: I think she did.

S2: 'Cause I think we had to tell Momma she died. I don't know.

S1: I think it was still though . . . when her sister passed away. I think that's when we began to notice.

Other accounts mark beginnings with events such as the death of a spouse, a child, or a major illness in the family.

In developing accounts of how family members come to be placed in nursing homes, establishing a point of departure is important. Whether directly or indirectly related to the family member's illness, the beginning point frames the experience, providing some indication of which events and circumstances are relevant, how they are related to one another, and how they ultimately lead to the institutionalization decision. Establishing a beginning helps make meaningful the course of experience and reasoning that leads to nursing home placement, allowing respondents to produce an account that makes sense to them and the interviewer. The data also suggest that the matter of placing a family member in a nursing home can be "a long story," encompassing a multitude of family changes and life events, occurring over lengthy time periods. In this regard, the effort to describe the decision-making process as predictable from a limited set of variables related to illness events or social support networks may severely distort the experience's subjective reality. Family members' stories of the institutionalization process can convey much wider temporal boundaries than predictor studies suggest.

Conclusion

This chapter has sought to show how life stories can be used in aging research, characteristically to tap the subjective side of being and growing old. What should be stressed is the ability of life story methodology to address human experience at a variety of levels, much of which is inaccessible through more conventional research techniques. As the life story method grows in importance in gerontological research, the narrative boundaries, contents, and contours of the aging experience probably will be sorted and organized much as have the experience's objective properties.

References

Bertaux, D. (Ed.). (1981). *Biography and society.* Beverly Hills, CA: Sage.
Bertaux, D., & Bertaux-Wiame, I. (1981). Life stories in the bakers' trade. In D. Bertaux (Ed.), *Biography and society* (pp. 169-190). Beverly Hills, CA: Sage.

Bertaux, D., & Kohli, M. (1984). The life story approach: A continental view. *Annual Review of Sociology, 10*, 215-237.

Brody, E. (1978). The aging family. *Annals of the American Academy of Political and Social Science, 438*, 13-27.

Bruner, J. (1986). *Actual minds, possible worlds*. Cambridge, MA: Harvard University Press.

Bruner, J. (1987). Life as narrative. *Social Research, 54*, 11-32.

Climo, J. (1992). *Distant parents*. New Brunswick, NJ: Rutgers University Press.

Cohler, B. (1982). Personal narrative and the life course. In P. Baltes & O. Brim (Eds.), *Life-span development and behavior* (Vol. 4, pp. 206-241). New York: Academic Press.

Colerick, E. J., & George, L. K. (1986). Predictors of institutionalization among caregivers of patients with Alzheimer's disease. *Gerontologist, 28*, 318-324.

Denzin, N. (1970). *Sociological methods: A sourcebook*. London: Butterworth.

Denzin, N. (1978). *The research act: A theoretical introduction to research methods*. Englewood Cliffs, NJ: Prentice-Hall.

Denzin, N. K. (1984). *Interpreting the lives of ordinary people: Sartre, Heidegger, and Faulkner*. Paper presented at the 10th World Congress of Sociology, Mexico.

Glaser, B., & Strauss, A. (1967). *The discovery of grounded theory*. Hawthorne, NY: Aldine.

Gubrium, J. F. (1991). *The mosaic of care*. New York: Springer.

Gubrium, J. F. (1992). Voice and context in a new gerontology. In T. R. Cole, W. A. Achenbaum, P. L. Jacobi, & R. Kastenbaum (Eds.), *Voices and visions of aging* (pp. 44-63). New York: Springer.

Gubrium, J. F., Holstein, J. A., Buckholdt, D. R. (1994). *Constructing the life course*. Dix Hills, NY: General Hall.

Kaufman, S. (1986). *The ageless self*. Madison: University of Wisconsin Press.

Knight, B. (1985). The decision to institutionalize. *Generations, 10*, 42-44.

Kohli, M. (1981). Biography: Account, text, method. In D. Bertaux (Ed.), *Biography and society* (pp. 61-75). Beverly Hills, CA: Sage.

Kohli, M. (1986). Social organization and subjective construction of the life course. In A. Sorensen, F. Weinert, & L. Sherrod (Eds.), *Human development and the life course* (pp. 62-83). Hillsdale, NJ: Lawrence Erlbaum.

Lofland, J. (1971). *Analyzing social settings: A guide to qualitative observation and analysis*. Belmont, CA: Wadsworth.

Luborsky, M. (1990). Alchemists' visions: Conceptual templates and sequence formats as representations of subjectivities in life narratives. *Journal of Aging Studies, 4*, 17-29.

Luborsky, M. (forthcoming). In whose image does the life history empower?

Matthews, S. (1986). *Friendships through the life course*. Beverly Hills, CA: Sage.

McCrachen, G. (1988). *The long interview*. Newbury Park, CA: Sage.

Mishler, E. (1986). *Research interviewing: Context and narrative*. Cambridge, MA: Harvard University Press.

Morycz, R. (1985). Caregiver strain and the desire to institutionalize family members with Alzheimer's disease. *Research on Aging, 7*, 329-361.

Plummer, K. (1983). *Documents of Life: An introduction to the problems and literature of a humanistic method*. London: Allen & Unwin.

Plummer, K. (1990). Herbert Blumer and the life history tradition. *Symbolic Interaction, 13*, 125-144.

154   Life Stories

Poulshock, S. W., & Diemling, G. T. (1984). Families caring for elders in residence: Issues in the measurement of burden. *Gerontologist, 24,* 230-239.
Sarbin, T. (1986). *Narrative psychology: The storied nature of human conduct.* New York: Praeger.
Shapiro, E., & Tate, R. (1988). Who is really at risk of institutionalization? *Gerontologist, 28,* 237-245.
Smallegan, M. (1985). There was nothing else to do: Needs for care before nursing home admission. *Gerontologist, 25,* 364-369.
Soldo, B. J., & Manton, K. G. (1985). Health status and service needs of the oldest old: Current patterns and future trends. *Milbank Memorial Fund Quarterly, 63,* 286-319.
Spence, D. P. (1982). *Narrative truth and historical truth: meaning and interpretation in psychoanalysis.* New York: Norton.
Teresi, J., Toner, J., Bennet, R., & Wilder, D. (1980). *Factors related to family attitudes toward institutionalizing older relatives.* Paper presented at annual meeting of Gerontological Society of America, Washington, DC.
Wallace, J. B. (1990). *"The good old days": The construction and communication of life stories by the very old.* Unpublished doctoral dissertation, University of Florida, Gainesville, FL.
Wallace, J. B. (1992a). Reconsidering the life review: The social construction of talk about the past. *Gerontologist, 32,* 120-125.
Wallace, J. B. (1992b). *An analytic vocabulary for life narrative practice.* Paper presented at the annual meeting of Gerontological Society of America, Washington, DC.
Weber, M. (1949). *Max Weber on the methodology of the social sciences* (Ed. by E. Shils & H. Finch). New York: Free Press.
Wingard, D. L., Jones, D. W., & Kaplan, R. M. (1987). Institutional care utilization by the elderly: A critical review. *Gerontologist, 27,* 156-163.

10

Fieldwork in
Groups and Institutions

KAREN A. LYMAN

The experience of aging shapes and is shaped by daily participation in particular social worlds. Aging takes place in various group and institutional settings such as families, work groups, religious communities, volunteer associations, fitness clubs, informal widows' support groups, adult day care centers, and residential and long-term care facilities. The psychosocial and interpretive process of aging may be found in these places.

Research on aging in these natural settings opens the door to an understanding of the career of later life and its daily work: adapting to loss and dependency, building and rebuilding relationships, retaining and enhancing competency, and, above all, maintaining self-identity and self-worth. What is discovered through fieldwork is how meaning is constructed as individuals interact with others. So field research on aging reveals a process of creating and re-creating meaning in one's life, despite or because of changes associated with the passing years.

Fieldwork involves participant observation in a natural setting. The researcher becomes a temporary member of the setting to understand the place and the people from their perspective (Emerson, 1983; Gold, 1958; Schatzman & Strauss, 1973). It is inductive theory building from the bottom up rather than deductive, hypothesis-testing research (Charmaz, 1983; Glaser & Strauss, 1967; Gubrium, 1992b). Field research in group and institutional settings allows in-depth exploration of the meaning of a place to its members and of the effect of the place on the self. As with other research, there are limits to the insights provided

155

by field research. Ethnography is a process of cultural representation (Clifford & Marcus, 1986). There are partial truths and inevitable exclusions in depicting others' sociocultural worlds. The researcher herself is socially situated, which limits her interests and understandings. Yet much can be seen in fieldwork that remains invisible in other research on aging.

Fieldwork is uniquely appropriate for research on aging in natural social settings because of its flexibility. Field studies use a variety of research tools to explore social processes, tools that may be adapted to unanticipated or changing circumstances (Denzin, 1989; Gubrium, 1988, 1992b; Mechanic, 1991; Miles & Huberman, 1984; Strauss, 1987). Talking with people to elicit information and perspective may take place in structured interviews or informal guided conversations. Archival data such as written records and case files may be recorded. Various inventories, checklists, and assessment instruments may be employed to "count" characteristics or events of the people or place. Overheard conversation may be compared with public discourse. In short, fieldwork, like the daily work of living and aging in social settings, involves what Gubrium and others have called *definitional labor* (Gubrium, 1988; Gubrium, Holstein, & Buckholdt, 1994; Gubrium & Lynott, 1985). People do not simply attach meaning to life events and situations, they labor over the ongoing creation of meaning. The definition of social situations, and of the self, is an emergent process. In field research, both the members of social settings and the researcher are thus engaged in such definitional labor. In field research, it is possible that aging persons and people who conduct research on aging may develop common understandings about the aging experience.

The Contributions of Fieldwork to Aging Research

Three research questions will be examined here to demonstrate the contributions to aging research that may be expected from fieldwork in group and institutional settings. Two are questions that have already received considerable attention but are expected to remain hot issues in aging research in the 1990s: caregiver stress and quality of care. The third is an important issue that has received little attention: the importance of peer relationships and friendships to the experience of aging, particularly for institutionalized and other dependent elders. This question has seldom been investigated, primarily because it requires qualitative research, while quantitative research has dominated the study of most issues of aging and old age.

Caregiver Stress

The caregiver burden and strain literature has expanded rapidly during the past decade in recognition of the demographic, economic, and social changes that are occurring in chronic illness, aging, and family life at this point in our history. As more people live to older ages, more individuals and families are engaged as caregivers for frail or cognitively impaired family members for a larger period of their lives. Numerous studies have documented variables that account for health and mental health risks for caregivers, and more recent research has described variation in caregiver stress by gender, class, and ethnicity, as well as the effectiveness of various interventions intended to alleviate caregiver stress. Most of these findings are based on survey research.

Because it is by now virtually impossible for consumers of caregiver stress research to keep pace with its production, some principal investigators have recently asked, "Do we need more studies of caregiver strain?" (George, 1990; Zarit, 1989). In other words, are there unanswered questions yet to be investigated? Yes. In fact, there are questions seldom asked, questions that may require procedures that are not customary for most investigators of caregiver stress. For example, a recent discussion of caregiving argues that we need a *new paradigm* to reconceptualize caregiving in terms of how people construct meaning in their lives as caregivers rather than the more narrow view of caregivers coping with burden and strain (Farran, Keane-Hagerty, Salloway, Kupferer, & Wilken, 1991).

Understanding the "meaning" of caregiving is possible through field research in various group and institutional settings such as group care homes, day care centers, residential care facilities, caregiver support groups, and the homes of families. Fieldwork means "being there" during the ebb and flow of good days and bad days, participating in conversation with people who are structuring their lives around caregiving, and witnessing the frustrations, accommodations, and losses as well as the emergence of new skills, joys, and life priorities. Fieldwork offers the opportunity to experience the definitional labor of becoming a caregiver. This view provides more than a snapshot taken at one or two points in time. The camera is rolling during the entire process of fieldwork, and the researcher steps into the frame instead of standing behind the lens. What is possible, then, is understanding something beyond the quantifiable stressors and measurable health consequences of caregiving. Fieldwork offers the possibility of understanding how one's life is transformed in the process of becoming and being a caregiver, a transition that will be experienced by increasing numbers of people in the coming decades.

Perhaps more important, field research takes place in the context of group and institutional care settings and in the presence of care recipients. Thus field research on caregiver stress explores facets of the caregiving experience that have seldom been examined in this literature to date: the importance of *socioenvironmental conditions* in care settings as factors in caregiver stress and the reciprocal nature of stress in the caregiving relationship.

The literature on caregiver stress largely has described stress as one-sided, in models with one-way arrows from the stressors involved in providing care to the health and mental health outcomes for care providers. Pearlin's recent model of caregiver stress (Pearlin, Mullan, Semple, & Skaff, 1990) summarizes this approach, taking account of the background and context that must be acknowledged as a factor in stress. But this model, like most of the literature on caregiver stress, does not consider the daily process of caregiving as it takes place in socioenvironmental settings. The care setting is more than a background factor: It is part of the dynamic process of caregiving. For example, the daily work of caregiving may become frustrated by features of the physical environment that change over time, such as a fence that needs repair and no longer provides security for a person with Alzheimer's disease who has enjoyed walking in the fenced garden. Time required for supervision and anxiety about losing the person may increase while the fence remains unrepaired.

The Pearlin model and others also do not account for the reciprocal nature of stress for care providers and care recipients. In contrast, fieldwork in natural settings allows the researcher to observe and experience the dynamics of the caregiving relationship firsthand. Thus it is possible to walk around the one-way arrows to see the other side of the one-sided caregiver stress equation, discovering ways in which outcomes of caregiver stress include diminished care and distress for care recipients, which itself intensifies stress for care providers. Furthermore, fieldwork can capture the evolving meaning of caregiving as people move through periods of distress and frustration as well as competency and joy.

Another benefit of field studies of caregiver stress is that fieldwork may be conducted as *participatory research* (Bookman & Morgen, 1988; Hall, Gillette, & Tandon, 1982; Lather, 1986; Maquire, 1987) whereby research questions are generated by members of the social setting, and actions are taken on behalf of and with the members as a result of the research. Giving voice to people directly involved in caregiving promises valuable insights for both research and practice. Moreover, for people whose daily lives are constrained by the responsibilities of caregiving, stress may be mediated somewhat by the very act of empowering them to voice their own concerns.

Quality of Care

Concerns over quality of life and quality of care have become a priority in aging research as millions of people live longer lives with chronic conditions. Legislation has expanded patients' rights in residential and long-term care facilities, including the right to restraint-free care. But as restraints are untied and other steps are taken to increase the autonomy of frail and dependent elderly people, most of the research investigating the effects of these changes has employed quantitative measures of health and safety risks and benefits. This is vital research. It is very important, for example, to know that removing restraints in nursing homes does not increase the risk of injury from falls. But other important questions about quality of care require new research approaches, including *intervention and evaluation research* incorporating the perspective of people who live with impairment.

Field research offers the opportunity to generate new research questions and interventions based on direct observation and participation in the daily lives of people who live with chronic conditions. For example, what is the meaning of quality of care and quality of life, from the perspective of people who live with a chronic condition such as Parkinson's disease? What interventions to improve care are experienced as actual improvements in daily life from the viewpoint of people experiencing the intervention? As with caregiver stress, fieldwork concerning quality of care may be conducted as participatory research, providing a voice for people to identify their own concerns about their care. In the very process of empowering people to speak for themselves, quality of care may improve.

Peer Relationships and Friendships

Hochschild's (1973) field study of a San Francisco senior-housing complex reported the discovery of "unexpected communities" of older people who were largely invisible to outsiders, including most behavioral and social scientists engaged in aging research. The residents developed strong social ties that enabled them to face the assaults of later life experienced by older people in urban settings. This was a study of survivors. The strength, dignity, neighborly exchanges, humor, and other social resources apparent among these elders presented a model of aging contrary to the typically negative expectations for at-risk elderly.

Hochschild's study provides a model for investigating the importance of peer relationships and solidarity for older people who live in group and institutional settings, as well as those who live in a variety of rural, urban, and suburban communities. There is a body of research that suggests the importance of *social support* in maintaining health and mental health throughout the life cycle. But measures of social support often have been limited to frequency counts, without exploration of the meaning of various forms of support from the perspective of the person (Barker & Mitteness, 1990; Matthews, 1986). There is little research on how friendships are formed and maintained in later life or comparisons of the process and consequences of friendship for people living in institutional settings compared with those who age in their own homes. Field research provides an opportunity to discover to what extent unexpected communities are created in a variety of living arrangements, including places where social isolation and dependency might be expected to inhibit the formation of social support. For example, an increasing number of recent ethnographic studies of nursing homes explore these social relationships among residents and between staff and residents (Diamond, 1992; Gubrium, 1975; Kayser-Jones, 1981; Savishinsky, 1991; Shield, 1988).

An Illustration: Fieldwork in Alzheimer's Day Care Centers

For several years recently, I had the pleasure of spending two days a week conducting a field study of 8 Alzheimer's day care centers, including approximately 50 staff members and 150 people with dementia. The eight programs were part of a California Department of Aging project to determine the feasibility of outpatient care for people moderately to severely impaired by a dementing illness. The day care centers also were resource centers for the primary caregivers to enable them to continue providing care for the person in the community.

My initial interest was in the nature of stress for service providers in this new field of dementia care. But during the course of the study this evolved into a concern with the links between staff stress and quality of care, as well as the socioenvironmental conditions associated with distress for both staff and clients (Lyman, 1989a, 1989b, 1990, forthcoming). Only one of the eight programs provided health care (such as physical therapy and nursing services), and in each program clients were referred to as *participants* rather than as *patients*. But most of the eight programs were organized to some extent around the *medical model,* based on biomedical assumptions about the "behavior problems" of people with dementia. The daily routine in the eight day care centers was similar. They were organized as activity programs with both structured and informal group interaction. The structured activities included exercise, "current events," craft projects, music and dance, and cooking and eating.

There were several subgroups within the day care centers. Staff and clients came together for organized activities, informal conversation, and one-on-one intergenerational relationships. Service providers developed work group norms, teamwork, and friendships. And some of the participants established ongoing peer groups and intimate ties, despite short-term memory loss. However, all of these subgroup relations developed within the framework of institutional structure. In some settings, because of size, strict adherence to a planned schedule, or a preoccupation with staff authority in managing clients, few primary group ties developed between staff members and clients or among elderly peers. In other settings there was more flexibility and informality and more time for the development of personal relationships.

Procedures

This field study of dementia care provided an opportunity to experience caregiver stress and to observe firsthand the social and environmental context in which *cognitive decline* and *behavior problems* occur for people with dementia. There were several unique conditions in this field study that required adaptation of conventional field research methods. First, this was a multisite study. Between-site comparisons were of interest, regarding variation in the conditions associated with staff stress and quality of care. Also, data analysis was complicated by the sheer volume of field notes in eight different day care centers. Finally, many of the people with dementia were language-impaired to some extent, or confused about my role in the day care center, or changed over time in their involvement in social relationships with me or others. The impairment of the clients was the most relevant organizing feature of this particular field study, both because of its effect on the participation of clients and its ongoing interpretation by the day care staff. "Making sense" of both dementia and how staff members themselves make sense of dementia became central tasks in the definitional labor of fieldwork in the eight Alzheimer's day care centers.

Informed Consent

Legitimacy for any research with vulnerable elderly people requires rethinking the issues surrounding informed consent and the definition of *research subjects* (George, 1989). The intent of informed-consent requirements in social and behavioral science research is to protect vulnerable people. For this reason, many aging persons who live with cognitive impairment or depression may be viewed as inappropriate research subjects because they are assumed to be incapable of giving informed consent on their own behalf.

Informed consent generally is negotiated once as a preliminary step in conducting research. When subjects are identified as cognitively impaired or clinically depressed, someone with recognized authority speaks for the person, providing descriptive accounts of their illness and concerns, and assessing their ability to participate as research subjects. The spokesperson's considerations may have little to do with the ongoing interest or consent of the person during the course of the research. Furthermore, second-person proxy accounts are inherently suspect, especially when the proxy may have an interest in a particular definition of the situation.

True informed consent with people who are confused or depressed would require that, in every encounter with a researcher, the person indicates willingness to participate without coercion or manipulation and willingness to continue as the encounter proceeds. In fieldwork, this understanding of informed consent typically is inherent in the ongoing relationship between the researcher and members of the setting. For example, in this day care study, people had "good" and "bad" days that affected their participation in the study. People on a particular day were lucid or not and either indicated an interest in talking or withdrew from interaction. An understanding of this kind of variation over time is at the core of field research. The intention of informed consent clearly is served by fieldwork, and its flexibility opens the door to an understanding of older people otherwise neglected in aging research.

Access

The eight dementia day care programs selected for this study were more accessible than others might be because they were part of a state evaluation research project. The program administrators in each of these model programs were accustomed to visitors, and the state collected monthly descriptive data on programs and staff and semiannual standardized assessments of clients. Yet at most sites there was some protectiveness on the part of top administrators, necessitating the submission of letters of intent and some indication of benefit to the agency in return for their participation in the study. Because my interest in staff stress could be framed empathically rather than critically, it was easier to argue the potential benefits of this study than might be the case for other field research in these settings.

During the first year of my research, four of the eight sites lost their original program directors, which required renegotiating access. Administrators threatened to close their programs to "outsiders" during these difficult transitional periods. But in the end, at each site I was able to regain access—in large part because my research was funded by a private foundation that has credibility with people who work in this field (the Alzheimer's Disease and Related Disorders Association). It also was helpful to be able to refer to my previous acceptance by directors in three Alzheimer's centers that were part of the same state project. Also, I must have been seen as an experienced volunteer who might be found useful during these difficult periods. In the end, all eight program directors and staffs were very cooperative.

Concurrent Data Collection and Data Analysis

In this comparative field study, as in Jay Gubrium's comparison of two family therapy programs (Gubrium, 1992a), theory and research were intertwined. *Theory building* occurred on the job during data collection, and specific research procedures and conceptual categories were refined midstream because of insights acquired during the course of the study. For example, after the first two sites as the scale and complexity of between-site comparisons became apparent, I developed standardized procedures to record information on facility design and characteristics of the staff, clients, and program. (Problems such as these involved in managing large qualitative research projects are addressed in Chapter 6 in this volume.) Comparative tools included a face sheet to summarize information from an initial interview with the program director, a one-page client-information form to record sociodemographic and assessment data from client files, and a facility-design checklist developed in conjunction with an environmental gerontologist and a public policy researcher (Cohen, Lyman, & Pynoos, 1991; Lyman, Pynoos, & Cohen, 1993). These more structured procedures generally were used during first-day visits and toward the end of fieldwork at each site, to minimize intrusion on the emerging relationship with members of the setting.

The *measurement* of stress also was refined after fieldwork at the first few sites. Typical measures of occupational stress such as aggregate rates of absenteeism and turnover were abandoned in this study, because day care centers that varied widely in both observed and reported stress had similar rates of absenteeism and turnover. Furthermore, it became apparent that more subjective measures of stress at work were more important, and these measures were available in field research. One can see and hear frustration with co-workers, exasperation and punitive reactions to clients, and other comments indicating role distance, exhaustion, and depersonalization. In a field study, it is possible to observe and experience various "acute stressors and chronic strains" (Avison & Turner, 1988) in the work of dementia care.

Researcher Role

My interest in Alzheimer's disease and dementia care is rooted in several important life and career experiences as well as my academic training. First, two of my aunts have been diagnosed with Alzheimer's. One received care at home, the other is in an institutional setting. Second, I worked as a social worker for a public agency for a year, an experience that introduced me to some sources of stress for service providers. And third, my academic training has sensitized me to issues of power and inequality in all social relationships. These aspects of my social situation, and others of which I am less aware, are ground into lenses through which I view Alzheimer's care settings and caregiving relationships.

The eight research sites were scattered throughout California, which required considerable air travel and driving. I visited each day care center on variable days each week for approximately three months. I was present for routine activities, unexpected emergencies, and staff meetings. I sat in on mental status assessments of client functioning. I overheard staff gripe sessions as well as staff conversations that shared pride in acquired knowledge, successes in working with clients, and a sense of loss as clients declined.

My role was to become a part of these social worlds as much as possible, to overcome the status of outsider. I helped with the work of day care: serving and cleaning up after meals, walking with "agitated" people, directing confused people to a destination. I worked "on the floor" to assist one short-staffed center during a flu epidemic in which several clients died, including a man with whom I had danced the previous week. Also, I was drawn into the intimacy of these places: I had my hands warmed by a nonspeaking client who could still offer nonverbal gifts; sympathized with a worker who was separating from her husband; comforted one client who suddenly realized she did not know if her mother was alive; and reassured another who felt abandoned by family for a day that seemed forever.

Commuting Between Different Social Worlds

In settings such as dementia day care, the emotional demands for the researcher are high. It can be very draining to interact both with people who have dementing illnesses and with staff who seek understanding and support for their difficult work. Also, the role of a temporary outsider can be alienating after some months and several sites, particularly when the demands of the research and travel restrict contact with colleagues, friends, and family. After the third or fourth site, I was pulled between a temptation to withdraw into detached note-taking and the need to become more involved, to acquire friends of the moment, to belong.

Fieldwork in the eight Alzheimer's day care centers required frequent passage between radically different worlds of meaning. Situational normalcy became the definition of reality. As Goffman (1961) observed about the "sphere of sympathetic participation" in various mental hospital wards, overcoming social distance makes any social world meaningful. However, because my participation in dementia day care centers occurred only two days a week, at times it was difficult to travel back and forth between the world of dementia and more familiar communities of meaning.

Fully participating in the world of people with dementing illnesses required learning the new language of "dementia talk," adapting to the nonlinear time order of people with dementia, participating in inappropriate intimacy based on mistaken identity, and redefining adult behavior in a context in which older adults frequently were infantilized or treated as if they were children (Lyman, 1988). The result was firsthand experience of "the permeability of realities" (Mehan & Wood, 1975). It was difficult to reenter the so-called normal world several times each week after a day in a dementia care facility. I came to understand the frequently voiced comment of day care staff members that "outsiders don't understand."

Note-Taking

Because of the scale of this project, across eight sites and three years, detailed field notes became an essential tool. But note-taking inhibits participation and rapport. Some staff members and clients in each setting expressed suspicion or at least curiosity about my note-taking. People with dementia would ask, "Are you a student?" or make requests indicating they identified me as someone official. One confused man even stood by my chair with his hand on my shoulder, dictating "letters" to me as if I were his secretary.

Self-conscious staff members who were highly aware of my note-taking sometimes staged interactions "for the record." Some workers displayed frustration over the heads of clients (eyes rolling, sighs) or made humorous comments to clients about their personal quirks, clearly intended for me as the observer. Impression management at times was obvious; staff members were aware the cameras were rolling. For example, at one site a program aide caught himself midsentence: "They're all cra— . . ." A nurse bustled by on a slow day, wearing a stethoscope and carrying other medical props, telling me, "Busy day!" She then addressed a co-worker for my benefit: "I need to talk with you, but I'm rushing around. . . ." However, these rather transparent displays became less frequent as the research continued over several months and the staff members relaxed and began to see me as a temporary member.

I took care to overcome the artificial barriers of note-taking through reassurances, humor, volunteered labor, food sharing, and casual conversations with the notepad conspicuously left on the table. Soon at each site, my note-taking was accepted simply as something I needed to do so I would not forget important information, and there was joking about my short-term memory loss. Note-taking was a daily reminder to all that I was an outsider, which at times created barriers to be overcome, but which also allowed me to extricate myself from what could have become all-consuming volunteer tasks when I felt the need to record something.

One clear advantage of visible note-taking was that some people volunteered information they felt should be recorded. A social worker took me aside and said, "You should have been here yesterday. It was like a Chinese fire drill." She then recounted an important incident on a particularly difficult day. Another staff member volunteered many direct statements, often prefaced by "Just so you'll understand, . . ." or "For your notes, . . ." Just as note-taking may curtail some opportunities for information, it creates others.

Applied Research During Fieldwork

Day care centers are places where clients are struggling to maintain some dignity and meaning, and staff members are struggling to stay in control in work that involves considerable uncertainty and tension. These are places where the understandings derived from fieldwork have immediacy. "Doing something" to improve daily living for people with dementia and their care providers becomes a responsibility associated with "knowing something" about the connections between staff stress and quality of care and about stressful conditions in the social and physical environment. Sometimes the expectation of doing something was explicitly stated by members of the setting. One staff member told me that she saw me as an advocate for the needs of her program and staff, someone whom the administrative staff might hear because they did not listen to the paraprofessional staff. I agreed. I helped her develop a written rationale to argue with administrators for a higher staff to client ratio. Another program aide expressed her sense of powerlessness to effect change in some very difficult working conditions, including the fact that there often were only 2 staff members available to assist and care for 15 clients: "I'm glad you're around enough to see. . . . It seems like there's nothing we can do." I met with her program manager on my last day to offer observations about staff stress and quality of care.

At several day care centers, staff members offered unsolicited and candid exit interviews. They cited problems they hoped I might help resolve, which were the reasons they were quitting. On occasion, people with dementia sought me out as an advocate regarding a complaint about treatment by family caregivers or day care staff. In addition, several program managers asked me to present what I had seen at staff meetings, which I agreed to do with some trepidation. I needed to protect the confidentiality of staff members who had been candid about their concerns, and I needed to protect the integrity of my fieldwork as I continued at other day care centers whose directors knew one another.

On my last day at one site, the program manager specifically asked me for suggestions or criticism she could "grow" from. In another setting, I offered unsolicited suggestions to the program manager, because the level of staff stress and client care I had observed called for immediate reforms. In both of these centers, changes were made as a result of my suggestions, and I was able to protect my sources as well as continue fieldwork at the other sites.

Offering suggestions at the conclusion of fieldwork presents a delicate situation. Interactions between the field researcher and members of the setting must be carefully managed if observations are discussed with those observed. One worthwhile outcome is that immediate application generates feedback from staff, which lends validity to the field researcher's observations. This feedback from the members of the setting helps to bridge the gap between research and theory, as well as putting knowledge to use in generating institutional and social change.

Conclusion

Fieldwork in groups and institutions offers unique opportunities for the study of aging. Maddox (1979) has argued that later life is a "strategic site" for studying many pivotal issues of concern to social and behavioral scientists. Field research opens the door to an understanding of many of those issues of later life, especially of the meaning and experience of aging or being old. Understanding the social and environmental context in which aging occurs, including the context for dementing illness and dementia care, is crucial for social policy and the planning of services in the coming decades. In a period in which there will be a dramatic increase in the population of very old people, and an era of limited resources for both aging research and services, it is essential that researchers and planners "get it right." Fieldwork in group and institutional settings provides a reality check in the study of aging and later life, incorporating the voices and definitional labor of aging persons as well as their care providers.

References

Avison, W. R., & Turner, R. J. (1988). Stressful life events and depressive symptoms: Disaggregating the effects of acute stressors and chronic strains. *Journal of Health and Social Behavior, 29,* 253-264.

Barker, J. C., & Mitteness, L. S. (1990). Unvisible caregivers in the spotlight: Non-kin caregivers of frail older adults. In J. F. Gubrium & A. Sankar (Eds.), *The home care experience: Ethnography and policy* (pp. 101-127). Newbury Park, CA: Sage.

Bookman, A., & Morgen, S. (Eds.). (1988). *Women and the politics of empowerment.* Philadelphia: Temple University Press.

Charmaz, K. (1983). The grounded theory method: an explication and interpretation. In R. E. Emerson (Ed.), *Contemporary field research* (pp. 109-126). Boston: Little, Brown.

Clifford, J., & Marcus, G. E. (1986). *Writing culture: The poetics and politics of ethnography.* Berkeley: University of California Press.

Cohen, E., Lyman, K. A., & Pynoos, J. (1991). Adapting day care center settings for persons with Alzheimer's disease: Environmental design training for staff. *American Journal of Alzheimer's and Related Disorders Research, 6,* 25-32.

Denzin, N. (1989). *The research act* (3rd ed.). Englewood Cliffs, NJ: Prentice-Hall.

Diamond, T. (1992). *Making grey gold: Narratives of nursing home care.* Chicago: University of Chicago Press.

Emerson, R. M. (1983). *Contemporary field research.* Boston: Little, Brown.

Farran, C. J., Keane-Hagerty, E., Salloway, S., Kupferer, S., & Wilken, C. S. (1991). Finding meaning: An alternative paradigm for Alzheimer's disease family caregivers. *Gerontologist, 31,* 483-489.

George, L. K. (1989). Services research: Research problems and possibilities. In E. Light & B. D. Lebowitz (Eds.), *Alzheimer's disease treatment and family stress: Directions for research* (pp. 127-140). New York: Plenum.

George, L. K. (1990). Caregiver stress studies: There really is more to learn. *Gerontologist, 30,* 580-581.

Glaser, B., & Strauss, A. (1967). *The discovery of grounded theory.* Hawthorne, NY: Aldine.

Goffman, E. (1961). *Asylums.* Garden City, NY: Doubleday.

Gold, R. L. (1958). Roles in sociological field observations. *Social Forces, 36,* 217-223.

Gubrium, J. (1975). *Living and dying at Murray Manor.* New York: St. Martin's.

Gubrium, J. (1988). *Analyzing field reality.* Newbury Park, CA: Sage.

Gubrium, J. (1992a). *Out of control: Family therapy and domestic disorder.* Newbury Park, CA: Sage.

Gubrium, J. (1992b). Qualitative research comes of age in gerontology. *Gerontologist,* *32,* 581-582.

Gubrium, J., Holstein, J. A., & Buckholdt, D. R. (1994). *Constructing the life course.* Dix Hills, NY: General Hall.

Gubrium, J., & Lynott, R. J. (1985). Alzheimer's disease as biographical work. In W. Peterson & J. Quadagno (Eds.), *Social bonds in later life* (pp. 349-367). Newbury Park, CA: Sage.

Hall, B., Gillette, A., & Tandon, R. (Eds.). (1982). *Creating knowledge: A monopoly? Participatory research in development.* New Delhi: Society for Participatory Research in Asia.

Hochschild, A. R. (1973). *The unexpected community.* Englewood Cliffs, NJ: Prentice-Hall.

Kayser-Jones, J. (1981). *Old, alone and neglected.* Chicago: University of Chicago Press.

Lather, P. (1986). Research as praxis. *Harvard Educational Review, 56,* 257-277.

Lyman, K. A. (1988). Infantilization of elders: Day care for Alzheimer's disease victims. *Research in the Sociology of Health Care, 7,* 71-103.

Lyman, K. A. (1989a). Bringing the social back in: A critique of the biomedicalization of dementia. *Gerontologist, 29,* 597-605.

Lyman, K. A. (1989b). Day care for persons with dementia: The impact of the physical environment on staff stress and quality of care. *Gerontologist, 29,* 557-560.

Lyman, K. A. (1990). Staff stress and treatment of clients in Alzheimer's care: A comparison of medical and non-medical day care programs. *Journal of Aging Studies, 4,* 61-79.

Lyman, K. A. (1993). *Day in, day out with Alzheimer's: stress in caregiving relationships.* Philadelphia: Temple University Press.

Lyman, K. A., Pynoos, J., & Cohen, E. (1993). Occupational stress and workplace design: Evaluating the physical environment of Alzheimer's day care. *Journal of Architectural and Planning Research, 10,* 130-145.

Maddox, G. L. (1979). Sociology of later life. *Annual Reviews of Sociology, 5,* 113-135.

Maquire, P. (1987). *Doing participatory research: A feminist approach.* Amherst: University of Massachusetts.

Matthews, S. A. (1986). Friendships in old age: Biography and circumstance. In V. W. Marshall (Ed.), *Later life: The social psychology of aging* (pp. 233-269). Beverly Hills, CA: Sage.

Mechanic, D. (1991). Medical sociology: Some tensions among theory, method and substance. *Journal of Health and Social Behavior, 30,* 147-160.

Mehan, H., & Wood, H. (1975). *The reality of ethnomethodology.* New York: John Wiley.

Miles, M. B., & Huberman, A. M. (1984). *Qualitative data analysis: a sourcebook for new methods.* Beverly Hills, CA: Sage.

Pearlin, L. I., Mullan, J. T., Semple, S. J., & Skaff, M. M. (1990). Caregiving and the stress process: An overview of concepts and their measures. *Gerontologist, 30,* 583-594.

Savishinsky, J. (1991). *The ends of time.* New York: Bergin & Garvey.

Schatzman, L., & Strauss, A. (1973). *Field research.* Englewood Cliffs, NJ: Prentice-Hall.

Shield, R. R. (1988). *Uneasy endings.* Ithaca, NY: Cornell University Press.

Strauss, A. (1987). *Qualitative analysis for social scientists.* New York: Cambridge University Press.

Zarit, S. H. (1989). Do we really need another "stress and caregiving" study? *Gerontologist, 29,* 147-148.

PART IV

Forms of Analysis

11

Analyzing Talk and Interaction

JABER F. GUBRIUM
JAMES A. HOLSTEIN

When a teacher tells students to speak up because that is the way their thoughts will be known, they are not only being urged to participate in classroom discussion, but also being told of the general relationship between knowledge and schooling. Whatever the students' private thoughts, the teacher concretely encounters what they know in how it is conveyed. When the facilitator of a support group for caregivers of Alzheimer's disease sufferers urges group members to tell their stories and express their feelings, the facilitator also addresses the interplay between speaking and inner personal life. It is speaking of feelings as much as it is feelings in their own right that makes the group and its experiences what they are. Just as the classroom as a going concern coalesces through conversation, so the support group is constituted in the expression and sharing of feelings on behalf of members' self-help. In their respective talk and interaction, the teacher, students, facilitator, and support-group members literally "do" knowledge and feelings as matters of occasioned communication (Garfinkel, 1967).

Talk and interaction not only make visible the unseen personal realms of experience, but also embody social realms such as the family, home, and community. When the distressed mother of a drug-abusing daughter describes in poignant detail in family therapy what her daughter's habit does to the household and cries for an answer to the question of what her family has become, she virtually requests a construction of the troubled home as she pleads for help (Gubrium, 1992; Gubrium &

Holstein, 1990). What is relayed communicatively embodies what this realm—the troubled home—is for her and other family members over and above their individual lives. Describing the one realm (individual family members' thoughts and feelings) in considerable detail and contrasting that with the other realm (home life), the mother narratively distinguishes the personal and the social.

This chapter considers talk and interaction as a narrative venue embodying both the personal and the social as they bear on aging and old age (Gubrium, 1988). Although growing older, not being old enough, and being too old are believed to have both specific personal and public referents that researchers often treat as variables, we turn here to ordinary talk and interaction about the referents as a way of analyzing the aging experience (Gubrium, Holstein, & Buckholdt, 1994).

Approaches to Talk and Interaction

Talk and interaction are the stock-in-trade of qualitative researchers. The pages of qualitative research reports in journal articles and monographs present a variety of usages. Some reports contain pages of quotations from individual subjects, whose thoughts, feelings, and activities are presented in their own words. Rather than writing about subjects' experiences or attempting to paraphrase what was said in interviews, the qualitative researcher uses direct quotes to present the tenor of the world under consideration in subjects' actual voices. Talk is highlighted more than interaction. The author is a background voice on these pages, serving to frame, sort through, or draw connections between what is more vividly conveyed in the quoted material.

The pages of Sharon Kaufman's (1986) *The Ageless Self* exemplify this usage in the field of aging. The importance of the quotations derives from an argument about the "sources of meaning in late life," the book's subtitle. Kaufman argues that the elderly are not passive respondents to processes of aging but actively draw together and convey the meaning of their lives from two important sources: major events across the life course and the values that served to locate their desires and intentions.

As far as major events are concerned, Kaufman presents the testimony of Millie, Ben, and Stella, three key informants. Kaufman emphasizes that the elderly assemble the meanings of their lives on their own terms, thus justifying the presentation of informants' voices in their own words. They do not automatically convey an aged self in response to historical conditions. For example, a woman who started her own business during the Great Depression of the 1930s comments that, while the Depression affected the venture, her "taking" to prayer sustained her, the turn to religion, in retrospect, narratively making meaningful the related events in her life both at the time and since (p. 79). Kaufman orients to the woman's narrative as an interpretation of life, indicative of the active subject, one who relates to historical experiences by "making meaning." Similarly, Millie, Ben, and Stella "do not recall World War I or World War II as pivotal forces in their own lives" (p. 81). Stella, for one, centrally thematizes her life in terms of a continuing desire for education and her drive to accomplish. The wars are brought into focus as factors within, not as determinants of, narrative themes.

In contrast, Haim Hazan's (1980) book, *The Limbo People,* stresses interaction over talk. The book is a "study of the constitution of the time universe among the aged" in a day center for elderly Jews in Marlsden, a London borough. Hazan's presentation calls attention to the local cultural context that designs talk and interaction. The patterns portrayed are interpreted to show what is shared and how this reproduces a certain time universe. The voice of the subject here is not as important as it is in Kaufman's work because the center's time universe as described by Hazan itself gives voice to participants' experiences (Douglas, 1986).

Hazan shows how elders' lives before the Marlsden center are transformed when they become center participants, especially changes in the way the course of life is reckoned. Lifetime reckoning is not linear or developmental, with the past, present, and the future connected in a sequential manner. For center participants, the time world shrinks. In their precenter lives, the present was evaluated in terms of an alienated past and future; life at the center is a present-constricted limbo. Important elements of the past such as growing up in the East End of London are renounced, not used as a context within which to evaluate present concerns. At the center, the future is vague, not seriously considered or estimated. The few who dwell on the past or prognosticate the future are summarily called to task. As Hazan writes, "[It is] almost as though time does not exist in the center itself, but is capable of being a nuisance outside" (p. 89).

Jaber Gubrium's (1975) nursing home ethnography *Living and Dying at Murray Manor* takes a middle ground and presents talk in relation to interaction. Neither talk nor interaction is analytically privileged; their interplay is taken to be a process of social construction. The pages of

Chapter 2 especially, where the world of top staff members is described, are covered with scripts of communication between the staff members who participate in patient care conferences. From the general theme that the single administrative unit called a nursing home can be construed as three separate worlds of experience, Gubrium shows how top staff members' talk and interaction narratively constitute residents' lives to align those lives substantively with staff members' need to set short- and long-term treatment goals. Staff members' sense of residents' conduct and conditions is informed by the task at hand. What is said and communicated about residents in conferences is as much about top staff members' world and their talk and interaction as it is about the residents' lives in their own right.

Excerpts from the staffings of eight residents are presented to reveal how conference participants' *typifications* of residents establish locally useful contexts for discussing care needs. A natural feature of all communication (Schutz, 1970), typification takes the type of process that is talked about—say, the possibility that a particular resident, Joan Borden, sees herself as a leader—as a context for further consideration of the resident in formulating the care plan. Having established a discursive context (the type *leader*), ensuing talk and interaction construct the particulars of Borden's conduct and condition within the type's recognizable and emerging cognitive horizons. For example, acknowledging that the typical leader has a considerable sense of self-worth, conference participants are momentarily loathe to make glib decisions about where Borden should reside in the nursing home. As the manor's social worker remarks in relation to the typification, "That's why we better be careful about moving her, because we'd threaten her and she'd flip out" (p. 67).

Typification constructs what this particular resident is. Her identity and its broader social meaning emerge through discourse; they cannot be separated from talk. Continuing conversation establishes other typifications. Scripted excerpts from the care conferences indicate how, by means of words and from practical considerations, speakers construct care needs: in Borden's case, her character in the nursing home for purposes of care planning.

Some researchers, known as *conversation analysts,* focus on the organization of talk per se and analyze its properties (Atkinson & Heritage, 1984; Goodwin & Heritage, 1990; Heritage, 1984, chap. 8; Sudnow, 1972; Zimmerman, 1988). The property of turn-taking, for example, features talk as naturally organized in sequences of turns between speakers (Sacks, Schegloff, & Jefferson, 1974). This normal property of communication can be used, say, to display interactional incompetence. James Holstein (1988, 1993) illustrates how district attorneys in involuntary hospitalization hearings use the normal communicative pattern of taking turns in an orderly fashion to draw out the incompetence of candidates for commitment. For example, simply remarking "Oh?" in responding to a candidate patient's utterance establishes the conversational imperative for the candidate to say something in turn, providing an opportunity for him or her to reveal incompetence. There is a kind of catch-22 here. Saying nothing is as much a sign of incompetence as saying something deemed irrational. Also capitalizing on turn-taking, public defenders attempt to set up communication with the candidate so that he or she is minimally subject to the property; it is hoped that this will show both turn-taking adherence and substantive competence.

Because conversation analysts are concerned with the ongoing sequential organization and management of conversation, they need detailed records of talk as it actually occurs for their analyses. Discerning the social organization of sequential talk requires explicit attention to the natural flow of conversation, including the myriad imperfections that are typically glossed over in less-detailed records. The ordinary structures of talk—conversational initiations, solicitations, responses and refusals, false starts, repairs, gaps in continuous speech, overlapping talk, and other fine-grained details—are important features of coordinated interaction and as such become the focus of conversation-analytic studies. As a result, discourse must be recorded as accurately and in as much detail as possible. Conversation analysts generally tape record conversation, although videotaping is also used to capture the details of nonverbal interaction.

The intermediate step between tape recording conversation and data analysis is transcription. Although transcription of any kind is painstaking and time-consuming, it is especially tedious for conversation analysis because this form of discourse analysis aims to show how conversational regularities and preferences in their own right construct and manage the realities under consideration. In transcripts, it is important to record not only what is said but how it is said, utterance by utterance. A system of notation for transcription has been developed by Gail Jefferson and is described in detail in Atkinson and Heritage (1984). Potter and Wetherell (1987, pp. 188-189) provide an abbreviated system of notation based on Jefferson's work.

Recording What Speakers "Do With Words"

Although conversation analysis has flourished in many substantive areas, its use in aging research has been relatively limited (but see Boden & Bielby, 1983, 1986). Other analysts of talk and interaction are less concerned with conversational organization than with what speakers "do with words" in everyday life (Bernardes, 1987). The substance and practice of what is said and shared in interaction is emphasized as much as how what is said is communicatively managed. Jon Bernardes (1985), for example, has drawn parallels with rhetoric, arguing that the social order of the family is not a thing that can be located, described, and studied; rather, it is an ideology with widespread rhetorical value. Gale Miller (1991) has applied this line of reasoning to the social construction of jobs and labor markets. His discourse analysis of a work-incentive program treats rhetoric, also called *persuasive discourse,* as a signal feature of how front-line service workers construct the conditions of work situations, client skills, and client attitudes toward work in the service workers' interactions with clients in the program. Gubrium's (1986, 1987a, 1987b) study of the social construction of Alzheimer's disease highlights how caregiving troubles are "organizationally embedded" and thus assigned meaning according to the categories shared in the organizational contexts in which the troubles are presented and considered. Gubrium shows, for example, how the local cultures of different caregiver support groups provide particular vocabularies for speaking of, and related categories for thinking about, matters such as the meaning of family responsibility, the burdens of care, and the limits of concern (Gubrium & Lynott, 1987).

Much of the qualitative research focusing on talk and interaction in the field of aging has examined what people concretely do with words. For that reason, the remainder of this chapter will focus on this kind of analysis. The matter of recording talk and interaction in this vein is more ethnographically inspired than it is attuned to the sequential organization of conversation. Transcripts of talk and interaction are as likely to take the form of field notes as they are scripted from audio- or videotapings.

Because talk is conceived as constructive of experiential reality, it is a practical undertaking and thus located in time and space. Setting is an important consideration. It matters a great deal, for example, whether the social construction of agedness—such as construing possible dementia in the forgetfulness of a parent—is done in the context of being a chapter member of the Alzheimer's association or in the context of a family network that, as network members put it, "accept old people for what they are and take care of our own." Regardless of what may be correct in the matter, the same talk will not necessarily have the same meaning in both contexts. What may be talk of symptoms in the chapter setting and constructive of Alzheimer's disease, may be talk of aging in the family network and constructive of "really getting on in years." Setting-neutral transcripts—that is, those that do not take local understandings into account—would not necessarily reveal what is being done with words in one context as opposed to the other.

Recording talk and interaction as a way of writing field notes is sometimes called "doing" process notes. Such notes aim to represent in the form of a written script the process or course of talk and interaction. In settings where tape recording is routine, as it is in brief family therapy where videorecordings are the norm (Gubrium, 1992), the researcher need only seek permission to view or transcribe tapes. Of course, official recording priorities may not exactly coincide with research interests, for example, when the clinical focus is on client talk and interaction, while the research aims to capture staff considerations of client conduct in the same setting. Even when tape recording is routinely done, not all situations in a particular setting may be tape recorded. Such variations usually require a combination of tape transcriptions and handwritten process notes.

In some settings, there is no regular tape recording, if any at all. For example, although talk and interaction are the hallmark of caregiver support groups, there is little interest in recording what transpires. Participants target sharing and learning. The researcher, on the other hand, although not unsympathetic to this, has the goal of describing and understanding the groups' communicative dynamics. The researcher may seek permission to tape record group proceedings, although this raises the issue of whether tape recording produces a dynamic of its own that is not natural to the proceedings. (In this regard, video recording is natural to brief therapy because everyone expects it to occur; it is a mark of what makes brief therapy what it is.) Deciding against this option, the researcher may settle on taking handwritten notes. But even this may be obtrusive, especially in small settings and intimate or delicate situations. Of course, in some small or intimate settings, note-taking by, say, staff members or family members is common and as such allows for a limited amount of similar activity by the researcher.

Process note-taking poses certain difficulties because it is done by hand and sometimes necessarily after the proceedings of interest have transpired. Often the pace of talk and interaction is faster than handwriting. Attempting to obtain a written facsimile is unrealistic. However, facsimiles may be unnecessary for certain analytic purposes. For example, the researcher who aims to make visible caregivers' social construction of symptom onset in Alzheimer's disease does not require the communicative detail needed by the conversation analyst whose goal is to document sequences of discovery for onset as a communicative category.

Records of talk and interaction appropriate for ethnographically oriented analyses combine the traditional note-taking that describes courses of interaction with handwritten scripts of conversation, portions of individual testimony in progress, or even belated written reproductions of conversation or testimony. As the following notes show, the proceedings of a caregiver support-group discussion about symptom onset in Alzheimer's disease could take the form of brief scripts of conversation of a few lines interspersed by short written descriptions of what was said, considered, or debated in the time between.

Wife A: I never doubted for a moment that something was different [with her spouse], but I thought, well, he's getting up there [in years].

Wife B: I can't say I really knew what was the matter at first.

[Participants discuss at length the clarity of onset, presenting various explanations for why things became different. As before, consideration gradually zeros in on particular spouse's experiences as exemplary of general types. Wife C soon becomes a "perfect study" of what is quickly taken to be an onset beset with quandary.]

Wife A (to Wife C):   Yeah, now I see what you mean. That is different. You and Viv are a lot alike. As I said, for me, I jumped to conclusions right away, like Kitty and Betty did. [Elaborates.]

What is selected for scripting and what for description in field notes depends on the researcher's analytic aim and the pace and substance of the talk and interaction being recorded. If the analytic aim is to show the different ways onset is constructed by family members, then scripts of the process by which members identify onset would be useful narrative material. Still, as the above notes indicate, we can get a sense of the identification process without having a complete record of the wives' exchanges. The ethnographic note following Wife B's comment describes how what was actually said develops, interpreting that to show how it meaningfully fits with what came before and what is said afterward. We can read Wife A's second comment in relation to a communicative theme of subjective onset identification and categorization in interpersonal comparison. The ethnographic note also tells us that at the time much talk transpired about a particular topic and point of analysis—more than is necessary to make and illustrate the point and, more than likely, too much for handwritten transcription. Once a particular analytic point is made and has been illustrated in detail, its further narrative elaboration by subjects can be indicated by simply writing "elaborates" in recorded scripts, as shown at the end of Wife A's second comment.

This manner of recording data is not a panacea, but it is a manner appropriate to a particular approach to talk and interaction. It leaves out too much talk for conversation-analytic purposes, just as it may supply too much talk for certain ethnographic aims. As far as ethnography is concerned, if we were to argue, say, that support groups form separate local cultures of the caregiving experience, a description of contrasting group categories, vocabularies, and images might be sufficient to illustrate differences.

Two Examples

Consider two examples of the analysis of talk and interaction related to matters of age and aging. The first focuses on discourse about age in relation to personal troubles that can arise at any time of life. The second concerns discourse about aging minds encountered and considered by caregivers.

Holstein's (1990, 1993) fieldwork on involuntary mental hospitalization proceedings in mental health and legal settings examines how the discourse of age is used throughout the commitment process to influence commitment decisions. He argues that age is not a definite and informative characteristic of individuals that accrues with the passage of time. Instead, it is an interactional accomplishment; the meaning of age "cannot be divorced from the communicative procedures through which it is produced" (p. 115).

Holstein observed and interviewed extensively in metropolitan court in California, which hears only cases related to mental health, as well as in several other venues where civil commitment is considered. The study focused on the hearings that produced judicial commitment decisions. Psychiatric experts, attorneys, judges, and even candidate patients produced age-related rhetoric, invoking age to make sense of the case at hand as they interpreted candidate patients' traits, behaviors, and circumstances and advocating specific resolutions and outcomes.

When psychiatrists discussed their diagnoses, for example, they frequently cited candidate patients' ages to establish a framework for viewing particular behaviors as symptoms of specific categories of mental illness. They sometimes used age or life stage to interpret a candidate patient's behavior as inappropriate and hence psychologically unhealthy. One psychiatrist, a Dr. Haas, employed this usage in the following metropolitan court testimony about Jake Donner, a candidate patient:

> Jake has the, shall we say, the enthusiasm of a much younger man. His landlord says he's out every night, and sometimes doesn't come back until the next morning. When I examined Mr. Donner he made no secret of his, let's say, passion for members of the opposite sex. He was extremely distraught about being hospitalized because he said he was dating several women and they would all be upset if he stopped coming round to visit them. He said some pretty outrageous things for a man his age. He claimed that he needed to have sex at least once a day or he would, as he put it, lose his manhood. And he said these women were anxious to oblige him. Now, here's a man in his fifties—what is he, fifty-five, sixty—saying the kind of things you'd expect from some teenager bragging to his buddies, but I'd have to say they were clearly inappropriate from him. (Holstein, 1990, pp. 116-117)

Throughout the testimony, Haas elucidated much of Donner's symptomatology with reference to age. Haas argued, for instance, that Donner's tales of his sex life were "outrageous" for a "man his age." Sexual talk was not said to be intrinsically outrageous, only within the age context used to invoke impropriety. Haas further elaborated age's meaning by way of rhetorical "contrast structures" (Smith, 1978) that specified the appropriate images and expectations of persons at various stages of the life course. Donner's age and behavior were juxtaposed and compared with descriptions of behavior considered normal or appropriate for someone of a different age. Haas used this to document

Donner's mental disturbance, framing it as age-inappropriate behavior symptomatic of psychiatric distress. Although the age appropriateness of Donner's behavior was not the sole concern in the case, Haas clearly made age salient by using it as an interpretive framework for evaluating Donner's mental status, his testimony thus producing the relevance of Donner's age. The application of a different contrast structure, such as the presumed sexuality of all men in a particular ethnic group, would provide an opposite, more normalizing rhetoric if it could be successfully argued that Donner was a member of the group.

Gubrium's research on the social construction of Alzheimer's disease provides an example of an analysis of talk and interaction focused on family members' responses to the aging mind (Gubrium 1986, 1987a, 1987b). The presentation of members' talk and interaction is partially drawn from scripted records of support-group proceedings. Consider how the meaning of family responsibility develops in the support groups. An enduring working question in all groups is "What kind of family are we [family members] to each other [at home]?" The question may never have been raised in the household proper. For many participants, it is now addressed for the first time.

Support groups vary in the kinds of answers they provide to such questions, reflecting their local cultural differences. Some group cultures are highly structured and others loosely designed in their formulations (Gubrium, 1989). One group, facilitated by two experienced caregivers, had a well developed conception of the normal course of familial responsibility. It was conveyed in references to the burdens of the so-called 36-hour day that caregiving entailed, reminiscent of Elizabeth Kübler-Ross's (1969) stage model of dying with its chronology of denial and eventual realization (Gubrium, 1987a). Caregivers who participated in this support group sorted and organized their thoughts and feelings in relation to the stage model, just as caregivers in other support groups took account of their experience in relation to less-structured formulations.

In none of the groups were answers a wholesale process of enculturation. Rather, talk and interaction showed that practical reasoning mediated in different ways what participants were otherwise said commonly to encounter in their caregiving experiences. To illustrate, take a brief exchange between two facilitators (Anne and Ruth), a caregiver (Dee), and two other participants (Belle and Dora). The exchange follows an extended discussion between Anne, Ruth, and Belle about how similar the course of the home care experience has been for them.

Dee: I don't know, Belle. Sure, I can see what happened . . . why you decided to start looking for a place [nursing home] for Harold [Belle's demented husband]. I guess if I was in your shoes, I wouldn't fight it anymore either. You do have to start thinking about how you feel inside and what's happening to your family. God knows, the kids would have been ignored.

Dora (to Dee): Well, dear, what's your problem? We're all in this together. You're no different. You just think you are. I was like you once. [Elaborates.] I did everything. I had no time to think. It was get this, do that, and take of Ben [her husband] 24 hours a day. Well, I learned the hard way and nearly put myself in the hospital. Ben's on a waiting list [for nursing home placement] at Pine Crest. God help me, it won't come too soon.

Belle: I don't think I'm ready for that yet, but I know I'll have to pretty soon. I know it's coming. It's only a matter of time.

Dee: I don't think it's that simple, Belle.

Anne: Oh, come on, Dee. That's what it is in a nutshell. You have to start thinking about yourself. [Elaborates.] Look at you. You're all worn down and I'll bet you're feeling lonely and depressed.

Dee: No, that's what I was trying to explain last time. I'm really not lonely. I'm . . . .

Ruth: You're denying. We all try to deny it.

[At this point, there is an extended discussion of denial, its workings, and how it applies to specific caregivers, after which Dee continues, resisting the group's characterization of the caregiver.]

Dee: I don't think so. Seriously, if I was in the same situation as most people, maybe I'd be denying, but basically I'm here to learn how to cope with his [her husband] . . . you know, how to dress him and what's going to happen to him in the months ahead. [Elaborates.]

Anne: Dee, you're forgetting that we know all about this.

Dee: I know. I know that's the way it works. I understand that. But you're forgetting one thing, too: He's all I have. He's a friend, a companion, even if he forgets who I am sometimes. It doesn't

matter that much anyway because I know he knows in his heart that
it's me. [Elaborates.] If we had had kids, maybe it'd be different.
I'd probably be going through all the phases of this thing. [Elabo-
rates.] But I don't have kids, and his family's not around, and I
don't know who mine are. We've been pretty much on our own and
with each other all our lives. If I give him up, it'd be, well, giving
up on life. It's not like I'm going to get back to my life after he's
gone. What life are we talking about? Life with Gordon is all I've
ever really had. Gordon's my family.

Although Dee acknowledges the stage model's general validity, she
considers herself to be an exception to its developmental rule, not on
grounds of denial, but applicability. Adherents of the model assume that
there is a family life separate and distinct from the caregiver's relation
with the care receiver—a life jeopardized by caregiving and, it is hoped,
taken into account "before it is too late." According to the model, in the
normal course of caregiving, one eventually breaks the clutches of
denial. The group's two facilitators assume that one of their tasks is to
help others do just that. Dee, however, insists that her husband, Gordon,
is her family, indeed her life. Her responsibility to her family and to life
itself is equated with her responsibility to Gordon.

By untangling her care for Gordon from the prevailing model of
caregiver adjustment and tying care instead to the life she and Gordon
have built together without competing familial obligations, Dee assem-
bles rational and practical grounds for resisting local culture (Connell,
1987; Paules, 1991; Scott, 1985). She not only claims exception to the
general rule concerning responsibility and the borders of the familial,
but also simultaneously depathologizes her responses and provides a
separate and unique space for her well-being. All the same, her status
as an exception proves the rule guiding other participants, allowing
Dee's difference to stand rationally adjacent to the locally recognized
normal course of the caregiver's experience.

Conclusion

Highlighting both talk and interaction, analysis conveys how inven-
tive, localized, and organizationally embedded the meaning of age in
everyday life can be. As Holstein shows in narrative materials gathered in

involuntary commitment proceedings, it is possible to use and thereby construct age and life stage for a variety of purposes. In Dr. Haas's testimony, it is used to pathologize candidate patient Donner's conduct. Yet, as Holstein suggests elsewhere, others, such as public defenders, could use age to show evidence of exactly the opposite, namely, that an older man who presents younger than his years is not yet "over the hill" and commands considerable control over his life, as spicy as that might be. Likewise, Gubrium's analysis reveals the practical reasoning that mediates, and in Dee's case serves as a basis of resistance to, local understandings of the course of the caregiving experience. Although Dee is still attuned to local culture, she virtually invents personalized grounds for both taking into account and transforming what it means to care for a demented spouse.

As analysis does not focus exclusively on talk, but on talk in interactional context, it takes considerable accounting of circumstance, which is a strength of ethnography. Holstein's narrative material not only shows the situated construction of age, but the use of age for the practical purposes of a particular kind of court proceeding. In the context of the commitment hearings, age indexes matters of mental competence; its meaning is thus embedded in this particular organization's context of concerns. Gubrium's brief script of support-group communication indicates difference and resistance, although in relation to (or against) a distinct and local culture of understanding about how one responds as a caregiver to an aging mind. His narrative material suggests that less-structured local cultures provide a different context for inventiveness, one not as crystallized for resistance.

Attention to talk and interaction allows us to see how age and aging are brought into being as meaningful entities through everyday interaction and usage. The broader vocabulary of the life course—including childhood, adolescence, adulthood, stage, growth, maturation, and regression—operates the same way to assign meaning to personal experience in relation to ostensible times of life (Gubrium, Holstein, & Buckholdt, 1994).

References

Atkinson, P., & Heritage, J. (Eds.). (1984). *Structures of social action: Studies in conversation analysis*. Cambridge, UK: Cambridge University Press.

Bernardes, J. (1985). "Family ideology": Identification and exploration. *Sociological Review, 33*, 275-297.

Bernardes, J. (1987). Doing things with words: Sociology and "family policy" debates. *Sociological Review, 35,* 679-702.

Boden, D., & Bielby, D. (1983). The past as resource: A conversation analysis of elderly talk. *Human Development, 26,* 308-319.

Boden, D., & Bielby, D. (1986). The way it was: Topical organization in elderly conversation. *Language and Communication, 6,* 73-89.

Connell, R. W. (1987). *Gender and power.* Stanford, CA: Stanford University Press.

Douglas, M. (1986). *How institutions think.* Syracuse, NY: Syracuse University Press.

Garfinkel, H. (1967). *Studies in ethnomethodology.* Englewood Cliffs, NJ: Prentice-Hall.

Goodwin, C., & Heritage, J. (1990). Conversation analysis. *Annual Review of Anthropology, 19,* 283-307.

Gubrium, J. F. (1975). *Living and dying at Murray Manor.* New York: St. Martin's.

Gubrium, J. F. (1986). *Oldtimers and Alzheimer's.* Greenwich, CT: JAI.

Gubrium, J. F. (1987a). Organizational embeddedness and family life. In T. Brubaker (Ed.), *Aging, health and family: Long-term care* (pp. 23-41). Newbury Park, CA: Sage.

Gubrium, J. F. (1987b). Structuring and destructuring the course of illness: The Alzheimer's disease experience. *Sociology of Health and Illness, 9,* 1-24.

Gubrium, J. F. (1988). *Analyzing field reality.* Newbury Park, CA: Sage.

Gubrium, J. F. (1989). Local cultures and service policy. In J. Gubrium & D. Silverman (Eds.), *Politics of field research* (pp. 94-112). Newbury Park, CA: Sage.

Gubrium, J. F. (1992). *Out of control: Family therapy and domestic disorder.* Newbury Park, CA: Sage.

Gubrium, J. F., & Holstein, J. A. (1990). *What is family?* Mountain View, CA: Mayfield.

Gubrium, J. F., Holstein, J. A., & Buckholdt, D. (1994). *Constructing the life course.* Dix Hills, NY: General Hall.

Gubrium, J. F., & Lynott, R. J. (1987). Measurement and the interpretation of burden in the Alzheimer's disease experience. *Journal of Aging Studies, 1,* 265-285.

Hazan, H. 1980. *The limbo people.* London: Routledge.

Heritage, J. (1984). *Garfinkel and ethnomethodology.* Cambridge: Polity Press.

Holstein, J. A. (1988). Court order incompetence: Conversational organization in involuntary commitment hearings. *Social Problems, 35,* 458-473.

Holstein, J. A. (1990). The discourse of age in involuntary commitment proceedings. *Journal of Aging Studies, 4,* 111-130.

Holstein, J. A. (1993). *Court ordered insanity.* Hawthorne, NY: Aldine.

Kaufman, S. R. (1986). *The ageless self.* Madison: University of Wisconsin Press.

Kübler-Ross, E. (1969). *On death and dying.* New York: Macmillan.

Miller, G. (1991). *Enforcing the work ethic.* Albany: State University of New York Press.

Paules, G. F. (1991). *Dishing it out: Power and resistance among waitresses in a New Jersey restaurant.* New Brunswick, NJ: Rutgers University Press.

Potter, J., & Wetherell, M. (1987). *Discourse and social psychology.* Newbury Park, CA: Sage.

Sacks, H., Schegloff, E., & Jefferson, G. (1984). A simplest systematics for the organization of turn-taking for conversation. *Language, 50,* 696-735.

Schutz, A. (1970). On phenomenology and social relations. Chicago: University of Chicago Press.

Scott, J. C. (1985). *Weapons of the weak: Everyday forms of peasant resistance.* New Haven, CT: Yale University Press.

Smith, D. E. (1978). "K" is mentally ill: The anatomy of a factual account. *Sociology, 12*, 23-53.
Sudnow, D. (1972). *Studies in social interaction*. New York: Free Press.
Zimmerman, D. (1988). On conversation: The conversation analytic perspective. In J. A. Anderson (Ed.), *Communication yearbook* (Vol. 11, pp. 406-432). Newbury Park, CA: Sage.

12

The Identification and Analysis of
Themes and Patterns

MARK R. LUBORSKY

One hallmark of qualitative methods is the search for themes in human experience. The study of themes is traditionally seen as a simple chore of reading through notes and transcripts to identify recurrent statements or behaviors that are then labeled, described, and summarized to portray the person's most frequent—that is, most important—experiences or actions. Many pitfalls in this process are seldom noted.

Standard textbooks on qualitative research devote at most a few paragraphs to the procedures and fewer to critical issues in conducting thematic analysis (Bernard, 1988; Pelto & Pelto, 1978; Spradley, 1979, 1980; Strauss & Corbin, 1990; Werner & Schoepfle, 1987a, 1987b). The procedures for finding and analyzing themes have not received the kind of in-depth and critical examination as have other research techniques and concepts. A host of critical concerns remain incompletely understood, yet the importance of identifying and resolving these issues is urgent because the use of all qualitative insights and methods is growing.

This chapter has five objectives: (a) to consider the benefits of thematic analysis, (b) to outline the issues and dilemmas in the use and interpretation of themes and to suggest basic definitions, (c) to describe methods and potential pitfalls in the discovery and analyses of themes, (d) to specify guidelines for discovery, and (e) to discuss continuing challenges and unresolved issues. Although thematic analysis is applied to a wide range of materials and topics, the focus here is primarily on the analysis of themes in face-to-face conversations and in texts or transcripts. Such data are commonly elicited during in-depth interviews, focus groups, and semistructured interviews. But the concepts, issues, and procedures are broadly applicable, for example, to data from participant observation, literary texts, or popular literature and media.

The Benefits of Thematic Analysis

Enthusiasm for thematic analysis is well founded. Among its many notable benefits is its direct representation of an individual's own point of view and descriptions of experiences, beliefs, and perceptions. In contemporary terms, the qualitative study of themes gives more weight to the voices and experiences of the individual consumer or patient than to the expert observer or medical researcher. It exemplifies the goal of qualitative research, which aims to discover lived experiences and meanings—that is, the *emic* (Fry & Keith, 1986) or insider's view of the lived world (Mishler, 1986).

Themes can provide insight into the cultural beliefs and values that instill powerful experiences and motivations and shape how individuals plan, makes sense of, and respond to events. At the same time, thematic analyses illustrate key limitations in the current practice of some qualitative studies. For example, qualitative data on personal and cultural themes provide information that elude medical or psychiatric case diagnostic or standardized behavioral science measurements of traits that assign people to predefined generalized categories. These approaches do not capture the idioms and contents of an individual's views, experiences, and sentiments. As Gubrium (1988) carefully documents, some deeply felt kinds of experience, sentiments, and beliefs may remain inexpressible in the scientific format of direct questions and answers or professional literature, but they may emerge in other forms such as poetry (Abu-Lughod, 1985; Groves, Fultz, & Martin, 1992).

Themes can be readily described and coded. It is relatively easy to reduce a lengthy stretch of talk to a phrase or label that describes the main point or theme of the passage. The theme is then readily comparable with other stretches of talk by the same speaker or by other people. This amenability to coding and systematic comparison helps to explain the widespread use of theme analyses across diverse disciplines, in the arts, humanities, social sciences, mental health, and health research.

Thematic analysis and reports on themes are useful for qualitative researchers at a pragmatic level as well as in the discovery and analysis of information. Themes have a dual life, serving as qualitative and quantitative units of analyses. In one mode, themes can be discovered and reported in a way that preserves their richness of detail and contexts by using ethnographic description and interpretative approaches in examining transcripts and field notes as cultural texts for interpretation (DelVecchio Good, Good, Schaffer, & Lind, 1990; Geertz, 1973; Marcus & Clifford, 1986). In the second mode, themes can be coded into standardized categories and then counted and used for many kinds of quantitative analyses. Analyses of the reliability and validity of the methods and concepts can be provided more readily than for some other kinds of content and interpretive analyses. In this mode, the themes are decontextualized and standardized rather than richly described. Indeed, in this regard the use of themes to group informants together in terms of shared features suggests that themes stand as a kind of qualitative version of medical and psychiatric diagnosis categories.

The dual life makes them appealing to qualitative and quantitative researchers. For quantitative researchers, the analysis of themes brings the cold statistical presentations and researchers into closer proximity with the warmth of the expressed sentiments and experiences of the research population. For the qualitative researcher, themes provide a bridge to a mode of constructing scientific knowledge that is at once more objective, dispassionate, and less biased and thus credible, legitimated, and authorized because themes can be counted and share the aura of the numerical language of science.

Issues and Dilemmas in the Interpretation of Themes

The intuitive familiarity and wide appeal of thematic analysis belies a deeper cultural affinity and the need for a more critical understanding. The concept and practices in studying themes resonate with fundamental cultural ideals and taboos. Themes can be used by speakers to provide structure and coherence, a sense of order, and also an explicit point or meaning. Talk, writing, music, or poetry that lack some discernible theme or central point are typically judged negatively as incomplete or incoherent. During our century, major artistic and scientific innovations in literature, music, and mathematics came from those who challenged the deeply held Western sensibility or quest for patterned repetition, order, and wholeness (Ewing, 1990; Quinn, 1991). Think of the challenges presented by James Joyce, Jackson Pollock, John Cage, or physicists who propose that the universe is characterized by an underlying randomness or disorder rather than a unified master pattern. Yet these have not widely entered popular culture. The popular arts and entertainment remain highly thematic, with readily identifiable leitmotivs and repeated melodic patterns. The innovations remain labeled "experimental" and are believed to have limited popular appeal. Themes are a manifest part of our experiences as an explicit folk category in our daily life, not just a scientific construct.

What does that mean for qualitative researchers conducting thematic analysis? We must recognize that the search for themes is an activity and ideal we share with informants, one that is instilled early in life and reinforced in daily life. In other words, the concept and appeal of themes is rooted in widely shared sociocultural settings and not strictly limited to a rarefied objective scientific context. From this point of view, the vocabulary of science is plainly rife with culturally laden moral terms in that the same terms apply to ideals for individuals and research. We construct and carefully protect the "independent" and "dependent" variables, we design studies to provide the greatest statistical "power," we speak of "controlling" variables and of enhancing individuals' sense of control, we judge if constructs and data are right and valid or invalid (a slight phonetic shift leads to "invalid," the person who is not upright but is deformed or ill). Likewise, it is important to recognize that we share with informants the search for themes and coherence in life, and we normatively judge the performance of others in these terms.

It is precisely because themes are culturally laden that they are useful for qualitative research. We know that the concept of a theme is meaningful and important to the informants and is not solely a construct devised by researchers. Thus we need to be aware of the several possible ways to interpret the detection of a theme when it appears in speech and behavior. Themes may be explicitly important personal or sociocultural meanings to the informant; they may be produced situationally as part of a strategy for presenting a credible, coherent, understandable account; and they may be an artifact of the analyses without meaning to the informant.

An example of how these issues enter into working with themes is suggested by recent studies of life stories. Personal life themes are idealized as a natural resource for adaptation, coping, self-expression, and autonomy. Life review studies treat them as adaptive and developmentally normative (Kaufman, 1987; McAdams, 1988; Myerhoff, 1982;

Whitbourne, 1986). The view is related to the model of the singular, autonomous, coherent self that underlies Western psychology (Ewing, 1990; Geertz, 1986; Marsella & White, 1982; White & Kirkpatrick, 1985). Yet some studies report that reviewing life themes may inflame dormant conflicts or sadness rather than rejuvenate new meaning and identity; themes may embody unresolved conflicts and not be positive values for coping (Butler, 1968; Csikszentmihalyi & Beattie, 1979).

In two studies of how life history themes relate to well-being, themes were found among people experiencing distress. One study compared elderly Irish, Italian, and Jewish widowers two to seven years after the loss of their spouses and found strong relationship between explicit life themes and negative well-being, depression, and unresolved grief (Luborsky, 1990). The second study compared clinically depressed residents with nondepressed residents and again found that explicit personal life themes were prominent in the experience and talk of depressed elderly in contrast to nondepressed elderly (Luborsky, 1993). In brief, life stories organized around telling a personal theme ("I was successful," "times were hard") served to express unresolved grief, while stories that followed the cultural life course (e.g., birth, school, work, and marriage) were related to well-being.

The thematic stories focused on conflicts and struggles with others and within themselves and asserted a single personal identity (e.g., "I've always been the kind who tried to help") across the lifespan. Life course stories told of succeeding identities and blended social and personal life; that is, explicitly stated life themes represented a sense of disruption in the unfolding of the expected biography of life meanings or active biographical work to impose a sense of missing meaning (Bury, 1982; Cohler, 1982, 1991; Gubrium, Holstein, & Buckholdt, 1994; Williams, 1984). The quest for personal themes may not be an experience shared by everyone (Ewing, 1990; Luborsky, 1990). Life themes may reflect current experiences and mood as much as an enduring lifelong personal meaning. The lesson is that descriptions of interview themes should be carefully considered. Themes are markers of processes, not fixed structures. Outcome studies report little, no, or even adverse effects (Luborsky, 1993). Bury (1982) and Williams (1984) suggest that the experience of being ill from a chronic medical disease arises when the disease disrupts the expected trajectory of one's biography and life themes. Some researchers argue that a break in the sense of continuity in personal meaning (Becker, 1993) rather than any particular meaning (theme) precedes illness and depression (Antonovsky,

1987; Atchley, 1988; Huyck, 1988). Others argue that we need to focus on meaning making rather than specific meanings per se (Frankl, 1978; Gubrium, 1987; Myerhoff, 1984).

Relevant to thematic analysis, these studies raise questions that suggest two other alternatives. There may be no single cohesive cultural or personal theme to use as a Rosetta stone for deciphering the core meaning of an event or lifetime. Rather we need to define themes following Rosaldo's (1989) definition of culture as "multiple busy intersections" (p. 17) of collective ideologies, family and personal values, local situations, and conditions. Themes need to be conceptualized as such in a much richer fashion, not simply viewed as objects or artifacts frozen by researchers out of the continuous individual processes of meaning making. Themes are one mode for assigning meaning or situationally making a point through repetition.

First, we need to be aware of overgeneralizing the importance of themes in our studies. Alternatives to constant ever-meaningful lives include concepts of experiential flow (Csikszentmihalyi, 1990) as periods of intentional *mindlessness* and untutored pauses (Read, 1986) or as breathers (Lazarus, 1991) from constant meaning making and reflection. Yet even these ideas of mindlessness may be cultural (Silverman, 1985). By seeing meaning everywhere, qualitative researchers perpetuate their own enterprise and cultural paradigm. Second, we need to consider themes as emergent and changeable in their meaning and desirability to individuals over their lifetime. Ethnic identity in the preceding description of aged Irish, Italian, and Jewish widowers was found to be cherished as part of childhood socialization; it was to be submerged and neglected to aid separation and individuation as young adults; finally, it became a valuable resource during losses and isolation for life reorganization in old age (Luborsky & Rubinstein, 1987, 1990).

Methods and Pitfalls in the Study of Themes

Definitions

Basic terms must be defined so that we can outline methods and pitfalls in the study of themes. Because several terms used in thematic analysis are familiar and used interchangeably in everyday conversation, we must clearly specify how they will be used consistently for research purposes.

Three terms are distinguished here: *theme, pattern,* and *topic. Themes* are defined here as the manifest generalized statements by informants about beliefs, attitudes, values, or sentiments. The definition highlights two important facets of the task of identifying and elevating a particular statement to the level of an analytic theme. First, it helps to provide a clear orientation to work that seeks to understand and reflect the informant's own views and words. Analogously, organizing themes or *templates* (Luborsky, 1990; Thomas, 1992) serve as a metaphor that individuals use to unify separate elements and experiences into an overarching meaning. Second, the definition primarily uses manifest and explicit statements rather than inference and background knowledge about the person or situation (Agar, 1980). The definition of a theme follows from useful discussions by Holsti (1969), Krippendorff (1980), Agar and Hobbes (1982), and Gumperz, Aulakh, and Kaltman (1982). Themes can be further described as both personal and cultural to reflect the level of description and the extent to which they are shared or individualized.

In contrast, the term *pattern* may best be used to describe findings from the researcher's frame of reference. These are built from the researcher's observations and analyses of a regularity, structure, or inferences but without direct concern for their meaningfulness to the people being observed. As such, discussions of how to identify and analyze patterns in qualitative data are not addressed in this chapter. For example, Harbert, Vinick, and Ekerdt (1992) label as themes the results of their analyses of popular literature on marriage and retirement. The authors reviewed the texts, made notes of themes that emerged, and sorted their own observations and impressions into categories that synthesized their observations. Here it is suggested that the terms *patterns* or *dimensions* would be more accurate usage.

Similarly, for clarity the terms *topic* or *main points*, rather than theme, should be used when summarizing the content of replies by many people to a question. For example, in a study of ethnicity and bereavement we asked, "Since the death of your spouse, would you tell me how has your life changed?" Summaries of the replies by 45 informants identified several topics in people's answers: concerns about a sense of grief, of being isolated and lonely, and a sense of relief for the end to a the loved one's suffering. The main topics or areas of concern identified by informants are not described as themes.

Note that these definitions and suggested usages are intended as guidelines; we know of no absolute definition of a theme that can be formulated and separated from the specific contexts and topics of discussion in which they emerge. The consistent use of these definitions can help to extend the clarity of research, analyses, and discussions.

Theme Identification

There are two basic approaches to identifying themes. One is to seek those statements that occur most frequently or are repeated. The other approach is to look for those statements that are marked in some way as being of great meaning to a person(s). In the first case, the research and analytic task is weighted toward counting the most frequently occurring statements. Analysis starts with eliminating less frequent utterances. In the latter case, the research task is more interpretive, requiring the investigator to identify importance by criteria internal to the discourse and to the speaker's own sense of significance. The analytic task is to explain how the infrequent statement is highly significant to the speaker or writer as well as giving order and meaning to a wide range of phenomena. However, researchers must be alert to other causes for repeated or highly charged statements, such as those that might arise from the interactions in the interview setting.

Three Examples

The following three examples will illustrate the use of these definitions and concepts. The examples are drawn from several studies of elderly residents of a geriatric facility. The transcripts use punctuation to mark natural breaks or intonation units, which are referred to as *chunks* (Chafe, 1980; Coleman, 1974) or *meaning units*. A comma or period is used to mark pauses and rising or falling tone; they do not adhere to conventions for proper grammar. The advantage is that natural units of talk and meaning are presented (Benjamin, 1986; Chafe, 1980; Mishler, 1991) rather than artificially defined sentences. Each chunk starts on a new line.

Walter Sendak is an 84-year-old man who was born in Philadelphia, where he has lived his entire life. He has been married for 50 years. This example illustrates the research use of two approaches to identifying themes, repetition, and explicit meanings. Talking about his lifetime, he was asked to name the scenes or themes that would make up a mural or painting showing his whole life. The second scene he describes as follows:

1. The only other thing I can put down is the day I got married to my wife.
2. And we went to New York for our honeymoon.
3. And coming back we stayed one day here, one day there.
4. And away I went.
5. I spent about six months up there.
6. And right around Christmas time we got orders to move.
7. We get on a boat.
8. We go to Europe, North Africa.
9. So, I couldn't even tell my wife, things happened so fast.
10. What she did, she and another girl went all the way down south to this Georgia town.
11. (We) practicing how to kill a Japanese that time, self-defense.
12. And she got a job there working for the government so we could be together once in a while, you know.
13. So, uh, it's a shame I couldn't say goodbye to her.
14. So in 1945, in October, right before my birthday I found my wife two blocks from my wife's mother's house.
15. She was staying with her mother.
16. And, I went up there and they were having some kind of gathering.
17. All her friends there.
18. And, boy, were they surprised.
19. I couldn't tell her I was coming.
20. Well, that's the way it was.
21. So, uh, you could picture us, uh, getting married.
22. Picture us meeting again at her mother's house after I come out of the Army.
23. Two pictures there.
24. That's all.
25. Otherwise I have a very calm, quiet life.

Let us examine how the two approaches of identifying and analyzing themes can be applied to this example.

Repetition

Several forms of repetition occur in this segment of talk (Tannen, 1987, 1989). For example, there is the repeated use of the word *and* (e.g., lines 2, 3, 4, and 6). *And* is a discourse marker that identifies the start of a separate event or idea. More significantly it is well documented for the ways it serves to collect together specific events and ideas in service of a more general point (Schiffrin, 1987, p. 131). The larger point connected by *and* is the whole scene the informant wishes to encompass: that he was married only a short time when he was separated from his wife without being able to say goodbye.

The repetition of whole phrases conveys Sendak's theme or main point, that of his marriage. It also is clear that the repeated use of the phrases emphasizes and reinforces the affective tone of the theme.

A less-obvious repetition is the use of places; this fits the definition of a pattern rather than theme. The pattern of repeatedly enumerating interesting place names greatly dramatizes his story. He weaves in mentions of travel to places that are more exciting and exotic (New York, Europe, North Africa, Georgia) in contrast to the rest of his life. The allusions to foreign places, learning to kill (but in "self-defense"), and the reunion all convey a richer sense of the nuances of the story parallel with its development. Including the names of places he went with his wife serves to call more attention to the climactic moment and links it into a fabric of unusual events in his life. The excitement in his personal life (marriage) and the larger world (wartime) are combined to heighten the remarkable nature of the scene he tells. These are echoed in the final segments (lines 21 through 23), where he reiterates the main point, joining with his wife, first in marriage and then after separation by war and the army. The final segment (line 25) frames the main point by contrasting the excitement of dramatic separations and new activities in marriage and in war with "Otherwise I have a very calm, quiet life."

The elements of repetition in this story serve several purposes. The repetition of a word or phrase (e.g., *and*) cannot automatically be equated with a unit of meaning. Here the repetition serves to mark events as part of a larger idea. The recurrent phrases "I couldn't even tell my wife, things happened so fast" do embody the central meaning of the story, yet they also serve as structural framework providing coherence. In this example, their structural role is very important because the story is not told in the linear order in which the events took place. The characteristic feature of a narrative is that the order of the clauses follow in the same order as the events that are being told (Labov, 1972). Sendak first tells of leaving to the war front (lines 7 and 8); second, he backtracks in time to mention that his wife moved to be with him during basic training (line 10 and 12); next, he tells of returning.

Central Meaning

In contrast to discovering themes by means of listening or reading for repetition, central meaningful themes can be identified that present the informant's own view of what is important in direct statements at a variety of levels. These also occur at the word, clause, and story levels.

One set of helpful signposts includes the class of explicit discourse markers *so* and *because*. These are examples of words that identify beliefs about causes and meanings of events. Other kinds of markers are intensifiers such as *very* and *so fast* and exclamations such as *boy* (line 18). These markers highlight especially intense or meaningful events and thoughts. Again, these only suggest candidates for further consideration. There are no automatic rules; we must consider the contexts of these discourse markers and judge whether that particular marker points to a salient theme.

Evaluative clauses in narratives are those that step outside the flow of events and evaluate the topic or event (Labov, 1972; Linde, 1987; Price, 1987). These clauses are valuable for qualitative work because they express the speaker's reasoning, stance, beliefs, and judgments about the event or topic. Evaluative clauses can be identified by the expression of moral language. These include judgments about cause, responsibility, blame, guilt, and right and wrong actions or beliefs. Consider, for example, the statement "How could you do that? It's your fault they left." Such statements and judgments by informants give direct insights into the primary cultural and personal frameworks of value and belief that shape motivations and the ways people plan and react to events and conditions in their lives. For example, in line 12 Sendak states that his wife got a job in Georgia (the action or event) so they could be together (the evaluation or reasoning for her action).

At a higher level of discourse, the importance of the main theme is highlighted and reinforced by three separate brief stories (the wedding, being together during basic training, and the reunion). The conclusion of each story supports the main theme (lines 21 and 22). The closing counterpoint—"Otherwise I have a very calm, quiet life" (line 25)—uses contrast to restate the main theme in yet another way without the use of repetition.

Sarah Taylor is an 89-year-old widow. She has a large family. The following text is the entire narrative life story told by Mrs. Taylor. This example is presented to illustrate how we share an attentiveness to themes with our informants. The example further highlights the use of repetition and explicit meanings raised in Sendak's case.

1. There was nothing unusual about my life.
2. I grew up here.
3. Met my husband at a very, very young age.
4. But we didn't know that we were going to marry someday.
5. His sister, the one that sent me that note, was my Sunday school teacher.
6. And he was also in my class, I knew his brother very well.
7. His brother was dating my girlfriend.
8. And, through him, I started going out with my future husband.
9. And we married at a very young age.
10. And we had a wonderful, wonderful life together.
11. We had two sons.
12. We . . . they married at young age too,
13. and I would say that they are now undergoing the same type of life that my husband and I had.
14. I have five grandchildren.
15. I have eight great-grandchildren.

Her story exhibits the elements we saw in Sendak's. In terms of repetition, candidates for themes also can be identified at several levels: discourse markers (*and,* lines 6, 8, 9, 10, and 13) conjoin several elements into the overarching theme of "a wonderful life" and the recurrent talk around the topic of meeting and marrying her husband. In terms of manifest content, she frames the start and close of the story by stating that she is typical: "nothing unusual about my life" (line 1). This echoes her theme of having led a conventional life shared with a good family. She then substantiates the claim by outlining her progress through the traditional female normative life stages from birth, to school, dating, marriage, and then children and grandchildren.

However, her opinion that her children are "undergoing the same type of life" (line 13) is a most powerful statement. It provides strong evidence to substantiate an interpretation that this is a key theme. This evaluative clause illuminates her reasoning, values, and expectations for the social life course. Indeed, her false start "We . . . they" reinforces the sense of similarity she feels between her life course and the ones her children are living.

Earlier I described studies where we found explicit themes associated with depression, which suggested we needed to attend to the informant's stance or affective tone. Taylor uses superlatives, a "wonderful, wonderful life." Since the loss of her husband, she has been separated from this cherished orienting theme in her life; she was clinically depressed at the time we spoke. In this instance, were a researcher to lift the theme "a wonderful, wonderful life" out of the wider context of her present life, it would lead to an entirely misleading interpretation about the current value and meaningfulness of that theme.

An important analytic point in the telling of her life story was that Mrs. Taylor was attentive to identifying and describing themes. This account exemplifies the cultural embeddedness of the notion of a theme. The search for meaningful themes is a part of the researcher's aims and methods and the informant's way of organizing and interpreting as meaningful her whole lifetime and those of her children.

Horace Vetch provides a third example. The example shows that simply tabulating repeated statements or highly evaluative judgments will be misleading if the context of the statement or discussion is not given adequate consideration. As part of a longitudinal clinical study of daily changes in mood, research subjects were asked a set of 10 structured questions every day for 30 to 90 days. In the following extract, Vetch is answering the questions on the 62nd day. He has just replied that he is "in excruciating pain" and is now asked, "Right now, are you feeling sad?"

1	Researcher:	You answered you felt sad. Is it
2		extremely sad, a little bit?
3	Mr. Vetch:	It
4		ain't bad. You know when you, you
5		ask me questions but, but **when**
6		**something hurts you, how could you**
7		**feel happy?**
8	Researcher:	It depends on the person.
9		It is such a personal thing.
10	Mr. Vetch:	Must be
11		you are a *stupid* person to feel good!
12	Researcher:	Not necessarily, there are different
13		reasons. Some people have a lot of
14		reasons to feel bad.
15	Mr. Vetch:	You know *I am not stupid!*

Repetition here indicates a point of heated contention. The dialog is structured by a clinician conducting a standardized test. The clinician aims to elicit statements about personal experience and then transform them into the format of standardized scientific data. The interaction is problematic and contentious. Using parody, Vetch challenges the researcher's authority and the basic rationality of the questions, "How could you feel happy . . ." and "Must be you are a stupid person to feel good." At the same time he claims his reply is more reasoned and intelligent, "You know I am not stupid!" and sensible than the clinician's. At best it is unclear if the final statement here is indeed a salient personal theme or a research subject losing his patience.

General Guidelines for Discovery

The discovery of themes begins most appropriately during the interviews and fieldwork using direct discussions and observations, not just during armchair review of completed field notes, transcripts, or other media. The active pursuit of themes during the research interviews provides for direct feedback from the informant. They can be enlisted into evaluating candidates for themes that emerge during the research. It is important to avoid a one-sided approach that relies heavily on transcripts. That approach lends itself to the noble conceit of an omniscient analyst divining meanings that are unknown to the research subjects; such practices can occur in qualitative research, not just biomedical and behavioral research (Luborsky, 1990). The discovery and exploration of themes with an informant is important because we have no absolute abstract criteria for themes. Rather, the assessment of themes is emergent in the expressions of informants about specific topics and events.

An equal emphasis on direct discussion and observation is needed because verbatim texts leave out large chunks of vital information. Mishler (1991) argues that the presumption that a verbatim transcript captures a complete and objective representation of a speech event is a seductive fallacy. Ambiguities may be introduced because entire channels of information are not encoded: body postures, gestures, eye contacts, and speech qualities (tone, speed, pitch, cadence) that express information about the speaker's attitude toward what he or she is saying. The absence of these in even the most meticulous transcripts supports the need for keeping contemporaneous field notes and actively talking with informants instead of relying on armchair methods of text analyses.

Astute interviewers are alert to asking for elaboration, such as, "Is this idea or statement an important theme or central thread in your life?" The ensuing talk and follow-up discussion will be a useful guide to ground later interpretations. The informant can be guided to describe the relative importance of topics, the affective feel, the source of the theme (e.g., individual, family, others), and its strength and pervasiveness in his or her life. These statements will provide direct feedback to help in the analysis of transcripts and field notes.

An aid to discovering themes and patterns is a worksheet on which a running log of topics is noted. It can be used for interviews and observations and while reviewing transcripts. Use it to track recurrent topics and phrases of importance to the subject. With a little practice, the list of topics can be used as a springboard to exploring topics and concerns during discussions. The worksheet is simply a page with one wide and one narrow column. Use the wide column to jot down key words and phrases to outline the flow or sequence of topics as they occur. The narrower column is a parallel list for the interviewer to check off recurrent topics and strong assertions or important meanings. The interviewer can then refer to these to pose additional questions and probes, such as "While we were talking, it seems that family came up a lot. Can you tell me more about what that means to you?" Or, "You said hard work is very important to you. Was it always?" The worksheet is also useful as a skeleton outline for write-ups and as a brief index to refresh your memory at a later time.

Procedures for discovering and documenting themes can be broadly outlined. These share with other forms of content analyses the need to be systematic and to document closely topics and conclusions.

Several readings of the texts or field notes are conducted to locate recurrent or important topics and to summarize and describe them. Start by simply reading the complete set of materials to get acquainted with them. No notes need be taken. A second reading is conducted to identify main points and topics. Be alert to striking points and assertions. Write marginal notations on the text or in a notebook as appropriate. Try to summarize the gist of the major topics with a phrase. These can be used later as code words or descriptive labels. These phrases serve as a list of candidate themes for further study. Next, narrow down the field of candidates using the twin approaches of frequent and recurrent topics and of importance as outlined in the previous section.

After a series of candidate themes are identified, the main themes can be analyzed using both analytic definitions in combination. To identify themes in terms of frequency, it is a straightforward task to count up all the topics and themes and pick the most frequent ones. To identify the most salient or important candidates, use frequency as a secondary concern. Look for the markers illustrated earlier in terms of direct statements, evaluative clauses, and discourse markers, including connectives and intensifiers. Other criteria to consider include the pervasiveness or importance of a theme across many different discussion topics and social settings. As part of differentiating among candidate themes, be alert to alternative sources for repeated statements or strong assertions (e.g., situations, factors, ethnic differences in speech style, individual health and living conditions) or to repeated turns away from a topic that may be painful to discuss.

The adequacy of insights needs to be judged for both the interview discussions and later reflective interpretation. There are at least two tactics. The first is to judge which themes and interpretations seem best at capturing the meanings and actions voiced by the informant or your observations of the social scene. If after continuing discussions with informants or rereadings of the texts no further information or new topics are apparent, then it can be assumed that the portrait or summary is relatively complete. This approach is defined as *pattern saturation* (Bertaux, 1981) or *theoretical saturation* (Strauss & Corbin, 1990).

A second tactic is to look for negative examples or instances when the informant directly refutes or contradicts the interpretation. Here, in addition to compiling examples that confirm your conclusion, you work to find statements or instances of behavior that contradict the theme or pattern. The negative examples will either help to substantiate your conclusion or directly challenge it. When reporting findings, a fundamental mandate of theme analysis is to make explicit the basis for the conclusions. A blizzard of verbatim quotes without contexts and other information does not establish veracity; these serve merely to illustrate a researcher's assertion. Indicate the extent to which recurrence and frequency and salience formed the basis for your conclusions. Make explicit the basis for deciding which topics were themes. It is especially important to limit the use of vague quantifiers (e.g., *most, some, typical*). Without overt statements, the quantifiers may mislead readers as to the nature of the analyses or data or reveal the researcher's vested interests or wishes. Again, we lack objective standards for gauging levels of importance or significance solely by frequency or by the presence or absence of certain topics or meanings. We also may lack normative baselines to use for reference in assessing particular findings.

Continuing Challenges and Issues

The study of themes is fundamental to qualitative methods. It offers benefits and carries limitations. The main contribution is to provide descriptions of salient concerns and experiences from the informant's own viewpoint. Thematic analysis aims to identify and describe the contents of an individual's perceptions, ideals, and values. It can contribute information on the nature of a people's life within a society, or of living with a disease, or of life transitions. These data are needed to complement and to extend into new areas the behavioral science and biomedical approaches to building knowledge. Studies of personal and social themes provide multiple perspectives on events and issues and document the situatedness of medically defined topics such as illness and health, the family, and age. It thus helps us to keep a fresh curiosity about many taken-for-granted concepts and values.

Pragmatically, thematic analysis is an effective way to communicate across the boundaries between professional disciplines. It partakes of the shared language of science in its attention to numbers via the underlying cultural usage of theme as indicative of frequently occurring phenomena. Thematic analysis lends an aura of legitimacy, replicability, and predictability to qualitative findings. The use of themes also poses several dilemmas and challenges. Many of these remain largely unresolved. These can best be stated as questions for further study.

When is thematic analysis appropriate? It may not be appropriate to all kinds of data or research questions. We find that the term *theme* is used loosely to describe a spectrum of methods and data ranging from those that are based solely on the observer's inferences to those that elicit a brief sentence or two from many subjects and to multiple in-depth interviews. How do the themes we as researchers identify relate to informants' own sense of their lives and subjective experiences? To minimize some potential ambiguities, this chapter suggested conceptual distinctions among *themes, patterns,* and *topics* or *dimensions*. Themes may be overused or misused even when built from meticulously transcribed conversations. A familiar case occurs when a large number of research subjects are asked standardized open-ended questions and the replies are summarized to identify the one main topic and then reported in the aggregate as the main themes. That approach does not preserve the diverse interpersonal and discourse contexts in which the theme or topic was a personally and culturally meaningful statement.

Is it appropriate to presume that all informants are equally interested in searching for themes to their experiences in specific settings or for an all-encompassing life theme? The discussion of the prevalence of explicit life themes among depressed elderly suggested that the presence of a theme is not always a sign of well-being; it may be a sign of troubles in finding acceptable meanings. We need to inquire continually about the varieties, sources, and feelings associated with a theme. These may include situational sources, such as interactions between the speakers.

The complex nature of many of our most basic analytic research terms that resonate deeply with Western cultural ideas and values was noted. Terms such as *theme, control, power* (statistical and personal), *independence, dependence,* and *validity* are highly charged and important for judging the quality of one's own daily life, not just scientific studies. Similarly, a pragmatic device such as repetition is used to convey importance, emphasize a point, or provide coherence that is highly prized as a sign of competent speech behavior. Yet, too, overly repetitive talk is viewed negatively by others. In brief, our language is redolent with concepts and concerns that we are socialized into as children and continually monitored in daily interactions throughout life. We need to increase our awareness of the potential confounds they introduce into our "objective" processes of discovery of meanings and patterns.

One reason theme analysis has wide currency in qualitative, quantitative, and medical studies is that it communicates a wealth of information with a simple, standardizable label. Themes can be readily counted, entered into statistical tests, and thus satisfy several of the tenets of the doctrine of operationalism. Despite the familiarity of thematic analysis to qualitative researchers, a troublesome critical quality is less recognized. By their very nature as condensed meaning, themes carry us toward a reductionism or simplification that strips away the explicit contexts, complexity, and richness of the original expression. Reports of themes need to be carefully presented to minimize the decontextualization of themes from the settings in which they are meaningful statements. Themes are about the speaker's experiences of the past, present, and anticipated future set within an extended dialogue with its own history of give and take between speakers (as the third example illustrated).

Although thematic analysis is widely used, much work remains to be done. This chapter provided insights into such issues, including an appreciation of the cultural roots of the concept, a set of working definitions and usages for key terms, and illustrations of the application of theme analyses to life story and discourse data. It outlined the two approaches to studying themes: identifying repetition and identifying central meaning. Criteria at the level of discourse markers, evaluative clauses, and explicit statements by speakers were highlighted. The chapter has clarified the substance and nature of themes in the specific settings of the dialogues in which they occur. Considerations of multiple alternative candidate themes, complexity, communicative contexts, and speakers are vital elements to be documented.

As yet we have no absolute criteria for automatically identifying a theme or its meaningfulness to a person. Instead, themes are emergent in the process of communication and of analyses and require a systematic approach that blends interpretation with explanation. The analysis of themes remains an important but challenging part of research. A great many opportunities for further critical work beckon.

References

Abu-Lughod, L. (1985). Honor and the sentiments of loss in a Bedouin society. *American Ethnologist, 12*, 245-261.

Agar, M. (1980). Stories, background, knowledge and themes: Problems in the analysis of life history narratives. *American Ethnologist, 7*, 223-235.

Agar, M., & Hobbes, J. (1982). Interpreting discourse: Coherence and the analysis of ethnographic interviews. *Discourse Processes, 5*, 1-32.

Antonovsky, A. (1987). *Unraveling the mystery of health.* San Francisco: Jossey-Bass.

Atchley, R. (1988). A continuity theory of aging. *Gerontologist, 29*(2), 183-190.

Becker, G. (1993). Continuity after a stroke: Implications of life-course disruptions in old age. *Gerontologist, 33*(2), 148-158.

Benjamin, L. S. (1986). Operational definition and measures of dynamics show in the stream of free associations. *Psychiatry, 49*, 104-129.

Bernard, H. R. (1988). *Research methods in cultural anthropology.* Newbury Park, CA: Sage.

Bertaux, D. (Ed.). (1981). *Biography and society.* Beverly Hills, CA: Sage.

Bury, M. (1982). Chronic illness as biographical disruption. *Sociology of Health and Illness, 4*(2), 167-182.

Butler, R. N. (1968). The Life review: An interpretation of reminiscence in the aged. In B. Neugarten (Ed.), *Middle age and aging.* Chicago: University of Chicago.

Chafe, W. (1980). The deployment of consciousness in the production of a narrative. In W. Chafe (Ed.), *The pear stories: Cognitive, cultural, and linguistic aspects of narrative production.* Norwood, NJ: Ablex.

Cohler, B. (1982). Personal narrative and life course. In P. Baltes & O. Brim (Eds.), *Life-span development and behavior* (Vol. 4). New York: Academic Press.

Cohler, B. (1991). The life story and the study of resilience and response to adversity. *Journal of Life History and Narrative, 1*(2,3), 169-200.

Coleman, P. G. (1974). Measuring reminiscence characteristics from conversation as adaptive features of old age. *International Journal of Aging and Human Development, 5*(3), 281-294.

Csikszentmihalyi, M. (1990). *Flow: The psychology of optimal experience.* New York: Harper & Row.

Csikszentmihalyi, M., & Beattie, O. (1979). Life themes: a theoretical and empirical exploration of their origins and effects. *Journal of Humanistic Psychology, 19*(1), 46-63.

DelVecchio Good, M. J., Good, B., Schaffer, C., & Lind, S. E. (1990). American oncology and the discourse on hope. *Culture, Medicine, and Psychiatry, 14,* 59-79.

Ewing, K. (1990). The illusion of wholeness: Culture, self, and the experience of inconsistency. *Ethos, 18*(3), 251-278.

Frankl, V. (1978). *The unheard cry for meaning.* New York: Simon & Schuster.

Fry, C., & Keith, J. (1986). *New methods for old age research.* Boston: Bergin & Garvey.

Geertz, C. (1973). *The interpretation of culture.* New York: Basic Books.

Geertz, C. (1986). Making experience, authoring selves. In V. Turner & E. Bruner (Eds.), *The anthropology of experience.* Chicago: University of Illinois Press.

Groves, R., Fultz, N., & Martin, E. (1992). Direct questioning about comprehension in a survey setting. In J. Tanner (Ed.), *Questions about questions: inquiries into the cognitive bases of surveys.* New York: Russell Sage.

Gubrium, J. (1987). Structuring and destructuring the course of illness: The Alzheimer's disease experience. *Sociology of Health and Illness, 3,* 1-24.

Gubrium, J. F. (1988). Incommunicables and poetic documentation in the Alzheimer's disease experience. *Semiotica, 3*(4), 235-253.

Gubrium, J., Holstein, J., & Buckholdt, D. (1994). *Constructing the life course.* Dix Hills, NY: General Hall.

Gumperz, J. J., Aulakh, G., & Kaltman, H. (1982). Thematic structure and progression in discourse. In J. J. Gumperz (Ed.), *Language and social identity.* New York: Cambridge University Press.

Harbert, E., Vinick, B., & Ekerdt, D. (1992). Analyzing popular literature: emergent themes in marriage and retirement. In J. Gilgun, K. Daly, & G. Handel (Eds.), *Qualitative methods in family research.* Newbury Park, CA: Sage.

Holsti, O. (1969). *Content analysis for the social sciences and humanities.* Reading, MA: Addison-Wesley.

Huyck, M. H. (1988). Give me continuity or give me death. *Journal of Gerontology, 29*(2), 148-149.

Kaufman, S. (1987). *The ageless self: Sources of meaning in late life.* Madison: University of Wisconsin Press.

Krippendorff, K. (1980). *Content analysis: An introduction to its methodology.* Beverly Hills, CA: Sage.

Labov, W. (1972). *Language in the inner city.* Philadelphia: University of Pennsylvania Press.

Lazarus, R. (1991). *Emotion and adaptation.* New York: Oxford University Press.

Linde, C. (1987). Explanatory systems in oral life stories. In D. Holland & N. Quinn (Eds.), *Cultural models in language and thought.* Cambridge, UK: Cambridge University Press.

Luborsky, M. (1990). Alchemists' visions: Cultural norms in eliciting and analyzing life history narratives. *Journal of Aging Studies, 4*(1), 17-29.

Luborsky, M. (1993). The romance with personal meaning in gerontology: Cultural aspects of life themes. *Gerontologist, 33*(4), 445-452.

Luborsky, M., & Rubinstein, R. (1987). Ethnicity and lifetimes: Self concepts and situational contexts of ethnic identity in late life. In D. Gelfand & D. Barresi (Eds.), *Ethnic dimensions of aging*. New York: Springer.

Luborsky, M., & Rubinstein, R. (1990). Ethnic identity and bereavement in later life: The case of older widowers. In J. Sokolovsky (Ed.), *The cultural context of aging: Worldwide perspectives*. New York: Bergin & Garvey.

Marcus, G., & Clifford, J. (1986). *Writing culture: The poetics and politics of ethnography*. Berkeley: University of California.

Marsella, A., & White, G. (1982). *Cultural conceptions of mental health and therapy*. Boston: Reidel.

McAdams, D. P. (1988). *Power, intimacy, and the life story: Personological inquiries into identity*. New York: Guilford.

Mishler, E. G. (1986). *Research interviewing: Context and narrative*. Cambridge, MA: Harvard University Press.

Mishler, E. G. (1991). Representing discourse: The rhetoric of transcription. *Journal of Narrative and Life History, 1*(4), 255-280.

Myerhoff, B. (1982). Life history among the elderly: Performance, visibility, and remembering. In J. Ruby (Ed.), *A crack in the mirror: Reflexive perspectives in anthropology*. Philadelphia: University of Pennsylvania Press.

Myerhoff, B. (1984). Rites and signs of ripening: The intertwining of ritual, time, and growing older. In D. Kertzer & J. Keith (Eds.), *Age and anthropological theory*. Ithaca, NY: Cornell University Press.

Pelto, P., & Pelto, G. (1978). *Anthropological research: The structure of inquiry* (2nd ed.). Cambridge, UK: Cambridge University Press.

Price, L. (1987). Ecuadorian illness stories: cultural knowledge in natural discourse. In D. Holland & N. Quinn (Eds.), *Cultural models in language and thought*. Cambridge, UK: Cambridge University Press.

Quinn, N. (1991). The cultural basis of metaphor. In J. Fernandez (Ed.), *Beyond metaphor: The theory of tropes in anthropology*. Stanford, CA: Stanford University Press.

Read, K. (1986). *Return to the high valley: Coming full circle*. Berkeley: University of California Press.

Rosaldo, R. (1989). *Culture and truth: The remaking of social analyses*. Boston: Beacon.

Schiffrin, D. (1987). *Discourse markers*. New York: Cambridge University.

Silverman, D. (1985). *Qualitative methodology and sociology*. London: Grover.

Spradley, J. P. (1979). *The ethnographic interview*. New York: Holt, Rinehart & Winston.

Spradley, J. P. (1980). *Participant observation*. New York: Holt, Rinehart & Winston.

Strauss, A., & Corbin, J. (1990). *Basics of qualitative research: Grounded theory procedures and techniques*. Newbury Park, CA: Sage.

Tannen, D. (1987). Repetition in conversation: Toward a poetics of talk. *Language, 63*(3), 574-605.

Tannen, D. (1989). *Talking voices: Repetition, dialogue, and imagery in conversational dialogue*. Cambridge: Cambridge University Press.

Thomas, J. (1992). *Doing critical ethnography*. Newbury Park, CA: Sage.

Werner, O., & Schoepfle, G. M. (1987a). *Systematic fieldwork. Vol. 1: Foundations of ethnography and interviewing*. Newbury Park, CA: Sage.

Werner, O., & Schoepfle, G. M. (1987b). *Systematic fieldwork. Vol. 2: Ethnographic analysis and data management*. Newbury Park, CA: Sage.

Whitbourne, S. K. (1986). *The me I know: A study of adult identity*. New York: Springer-Verlag.

White, G., & Kirkpatrick, J. (Eds.). (1985). *Person, self, and experience*. Berkeley: University of California Press.

Williams, G. (1984). The genesis of chronic illness: Narrative reconstruction. *Sociology of Health and Illness, 6*(2), 175-200.

13

Analyzing Personal Journals
of Later Life

HARRY J. BERMAN

When a question arises, it breaks open the being of the object.
Gadamer (1992, p. 363)

The work described in this chapter originates in this question: What is it like to be an older person? The question seems simple. Each word is readily understandable, and the grammatical form is straightforward. Yet the mere asking of this question raises issues that go to the heart of our lives as gerontological researchers.

The words *to be* in the question "What is it like to be old?" imply that the answer must be given in terms of descriptions of experience (being), rather than in terms of explanations of causes. The word *like* implies a process of interpretation, a series of linguistic approximations and metaphors, rather than objective measures.

The question calls for description rather than explanation, and words and metaphor rather than measurement. Perhaps for these reasons the question should be declared off limits, outside the pale, verboten as far as the serious, scientific work of gerontologists is concerned.

But what a loss that would be. Surely, among the many important things that gerontologists should be able to convey to our audiences of students, policy makers, and the general public is the sense of what it is like—what it means—to be old in this day and age.

Rather than abandon the question, it has been grounded in a line of thinking that centers on the investigation of lived experience. To provide answers to the question, we have used published personal journals (diaries) written in later life. Personal journals are particularly suitable sources of information about what it is like to be an older person; in them authors attempt to fixate the meaning of the day-to-day flow of experience. They are effective at capturing changes of mood and the subjectivity of the moment, but they also go beyond the moment and embed the flux of experience in larger contexts of meaning.

The Philosophical Grounding: Human Science Research

The Philosophical Tradition of Human Science

The idea that the effort to understand lived experience is a proper scholarly activity can be traced to the work of Wilhelm Dilthey (1833-1911), a German philosopher who worked in the tradition of hermeneutics, the science of interpretation. Dilthey used the term *human science* (*Geisteswissenschaft*) to characterize the area of inquiry whose subject matter consists of meanings and signifiers as opposed to nonintentional events.

Doing Human Science Research

The life world, the world of lived experience, is both the source and object of human science research (Van Manen, 1990). The data of human science are texts and text analogs that capture lived experience. Although the concept of data has quantitative overtones deriving from positivistic science, the term *datum* originally meant something given or granted. In natural science, data are drawn out of the objects of research. In contrast, human science uses data in the original sense of the term—that which has been given by subjects (i.e., self-interpreting beings).

The preferred methods of natural science involve detached observation, controlled experiment, and quantitative measurement. In contrast, the preferred methods of human science involve descriptions of lived experience, interpretation, and self-reflective or critical analysis. Natural science taxonomizes and explains; human science explicates meaning. Human science research methods involve particular researchers' encounters with texts and text analogs with the aim of producing historically and culturally rooted reflections on lived experiences.

Just as in natural science, human science involves a process of reasoning about data. In the natural sciences, reasoning involves the processes of induction and deduction so familiar to us from standard research methods courses. In the human sciences, reasoning involves a process of articulating meaning by focusing on the dialectical relationship between parts and wholes (Burke, 1992; Gadamer, 1992, p. 223). To assert that meaning inevitably involves reasoning about parts and wholes is to assert that meaning is contextual. Interpretation occurs within a circle in which parts are always interpreted within some understanding of the whole, which is in turn understood by understanding its constituent parts (Woolfolk, Sass, & Messer, 1988). A *fact* does not stand on its own, independent of the context or interpreter, but instead is partially constituted by them. The dialectical relationship between parts and wholes, which encompasses the relationship between knower and known, is referred to as the *hermeneutic circle*. What we understand is based on what we already know, and what we already know comes from being able to understand.

Recently published volumes of human science research (Packer & Addison, 1989; Thomas, 1989) exhibit the range of methods of gathering data that can be used to yield descriptions of lived experience. Thomas's collection includes analysis of written texts, participant observation, intensive case studies, and in-depth interviews. Packer and Addison's volume includes participant observation, case studies, audio and video recordings, and interviews. To these sources of data Van Manen (1990) adds the tracing of etymological sources and idiomatic phrases, experiential descriptions in literature and biography, and experiential descriptions in diaries or journals. It is the latter as a source of data about the experience of aging that is the subject of the following sections of this chapter.

Personal Journals

Diaries and journals are one source of data about lived experience. Following Fothergill (1974), I will use the term *personal journal* to designate journals and diaries in which the life of the author is the prime subject. These are distinguished from works in which the author is principally reporting external events, such as those describing travels or chronicling political affairs or diary records of special interests such as gardening or fishing. The terms *journal* and *diary* both express but are not strict about dailiness. Because there is no consistent difference in their use (Fothergill, 1974; Mallon, 1984), they can be used interchangeably.

The personal journal as a literary form has evolved over the past three centuries. Samuel Pepys's diary, written between 1660 and 1669, is a well known early example. By the beginning of the 19th century, diary writing began to be recognized as a literary activity open to both established and nonestablished writers.

The rise of the personal journal is part of a broad trend in Western culture that began in the Renaissance and continues to the present. This period has been characterized by an increasing focus on individuality and inner life (Cushman, 1990; Sampson, 1989; Weintraub, 1978). In effect, the form itself is an expression of Western individualism.

The potential held by personal journals for illuminating a variety of aspects of psychological functioning and social life has long been recognized (Allport, 1942; Plummer, 1983; Wrightsman, 1981). In his masterful discussion of the use of personal documents in psychology, Allport comments, "in its ideal form the diary is unexcelled as a continuous record of the subjective side of mental development" (p. 95). Yet little psychological or sociological research using diaries has been conducted. This is partly because the theoretical perfection of the diary is not often realized in practice. As Fothergill (1974) has noted, the great mass of diary writing is poor and does not fulfill the potential inherent in the form. The scarcity of research using diaries is also attributable to concerns about the validity or, more precisely, the authenticity of the accounts provided in diaries, an issue discussed later. The most significant factor, however, in accounting for the paucity of research using diaries has been the rejection by positivistically dominated behavioral and social sciences of the kind of knowledge that emerges from the study of the single case.

The mounting critique of positivism during the past three decades and the rise of qualitative research has led to a renewed interest in the use of personal journals in psychology. Two recent examples of research using personal journals are (a) the analytical studies by Haviland and Kramer (1991) of Anne Frank's diary for the relation between emotional expression and cognitive level and (b) the studies by Abigail Stewart and associates (Peterson & Stewart, 1990; Stewart, Franz, & Layton, 1988) of the diaries and novels of Vera Brittain for the Eriksonian themes of identity, intimacy, and generativity.

Personal Journals of Later Life

For several years, I have been examining published personal journals as one source of data about the question, "What is it like to be an older person?" (Berman, 1986, 1988, 1989, 1991, in press). The journals examined to date are those of contemporary authors, including Doris Grumbach (1991), Alan Olmstead (1975), May Sarton (1973, 1977, 1980, 1984, 1988), Florida Scott-Maxwell (1979), and Elizabeth Vining (1978).

Authenticity

Before proceeding to consider examples of the kind of information yielded by analysis of personal journals of later life, it will be helpful to reflect further on the question of authenticity. How confident can we be that the accounts in published journals of later life cited above accurately represent the author's thoughts and feelings about what it is like to be an older person. After all, because they are published documents perhaps they do not reflect the author's true feelings, but instead have been shaped by external forces (e.g., knowledge of future publication). Or, even if they are not actually false, perhaps the statements in the journals are not truly spontaneous. Or perhaps they have been edited and present a constructed rather than unpremeditated version of the self. In short, how can we know if the journal states what the author really feels?

The issue of the authenticity of published journals is fraught with difficulty. It raises questions such as the following: Is it ever possible to have completely spontaneous, unpremeditated communications about some aspect of inner life that is unshaped by external forces? How can we even trust what we say to ourselves about ourselves? Without presuming to have fully responded to these questions, it is possible to make several observations on the issue of authenticity.

First, the ideal of obtaining unrevised, unpremeditated expressions of the self, unmodified by any consideration of a possible audience, is an unachievable goal. All communications about the self are shaped by an interpersonal context. (Ricoeur, 1992, provides a thorough philosophical discussion of this point.) This is certainly true in the case of face-to-face interviews and questionnaires but is not less true in regard to diaries. Mallon (1984, p. xvi) provides an intriguing description of the way that an imagined audience seems to work its way into the writing of a diary.

A second point about authenticity is that statements about the self are always constructed and always premeditated. The idea of viewing the self as the result of a process of linguistic construction is in contrast to the implications of the prevailing term, *self-perception.* The self is not perceived, it is conceived. All we know of ourselves and others is the result of a process of interpretation, a process of constructing meaning (Gergen, 1985; Mahoney, 1991). Statements about the self are never merely read off in the manner of an EEG. A consequence of this line of thought is that a concern about the entries in a particular journal not being spontaneous, a concern about their being crafted or premeditated, is probably misplaced. All self statements are premeditated; that does not mean they are not authentic. All self statements are constructed accounts or representations of what is being experienced at a given moment. One attraction for me in studying diaries is that these texts closely reflect this process of meaning making; as Kegan (1982) so aptly states, this is the central activity of human beings. In the succession of entries, the reader of a personal journal witnesses an individual's attempt to make sense of his or her life, to integrate current events with the currently understood past and anticipated future.

A third point about the authenticity of journals is the author's stated intentions. Authors of published journals are typically explicit about their reasons for engaging in journal writing. For example, in *Being Seventy,* Vining says that she wants to record "the things I do for the last time or enjoy less keenly" (Vining, 1978, p. 5). At the end of *Journal of a Solitude,* Sarton (1973) states her purpose in keeping the journal: "The journal began a year ago with depression, with much self-questioning about my dangerous and destructive angers, with the hope that self-examination would help me to change" (pp. 206-207).

Elsewhere in *Journal of a Solitude,* Sarton makes a simple comment that applies broadly to the reasons writers keep journals: "My business is the analysis of feelings" (p. 44). Given the stated intentions of the authors, it is hard to believe the accounts would be any less credible than those of any other informant. In responding to texts created with the stated intention of providing accurate accounts, researchers may be well-advised to adopt what Schwartz and Jacobs call "the strategy of believing what you are told" (Schwartz & Jacobs, 1979, p. 72). More-over, given writers' skills at bringing experience into language, their accounts of the lived experience of aging should be viewed as especially valuable, analogous to accounts provided by key informants in research on topics such as needs assessment. For a gerontologically minded human scientist, finding a well-written personal journal of later life is like a paleontologist finding a completely intact human skeleton. Its uniqueness in no way detracts from its inherent worth.

Journal Analysis

The approach taken in my studies of personal journals of later life has consisted of close reading, the isolation and description of themes, and interpretation of those themes in terms of psychological concepts and developmental theories.

Reading Journals

Human science posits that all knowing is related knowing—that is, knowledge arises out of a relationship between the observer and the observed. Accordingly, it is helpful to try to characterize the reader's (i.e., researcher's) experience in doing the kind of reading required for human science research.

Wertz's (1984) description of the phenomenological method can be used to characterize the approach to be taken in analyzing personal journals. The reading begins with a bracketing or suspension of preconceptions and an immersion in the lived reality to which the text refers. In describing the change that aging has brought about in her reading habits, Grumbach (1991) unwittingly provides an excellent characterization of this method of reading: "It is hard work to read more slowly. . . . [W]hen I slow down, I interlard the writer's words with my own. I think about what they are saying, I consider their methods, I hesitate before their choices, I dilly-dally in their views instead of racing through their styles and subject matter" (p. 15).

The process of reading personal journals can be understood by analogy with the encounter between clients and therapists. The journals are a continuing report of life in the present, regardless of when that present was. The reader sees the days unfold much as a therapist would during a year of therapy. The analysis of the journals depends on being open to the feelings aroused by these texts as a basis for grasping the world of the other, much as therapists use the feelings generated by clients in them (i.e., countertransference) as therapeutic tools.

Isolating and Describing Themes

The purpose of hermeneutic phenomenological reflection is to try to grasp the essential meaning of something. As Van Manen (1990) has noted, to grasp meaning is both easy and difficult. People are always relating to the world in terms of the meanings they impart to events, but the explication of meaning is not straightforward.

To grasp the essential meaning of a text it is helpful to think of the phenomena described in the text as approachable in terms of themes. Reflecting on lived experience becomes a process of analyzing the thematic aspects of that experience. From a human science perspective, theme analysis does not consist of the application of predetermined categories to a text; grasping and formulating themes is neither a rule-bound process nor arbitrary. Rather, it is a disciplined application of the concept of the hermeneutic circle: Understanding of the whole arises from understanding of the parts (i.e., themes), but identification of the parts grows out of the emerging comprehension of the whole. Gadamer's (1992) description of the general process of interpretation can be used to clarify the process of thematic analysis. The relationship between the interpreter and the text is like that between speakers in a conversation. Just as in a conversation there is a dialogic process of questioning and answering, so in thematic analysis each emergent theme can be viewed as the answer to a question that the text puts to the reader: an answer that is then put into the conversation with the text and becomes the subject of further questions and answers.

The analysis of personal journals of later life is carried out through the selection and highlighting of statements in the journals that pertain to the experience of becoming an older person. Statements that relate to the same aspects of the overall experience of aging are grouped, and an attempt is made to express in writing the meaning of the selected group of phrases.

Interpretation

From a strict phenomenological perspective, the activities of close reading, the isolation of themes, and the crafting of texts articulating those themes constitute the activity of research. Put another way, the answer to the question "What does this text mean?" is given in the coherent articulation of its themes. Following this perspective, hermeneutic phenomenology becomes a science of examples. Evoking lived experience is the goal of research, not confirming or disconfirming universal laws. Accordingly, articulations of the themes in the personal journals of later life can be understood as providing answers to the research question "What is it like to be an older person?"

However, given that human science-oriented gerontologists are historically situated in a scientific culture that has been engaged in systematic discourse about human development for approximately 100 years, it is hard not to interpret the journals in the sense of relating their descriptions of aging to gerontological concepts and theories. In fact, because any reading is necessarily carried out in the context of the reader's forestructures of understanding, clarification of the reader's or researcher's response in terms of associations between themes in the text and prevailing gerontological thinking could be considered a necessary part of the overall human science research enterprise. The meaning of the text resides in its themes, but the meaning of the text also resides in its connections with the larger discourse of gerontology. A single text clearly does not prove one or another theory, but it can be placed in an imaginary dialogue in which it can be used to illustrate the theory or highlight aspects of the experience of aging not reflected in the theory. Theories that have proved useful in the interpretation of personal journals include Erikson's theory of psychosocial development over the life course (Erikson, 1950, 1982; Erikson, Erikson, & Kivnik, 1986), Levinson's conception of adult development as the evolution of the individual life structure (Levinson, 1986; Levinson, Darrow, Klein, Levinson, & McKee, 1978), and the existential approach to personal meaning elaborated by Frankl (1959) and Yalom (1980).

To summarize these points about journal analysis, the task for the human science researcher working with a journal of later life is first to read the journal and describe the account of the experience of aging captured in it, and second to interpret that account in terms of developmental theories. The terms *emic* and *etic* have been used to express the distinction between using the language of the individuals being studied versus using the language of the researcher (Denzin, 1989b; Spence, 1989). Emic data are expressed in the categories and meanings of the subject; etic data are expressed in the researcher's language or the categories of some theory. The emic-etic distinction parallels that between the description of themes in personal journals and their interpretation in terms of gerontological theory. In isolating themes, the effort should be directed at getting at the essence of the author's words. Subsequently, the isolated themes can be interpreted in terms of their consistency or inconsistency with theory.

Examples of Journal Themes

The focus of this chapter is on methodological considerations that underlie the analysis of personal journals of later life. Discussion of actual material from the journals thus will be very limited. For purposes of illustration, two issues that emerge in the journals will be briefly reviewed: felt age and the narrative, dialogical self. Felt age can be understood as an emic theme: It emerges from the author's recorded experiences and can be appreciated without regard to gerontological theory. The self as narrated and dialogical can be understood as an etic theme: It is seen through the lens of contemporary theory.

The Vicissitudes of Felt Age

The cliche "You're only as old as you feel" is not exactly true. Chronological age constitutes an aspect of reality that cannot be circumvented. It is not true that you are only as old as you feel. Yet the cliche does accurately reflect the possibility of a disjunction between chronological age and felt age. This disjunction is richly described in the journals. For example, Vining (1978) commented, "It isn't as if I feel old. I don't. Inside I feel often as gauche, as shy, as incapable of wise or effective action as I did at sixteen, or as surprised and delighted by unexpected beauty" (p. 4). Elsewhere she wrote, "Sometimes during the day [at the writers' colony at Ossabow Island, South Carolina] I thought about being old. I am older than anyone else in the group. I don't feel old and I don't feel sure of myself" (p. 108). The disjunction between chronological age and felt age is captured wonderfully in a statement Grumbach (1991) attributes to Satchel Paige: "How old would you be if you didn't know how old you was?" (p. 209).

The phenomenon of the lack of a correspondence between chronological age and felt age is demonstrated most interestingly in Sarton's journals. In various journal entries between 1974 and 1976, when she was ages 62 and 63, Sarton wrote of the coming on of old age, of preparing to die, and of feeling the heaviness of mortality. For example, in December 1974, she wrote, "It is not only the coming on of winter, but the coming on of old age that I shore up against these days" (1977, p. 35). The latter part of *The House by the Sea* records the lifting of this mood. In the entry the day after her 64th birthday (May 4, 1976) she wrote, "I found myself saying to everyone, 'Sixty-four is the best age I have ever been.' And that is what I feel" (p. 245). Three years later, late in the summer of 1979, now age 67, she again wrote about her sense that her life was over, that the timelessness at the end was approaching and that she was ready to let go of life (1980, p. 180). This was followed in the fall of that year with entries that record her sense of returning to a more vigorous state, of being alive and full of excitement. The sense of youthfulness present at the end of 1979 also pervades the next journal, covering the period of her 70th birthday. About halfway through the year following that birthday, she wrote, "It is quite incredible that I am seventy and that I feel so young" (1984, p. 272). Then, three years later, as recorded in *After the Stroke,* her stroke and a protracted intestinal illness have again led to a return to feeling old. She wrote, "The stroke has made me take a leap into old age, instead of approaching it gradually" (Sarton, 1988, p. 35). However, recovery reinstates feelings of youthfulness. "I am no longer the very old woman with a very old dog I was all spring and summer" (p. 188). This series of quotations reflects the oscillations in Sarton's felt age that occurred between her chronological ages of 62 and 74, which were brought about partly by external events, but also by what she terms changes in "the landscape of the heart."

Look Who's Talking

The personal journal form, with its succession of time-ordered entries, has an inherent narrative structure and is particularly valuable for exhibiting the narrative nature of self.

The idea of the narrative nature of self, the self as story, has been developed in psychology by Cohler (1982), Sarbin (1986), McAdams (1988), and Bruner (1990). From this perspective, the self is a literary production, a textlike entity, a narrative fiction, an account whose components are the continually reconstructed experiences of events that are believed to have occurred. The self story serves to *emplot* life events with meanings and to create followable narratives. The self story is not a fixed entity. It first emerges in recognizable form in late adolescence. At that age, people begin the activity of self-biography that continues for the rest of life. The process begins with development of a set of repudiations and assimilations of childhood identifications into a configuration that includes plot, character, settings, scenes, and themes. The initial story is continually reworked. The self story is constantly being created as it is lived; the meanings of the pieces change as new patterns are found (Denzin, 1989a).

Personal journals, like autobiography and life history, recount individuals' self stories. However, personal journals directly reflect certain aspects of the self that are only indirectly captured in autobiography and life history. Journals highlight the way that selves are temporal, with human temporality consisting of the presently remembered past, the experienced present, and the anticipated future. Journals highlight the way that selves are provisional, with all self stories subject to continual revision and constituting working models rather than fixed constructions. Finally, journals highlight the way that selves are dialogical (Hermans, Kempen, & van Loon, 1992), containing a multiplicity of "I" positions, consisting, for example, of the I who writes, the I written about, and other I's or possible selves (Markus & Nurius, 1986) that, depending on circumstances, may or may not emerge.

Especially intriguing are entries in which journal authors comment on and critique their own characterizations of themselves written earlier in the journal or in previous work. Such entries highlight not only that the self can be understood as narrative, but also that it is a continuously revised narrative. Two fascinating examples are found in the journals of Sarton and Grumbach.

Near the beginning of *Journal of a Solitude,* the first of her six journals, Sarton notes that her previously published memoir, *Plant Dreaming Deep,* had brought her many friends but also unwittingly conveyed a romanticized version of who she was. She complains that in *Plant Dreaming Deep* she comes across as a wise old party who is above it all. Through her narration of the story of her move to New Hampshire, Sarton in *Plant Dreaming Deep* constructed a coherent and plausible self for herself and her readers. In *Journal of a Solitude,* the earlier self story is sharply revised: "I have begun to realize that without my own intention, the book [*Plant Dreaming Deep*] gives a false view. The anguish of my life here—its rages—is hardly mentioned" (p. 12).

The subsequent entries in *Journal of a Solitude* make it clear that far from being above it all, Sarton, at that point in her life, was a far more involved, vulnerable, self-criticizing, conflicted person than had been revealed in her earlier work.

Another such revision of a self story occurs in Grumbach's (1991) journal. Toward the end of *Coming Into the End Zone,* Grumbach questions a version of her self presented earlier in the book: "If once I insisted that it was too late for me to lead a totally new life I may have been right, but I would like to try to prove I was wrong" (p. 209).

This passage can be interpreted in terms of a perspective on self that has been termed *dialogical* (Hermans et al., 1992). In this view, the self is conceptualized in terms of a dynamic multiplicity of I positions in an imaginal landscape. The I fluctuates among different and even opposed positions and has the capacity to imaginatively endow each position with a voice, so that dialogical relations among positions can be established. "The I in one position can agree, disagree, understand, misunderstand, oppose, contradict and even ridicule the I in another position" (Hermans et al., p. 28).

In the Grumbach quote, for example, there is an I that writes in the present, an I that had written in the past (and which may still be the "true" I), and a third I that may emerge and is being cheered on by the writing I.

One of the special powers of personal journals is to expose such multiple I positions and to make visible the dialogical aspect of the self (Nussbaum, 1988).

Conclusion: Research in a Hermeneutic Perspective

A question such as "What is it like to be an older person?" focuses inquiry on a state of mind. Through a series of ingenious interpretive experiments, Gergen (1989) has convincingly demonstrated that all research addressing mental conditions, regardless of methodological rigor or sophistication of statistical analysis, inevitably entails interpretations linked to conventions of sense making shared within an interpretive community. There are no objective timeless truths regarding mental states and conditions.

The validity of the descriptions of themes and interpretations of the personal journals of later life does not derive from the correspondence between the interpretations and some objective condition. Rather, valid interpretation emerges from dialogue about the meaning of texts within an interpretive community of like-minded readers.

Moreover, from the human science perspective, the purpose of scholarly accounts of experience is not to produce immutable truths but to contribute to the culture's resources for carrying out social life (Gergen, 1989). The products of human science are forms of intelligibility that enable people to live more enriched or fully potentiated lives. This is the hoped for result of research on personal journals of later life.

References

Allport, G. (1942). *The use of personal documents in psychological science.* New York: Social Science Research Council.

Berman, H. J. (1986). To flame with a wild life: Florida Scott-Maxwell's experience of old age. *Gerontologist, 26,* 321-324.

Berman, H. J. (1988). Admissible evidence: Geropsychology and the personal journal. In S. Reinharz & G. Rowles (Eds.), *Qualitative gerontology* (pp. 47-63). New York: Springer.

Berman, H. J. (1989). May Sarton's journals: Attachment and separateness in later life. In L. E. Thomas (Ed.), *Research on adulthood and aging* (pp. 11-26). Albany: State University of New York Press.

Berman, H. J. (1991). From the pages of my life. *Generations, 15*(2), 33-40.

Berman, H. J. (in press). The tree and the vine: Existential meaning and Olmstead's journal of retirement. *Journal of Aging Studies.*

Bruner, J. (1990). *Acts of meaning.* Cambridge, MA: Harvard University Press.

Burke, R. (1992). *Interpretive reasoning.* Paper presented at International Human Science Research Conference, June, Rochester, MI.

Cohler, B. J. (1982). Personal narrative and life course. In P. B. Baltes & O. G. Brim (Eds.), *Life span development and behavior* (pp. 205-241). New York: Academic Press.

Cushman, P. (1990). Why the self is empty: Toward a historically situated psychology. *American Psychologist, 45*(5), 599-611.

Denzin, N. K. (1989a). *Interpretive biography.* Newbury Park, CA: Sage.

Denzin, N. K. (1989b). *Interpretive interactionism.* Newbury Park, CA: Sage.

Erikson, E. (1950). *Childhood and society.* New York: Norton.

Erikson, E. (1982). *The life cycle completed: A review.* New York: Norton.

Erikson, E. H., Erikson, J. M., & Kivnik, H. Q. (1986). *Vital involvement in old age.* New York: Norton.

Fothergill, R. A. (1974). *Private chronicles: A study of English diaries.* London: Oxford University Press.

Frankl, V. E. (1959). *Man's search for meaning: An introduction to logotherapy.* New York: Washington Square.

Gadamer, H. G. (1992). *Truth and method* (Trans. by J. M. Weinsheimer & G. Donald) (2nd ed.). New York: Crossroad.

Gergen, K. J. (1985). The social constructionist movement in modern psychology. *American Psychologist, 40*(3), 266-275.

Gergen, K. J. (1989). The possibility of psychological knowledge: A hermeneutic inquiry. In M. J. Packer & R. B. Addison (Eds.), *Entering the circle: Hermeneutic investigation in psychology* (pp. 239-258). Albany: State University of New York Press.

Grumbach, D. (1991). *Coming into the end zone.* New York: Norton.

Haviland, J. M., & Kramer, D. A. (1991). Affect-cognition relationships in adolescent diaries: The case of Anne Frank. *Human Development, 34*, 143-159.

Hermans, H. J. M., Kempen, H. J. G., & van Loon, R. J. P. (1992). The dialogical self: Beyond individualism and rationalism. *American Psychologist, 47*, 23-33.

Kegan, R. (1982). *The evolving self.* Cambridge, MA: Harvard University Press.

Levinson, D. J. (1986). A conception of adult development. *American Psychologist, 41*, 3-13.

Levinson, D., Darrow, C. N., Klein, E. B., Levinson, M. H., & McKee, B. (1978). *Seasons of a man's life.* New York: Knopf.

Mahoney, M. (1991). *Human change processes: The scientific foundations of psychotherapy.* New York: Basic Books.

Mallon, T. (1984). *A book of one's own: People and their diaries.* New York: Ticknor & Fields.

Markus, H., & Nurius, P. (1986). Possible selves. *American Psychologist, 41*(9), 954-969.

McAdams, D. P. (1988). *Power, intimacy and the life story.* New York: Guilford.

Nussbaum, F. A. (1988). Toward conceptualizing diary. In J. Olney (Ed.), *Studies in autobiography* (pp. 128-140). New York: Oxford University Press.

Olmstead, A. H. (1975). *Threshold: The first days of retirement.* New York: Harper & Row.

Packer, M. J., & Addison, R. B. (Eds.). (1989). *Entering the circle: Hermeneutic investigation in psychology.* Albany: State University of New York Press.

Peterson, B. E., & Stewart, A. J. (1990). Using personal and fictional documents to assess psychosocial development: A case study of Vera Brittain's generativity. *Psychology and Aging, 5*, 400-411.

Plummer, K. (1983). *Documents of life.* London: Allen & Unwin.

Ricoeur, P. (1992). *Oneself as another* (Trans. by K. Blamey). Chicago: University of Chicago Press.

Sampson, E. E. (1989). The deconstruction of the self. In J. Shotter & K. J. Gergen (Eds.), *Texts of identity* (pp. 1-19). Newbury Park, CA: Sage.

Sarbin, T. R. (1986). The narrative as root metaphor for psychology. In T. R. Sarbin (Ed.), *Narrative psychology: The storied nature of human conduct* (pp. 3-21). New York: Praeger.

Sarton, M. (1973). *Journal of a solitude.* New York: Norton.

Sarton, M. (1977). *The house by the sea: A journal.* New York: Norton.

Sarton, M. (1980). *Recovering: A journal.* New York: Norton.

Sarton, M. (1984). *At seventy: A journal.* New York: Norton.

Sarton, M. (1988). *After the stroke.* New York: Norton.

Schwartz, H., & Jacobs, J. (1979). *Qualitative sociology: A method to the madness.* London: Collier-Macmillan.

Scott-Maxwell, F. (1979). *The measure of my days.* New York: Penguin.

Spence, D. P. (1989). Rhetoric vs. evidence as a source of persuasion: A critique of the case study genre. In M. J. Packer & R. B. Addison (Eds.), *Entering the circle: Hermeneutic investigation in psychology* (pp. 205-221). Albany: State University of New York Press.

Stewart, A. J., Franz, C., & Layton, L. (1988). The changing self: Using personal documents to study lives. *Journal of Personality, 56*, 41-74.

Thomas, L. E. (1989). The human science approach to understanding adulthood and aging. In L. E. Thomas (Ed.), *Research on adulthood and aging: The human science approach* (pp. 1-7). Albany: State University of New York Press.

226   Analyzing Personal Journals

Van Manen, M. (1990). *Researching lived experience*. London, Canada: Althouse.
Vining, E. G. (1978). *Being seventy: The measure of a year*. New York: Viking.
Weintraub, K. (1978). *The value of the individual: Self and circumstance in autobiography*. Chicago: University of Chicago Press.
Wertz, F. (1984). Procedures in phenomenological research and the question of validity. In M. Anastoos (Ed.), *Exploring the lived world: Readings in phenomenological psychology* (Vol. 23, pp. 29-48, of Studies in the Social Sciences). Carrollton, GA: West Georgia College.
Woolfolk, R. L., Sass, L. A., & Messer, S. B. (1988). Introduction to hermeneutics. In S. B. Messer, L. A. Sass, & R. L. Woolfolk (Eds.), *Hermeneutics and psychological theory* (pp. 2-26). New Brunswick, NJ: Rutgers University Press.
Wrightsman, L. S. (1981). Personal documents as data in conceptualizing adult personality development. *Personality and Social Psychology Bulletin, 7*, 367-385.
Yalom, I. D. (1980). *Existential psychotherapy*. New York: Basic Books.

14

Historical Perspectives on Caregiving: Documenting Women's Experiences

EMILY K. ABEL

As research on family care of the frail elderly proliferates, a growing number of commentators express dissatisfaction with the dominance of quantitative methods. The typical study presents a statistical analysis of structured interviews that focuses on two issues that lend themselves to quantification: the chores caregivers performed and the stresses they experience.

Both issues are important, but critics charge that if we continue to restrict our scrutiny to these topics, we will miss essential aspects of the caregiving experience. Fortunately, some researchers are beginning to examine caregiving more broadly. They investigate areas previously dismissed as "soft," using both qualitative and quantitative methodologies and incorporating the theoretical insights of a wide range of disciplines (Abel, 1991; Abel & Nelson, 1990; Gubrium & Sankar, 1990).

Historical studies, however, remain notable by their absence. Although it is commonplace to stress the importance of understanding the historical context in which caregiving occurs, we know little about how the work of care has changed over time. This chapter shows that women's diaries and letters provide a rich source of data on caregiving throughout the 19th century. The great majority of 19th-century women routinely engaged in caring for the sick and the dying and filled their personal writings with accounts of those activities. These accounts provide a unique perspective from which to examine caregiving today.

19th-Century Caregiving

Caregiving consumed women's energies for several reasons. One was the high incidence of disease and disability. Although improved nutrition had decreased susceptibility to many infectious diseases by the late 18th century, the growing urban areas remained breeding grounds for disease. Epidemics of yellow fever, cholera, and smallpox occasionally swept through the major industrial cities along the East Coast. Even more common killers in the 19th century included pneumonia, typhus, whooping cough, dysentery, and tuberculosis (Leavitt & Numbers, 1985).

Although some men participated in nursing care, the reigning ideology assigned the work of caring exclusively to women. Between 1820 and 1865, popular writers expounded a new doctrine that exalted women's special sphere. At the heart of this ideology lay the belief that women were innately different from men. The traits that are central to caregiving—including responsiveness to the needs of others, patience, and an ability to adapt to individual change—became part of a new cultural definition of womanhood (Cott, 1983; Ryan, 1982; Welter, 1964). Women also were believed to have a special obligation to safeguard the health of their families (Motz, 1983; Verbugge, 1979).

Few medical services relieved women's burdens. As Rosenberg (1987, p. 18) writes, "Most Americans in 1800 had probably heard that such things as hospitals existed, but only a minority would ever have had occasion to see one." The situation had not changed greatly 70 years later. When the first government survey was conducted in 1873, the nation boasted only 120 hospitals, most of which were custodial institutions serving the deserving poor (Vogel, 1980). Middle-class patients rarely entered hospitals. Although low-income people had few options, those with families to care for them avoided these institutions whenever possible. Even surgeries were performed at home, most frequently in the kitchen (Rosenberg, 1987; Starr, 1982).

Other institutions also were sparse. Although tuberculosis was common throughout the century, the sanitarium movement was not launched until the 1880s (Bates, 1992). Reformers began to establish special institutions for the mentally ill as early as the 1820s and 1830s, but many families were reluctant to entrust ill relatives to their care (Dwyer, 1987; Grob, 1973; Rothman, 1971; Tomes, 1984). In the absence of nursing homes, the sole facilities for the elderly were poorhouses; only the most desperate, however, sought refuge within their walls (Katz, 1986).

Family members also received little help from health professionals. Skepticism about medical interventions deterred some caregivers from relying on physicians. Throughout the 19th century, many women had little confidence that physicians could deliver better care than they themselves. In addition, some families could not afford the fees that physicians charged. For those without telephones and automobiles, summoning a physician involved considerable time and effort. Outside urban areas, physicians frequently were inaccessible (Blake, 1977; Cassedy, 1977).

Family caregivers had even less contact with nurses. Nursing did not begin to organize as a profession until after the Civil War. Most graduates of the first nursing schools worked as private-duty nurses providing care to patients' individual households. But hiring nurses was an option only for the very affluent (Reverby, 1987).

The Value of History

Of course, one could argue that the vast differences between the 19th century and the late 20th render irrelevant the experiences of 19th-century women for those who wish to understand contemporary caregiving. Because infectious diseases were rampant and antibiotics nonexistent, most 19th-century caregivers tended children with acute illnesses rather than elderly people with chronic health problems. To be sure, many women did have extensive responsibilities for both spousal and parental care. But because life expectancy was less than 50 years throughout the century (Siegel & Taeuber, 1986) women often cared for husbands and parents long before they reached old age.

Nevertheless, an exploration of caregiving in the past can highlight some of the distinctive features of modern caregiving. In addition, the history of caregiving raises several questions that have contemporary significance. What skills must caregivers develop? To what extent is this activity associated with qualities typically defined as feminine? To what extent does it simultaneously encompass affective relations and instrumental tasks? Historical analysis also can help us reassess the value of care. Using an economic model, most researchers assume that caregivers are rational calculators who make decisions about how much care to deliver on the basis of the costs and benefits of various alternatives. We need other ways of understanding the endeavors of caregivers.

Diaries and Letters

The interest in women's social history during the past two decades has drawn unprecedented attention to diaries and letters. Two excellent guides to women's writings are Hinding and Chambers's *Women's History Sources* (1979) and Joyce Goodfriend's *The Published Diaries and Letters of American Women* (1987). Among the many recent historians who have drawn on diaries and letters to enlarge our understanding of the thoughts, feelings, beliefs, and concerns of various groups of 19th-century women, are Faragher (1979), Glenn (1990), Hoffert (1989), Leavitt (1986), McMillan (1990), Osterud (1991), and Premo (1990); their bibliographies also provide useful information about both published and unpublished sources. In addition, several historians have edited and published full-length journals, most notably those of Martha Farnsworth (Springer & Springer, 1986) and Emily Hawley Gillespie (Lensink, 1989).

Diaries and letters have limitations as well as advantages. Many journal entries and letters consisted of short, matter-of-fact statements that chronicled daily events rather than revealing intimate thoughts. Because caregiving was often too commonplace to warrant detailed descriptions, many women simply noted that they had "visited" the sick or "sat up" with the dying. When they were most intensively involved in rendering care, women often failed to write at all. Because some women used diaries and letters to justify their actions or construct ideal self-images, we cannot accept their statements at face value. Although some full-length diaries are available, many journals are too fragmentary to enable us to place the entries in a meaningful context. An even more serious problem is that diary and letter writers tended to be overwhelmingly white, middle-class, and Eastern. A variety of historians have sought to correct this imbalance by uncovering the accounts of pioneer women, immigrant women, and women of color, but members of the most impoverished and oppressed groups remain seriously underrepresented. Finally, those who use the past to understand events today court the danger of "presentism." As Fee and Fox (1988) explain, this means "distorting the past by seeing it only from the point of view of our own time, rather than using primary sources to understand how other people organized and interpreted their lives" (p. 4).

Without ignoring the unique features of historical inquiry or oversimplifying the task of interpreting diaries and letters, I wish to suggest that at least some of these problems are familiar to qualitative researchers in other disciplines. Like historians, such researchers pay close attention to the particular to create complex descriptions of events. Many have developed techniques for interpreting the self-presentations of respondents. Rather than imposing their own definition of reality, qualitative researchers seek to be sensitive to the perspectives of their subjects. Their experiences can serve them in good stead when they approach historical material.

Analyzing Documents

What follows first relies on assorted diaries and letters to delineate distinctive elements of 19th-century caregiving and then discusses how changes since 1900 have altered various components of care.

The Content of Care

When policy makers idealize the care delivered by family members, they often are thinking primarily about its emotional dimension. Because relatives have a close bond with a patient, they are believed to be especially well qualified to comfort and reassure. This also is the aspect that brings the greatest gratification to caregivers. In the 19th century, as in the late 20th, some women found satisfaction in catering to their patients. "I had the great pleasure of supplying all her needs and fancies," wrote Louisa May Alcott when her beloved mother was ill in 1874 (Cheney, 1982, p. 272). After her mother's death three years later, Alcott wrote in her journal, "My only comfort is that I could make her last years comfortable, and lift off the burden she had carried so bravely all these years" (Cheney, 1982, p. 300). To a friend she commented, "I could not let anyone else care for the dear invalid while I could lift a hand for I had always been her nurse & knew her little ways" (Myerson & Shealy, 1987, p. 230). The century's attitudes about the significance of personal ties helped to elevate the emotional component of care. According to dominant medical beliefs, the mind and the body were closely related. The solace that family members offered could not only facilitate healing, but also ensure a peaceful death (Rosenberg, 1979).

Care of the soul was as important as care of the psyche. Women sought to ensure that the dying were adequately penitent, "sensible" of their situation, and prepared to face death openly (Saum, 1975). In the summer of 1863, Eliza Webber, her sister Emma, and her brother Alpha left their home in Glover, Vermont, to seek their fortunes as itinerant booksellers in upstate New York. When typhoid fever struck Alpha soon after their arrival, Eliza wrote to reassure her parents: "I think him perfectly prepared to die, we read in the Bible everyday to him. The Methodist and Presbyterian Ministers have been in a number of times and have prayed with him. He is so patient and satisfied with all that we do" (letter of Eliza Roxanna Webber Denny, July 22, 1863).

Women were especially likely to consider themselves entrusted with responsibility for their husbands' spiritual well-being. The wife of a merchant in Fulton, Missouri, Samuella Curd was more successful than many women in exerting a pious influence over her husband. She had been married for two years and had just given birth to her first child when her husband entered the final stages of tuberculosis. The pleasure she took in her husband's growing faith helped to mitigate her deepening gloom about his physical deterioration. After noting that she had heard "a most excellent sermon to the converted" on October 20, 1861, she commented, "Oh! that Mr. Curd might be made to consider & not harden his heart" (Arpad, 1984, p. 103). A few months later, her efforts to bring her husband into the church began to bear fruit: "To night I had a talk with him upon the subject of religion," she wrote in January 18, 1862. "It was gratifying" (Arpad, 1984, p. 112). On March 17, she was able to proclaim her enterprise a success. After getting up in the middle of the night to rub her husband's legs, "We got to talking on religion to my great delight said he would join the Church very soon. I believe him a genuine Christian" (Arpad, 1984, p. 124). Five days later he was "received into the Church." On March 30, she wrote, "Oh! it did delight my heart, to see him in his weakness give himself up to God" (Arpad, 1984, pp. 124, 126).

When caregivers provided spiritual and emotional support, they acted in accordance with prevailing conceptions about women's roles. But most aspects of care were less compatible with reigning notions about female identity. In many cases, caregiving entailed arduous and unpleasant physical labor. "It is hard to have the care of a poor sick man day after day, week after week," wrote Mary Ann Webber to her son in 1871 when her husband was seriously ill (letter of Mary Ann Webber to Alpha Webber, 1871). She had to dress him, help him in and out of bed, assist him in walking, and bathe him. As he grew progressively weaker, her burdens multiplied. Although she was familiar with heavy farm work, lifting a bedridden man several times a day taxed her strength.

Caregiving also involved what frequently is called "dirty work" (Douglas, 1966). Caregivers cleaned up excrement and vomit, washed bloodstained sheets and bedclothes, and removed chamberpots, "the most disagreeable item in domestic labor," according to one influential writer of household treatises (Catharine Beecher, quoted in Strasser, 1982, p. 95). Lucy Sprague Mitchell (1953, p. 105) later described one of the tasks entrusted to her when she nursed her tubercular father and aunt:

> I began to empty the cuspidors. Every room except mine had at least one cuspidor partly filled with water. . . . I knew cleaning the cuspidors was dangerous work, for no maid was ever allowed to touch one. . . . I half resented this job, but who else was there? I thought. It was an unpleasant job, too, and I often sent my breakfast down the toilet as a finish.

In addition, caregiving augmented the demands of household labor, which were staggering even in the best of times. Without indoor plumbing and major appliances, housework was difficult and unremitting. Family sickness meant that women had to cook special meals, haul additional water, and carry extra loads of wood. Moreover, because health advocates preached the virtues of cleanliness in the sickroom women's household chores were considered critical ingredients of medical therapeutics. Before the acceptance of the germ theory, scrubbing the sickroom and thoroughly washing patients' sheets and clothes were considered the best defenses against infection. But laundry was the most hated task of women. It was a day-long ordeal that demanded that women carry 50 gallons of water, lug pails of wet clothes, scrub each item, expose their hands to caustic soaps, and rinse and hang the laundry to dry (Strasser, 1982, p. 195).

In October 1884, Sarah Gillespie described her workload when caring for her brother, who had suffered a serious accident:

> I can't tell how many washings & ironings I have done. But a doz. pillow slips had to be changed each day besides sheets & clothes & I [remember] washing & ironing 23 slips one day when I came home & then baking a doz pumpkin pies & making cake & washing all the dishes making the beds & to see to everything else. (diary of Sarah Gillespie Huftalen [SGH; State Historical Society of Iowa in Iowa City], Oct. 19, 1884)

Marian Louise Moore (1977, p. 176), an Ohio homesteader, remembered her experience nursing her mother:

> In the Spring of the year 1872 . . . she was sick three months, part of the time helpless, typhoid inflammatory rheumatism. . . . This sickness of hers brought more work upon me, washing and other work, when I had more work of my own than I could possibly do well.

Caregivers also performed work that we now consider the exclusive province of skilled medical providers. The words women chose to describe their activities suggest that they saw themselves functioning as doctors and nurses. "We doctored her ourselves and got her all right in two or three days," wrote Gwendoline Kincaid of her daughter Cora in 1899 (Hampsten, 1979, p. 26). When her sister lay dying in 1842, Catharine M. Sedgwick commented, "We are all by turns her nurses" (Dewey, 1871).

Because surgeries were performed at home rather than in hospitals, women frequently served as assistants. In 1871, a physician operated on the thumb of a woman who was staying at a friend's home in Idaho. The friend later commented, "By the time it came to the tying of the stitches she struggled so that the doctor asked me to tie them while he held her and I did" (Reid, 1923, p. 52).

In most instances, however, women did not act as subordinates of physicians. I have noted that many women had no more than fleeting contact with doctors. Even women who summoned physicians regularly relied extensively on their own medical knowledge and skills. Alone, or with the assistance of family and friends, women dressed wounds, applied poultices and plasters, dispensed drugs, and administered special tonics. Two weeks before the death of her mother in March 1888, Sarah Gillespie wrote in her diary,

> Her bed-sores are very painful—one which is a trifle better now is 3 in. deep & 2½ in. in diameter. I have to cut out the "puss" & cleanse them often & it fairly makes my veins refuse to carry the blood sometimes. (SGH, March 15, 1888)

Because there was a wide variety of medical beliefs and practices in the 19th century, caregivers embraced a range of therapies, including both herbal remedies and patent medicines. What caregivers shared was confidence in whatever treatments they used and pride in their ability to exercise their own judgment.

When patients were seriously ill, "watching" was a crucial component of caregiving. The watcher sat by the patient's bed, looking for signs that might indicate the approach of death or the need to administer new treatment. In the absence of stethoscopes and thermometers, it was necessary to monitor changes in the color of the skin, the rapidity of the pulse, and the character of the breathing. After her mother suffered a stroke in the spring of 1886, Sarah Gillespie frequently "sat up" to forestall more "sinking spells." She often slept just one or two hours. On June 2, she slept from 11:30 p.m. to 12:30 a.m. and from 2:15 to 3:45 a.m. (SGH, June 3, 1886). On June 28, she wrote that she undressed and went to bed for the first time in six weeks (SGH, June 28, 1886).

Caregiving responsibilities continued after the patient's death. Although family and friends hoped for an eternal life of the soul, they themselves had to take care of the corpse. Because professional funeral services were not available until the end of the century (Farrell, 1980), many women found themselves responsible for laying out the dead. The wife of a small farmer in Arkansas, Nannie Jackson visited her friend Mrs. Hornbuckle for a few hours after the death of her son on April 13, 1891. After dinner, Nannie went back to the home of the bereaved mother to "sit up" with the body. Returning home before breakfast the following day, she again "went up to Mrs. Hornbuckles & stayed a few minutes [and] got the material." Nannie then went to the home of another friend, who helped her "make the pillow and face cover" for the coffin (Bolsteri, 1982, pp. 66-67). Edith White had this memory from her childhood in frontier California in the 1860s: "My parents were always ready to help their neighbors in trouble. . . . In those days everybody who died must be wrapped in a shroud to be properly prepared for burial. Mother made many a shroud for her neighbors, and sat up all night doing it. She washed and dressed them and helped to put them into the home-made wood coffins covered with black cloth. Those were sad times for the whole town" (White, 1977, p. 276).

We can see that women who delivered care during the 1800s were not simply angels of mercy. Caregiving demanded strength, resourcefulness, and skill, not just warmth and compassion. Although women found fulfillment in responding to the needs of intimates, they also exercised medical judgment, lugged heavy pails of water, and prepared corpses for burial. The prodigious labor required by households with sick members occasionally left little time for ministering to patients' emotional and spiritual needs. Even when physicians were accessible, women controlled medical decisions. And despite widespread notions of female modesty, women routinely cleaned up excreta, vomit, and blood. In short, the demands of caring for sick and disabled people in the 19th century required women to develop high-level skills and brought them into sustained contact with some of the most fundamental aspects of human existence. Women's experiences during the 19th century add weight to the recurrent feminist argument that we should accord greater recognition to the work of care.

Continuity and Change

A series of historical changes have profoundly altered the content and meaning of care since 1900. The growing secularization of society has meant that women devote less attention to safeguarding the spiritual health of the dying. Because many infectious diseases have disappeared and the lifespan has lengthened, caregivers are much more likely today to focus on elderly people suffering from chronic conditions. With the advent of mass-produced labor-saving devices, few contemporary caregivers have such difficult and unremitting household chores as 19th-century women. The emergence of a formal system of health care delivery has simultaneously lightened many aspects of caregiving and undermined the sense of mastery that women previously enjoyed.

But historical analysis can reveal continuity as well as change. Although hospitals and funeral homes isolate family members from some aspects of sickness and death, caregivers still must confront basic life experiences. Despite the decreased prominence of religion, many family members continue to try to ease dying people into acceptance of the inevitable. And even though family caregivers today are far less likely than their 19th-century counterparts to draw on their own fund of medical knowledge, their work still requires considerable skill. In a study of adult daughters caring for frail elderly parents, I found that the women emphasized their desire to protect individuality and self-respect. The daughters worked toward this end in various ways. When the parents suffered little or no mental impairment, daughters defined their goal as respecting their parents' autonomy and encouraging them to remain in control of their lives. When dementia progressed, the women increasingly viewed their mission as pretending that nothing had changed. One woman who spoke emphatically about the need to respect her mother's dignity explained that this meant preventing her mother from realizing that she had lost control over decisions affecting her life. The daughters also tried to conceal other changes in their parents' status. Women whose parents had been professionals sought to create the illusion that the parents continued to command the respect they previously had enjoyed. Women caring for mothers who had been house-wives encouraged their mothers to believe that they still could make valuable contributions to household services (Abel, 1991).

In trying to preserve their parents' sense of competence and unique-ness, the caregivers used a distinctive pattern of thought that differs sharply from scientific rationality but nevertheless requires discipline and attention. Although they applied knowledge gained from experience and intimate understanding of a particular individual, they formulated and adhered to rules, honed skills, and sought to fulfill an ideal (Rose, 1986; Ruddick, 1982; Waerness, 1987).

Conclusion

One virtue of historical analysis is that it compels us to ask new questions about the present. During the past 10 years, a new research industry has emerged that is dedicated to documenting the stresses ex-perienced by caregivers of the frail elderly. Such studies foster healthy skepticism about the direction of contemporary social policies. Govern-ment officials repeatedly emphasize the need to save money by reim-posing care for sick and disabled people on individual households. Researchers respond that such decisions are not costless for women. Caregiving responsibilities reignite family conflicts, impose financial strains, and encroach on both paid employment and leisure activities; caregivers experience stress because they perceive their obligations as burdensome. Nevertheless, the focus on stress seriously restricts our understanding of the experience of care and narrows policy concerns (Abel, 1991).

Women's letters and diaries suggest an alternative way of viewing the work of care. Rather than focusing solely on the problems that caregiv-ing creates, we could challenge the social devaluation of this activity. The absence of universally accessible, publicly funded long-term care programs reaffirms the low status accorded to care of the frail elderly. The coping strategies of many women suggest that they also trivialize this endeavor. Instead of pressing demands for support, some women express gratitude that others tolerate their involvement in care and seek to shield bosses, co-workers, and other family members from the con-sequences. Some women also devalue caregiving by skimping on the wages paid helpers or denying the real skills these workers also bring to their jobs (Abel, 1991). An understanding of the content of care in different eras reclaims the importance of an endeavor too often denigrated. Caregiving deserves reward and esteem not only because it creates stress but also because it is an essential human activity that demands a high level of skill.

References

Abel, E. K. (1991). *Who cares for the elderly? Public policy and the experiences of adult daughters.* Philadelphia: Temple University Press.
Abel, E. K., & Nelson, M. K. (1990). *Circle of care: Work and identity in women's lives.* Albany: State University of New York Press.
Arpad, S. S. (Ed.). (1984). *Sam Curd's diary: The diary of a true woman.* Athens: Ohio University Press.
Bates, B. (1992). *Bargaining for life: A social history of tuberculosis, 1876-1938.* Philadelphia: University of Pennsylvania Press.
Blake, J. B. (1977). From Buchanan to Fishbein: The literature of domestic medicine. In G. B. Risse, R. L. Numbers, & J. W. Leavitt (Eds.), *Medicine without doctors* (pp. 11-30). New York: Science History.
Bolsteri, M. J. (Ed.). (1982). *Vinegar pie and chicken bread: A woman's diary of life in the rural south 1890-1891.* Fayetteville: University of Arkansas Press.
Cassedy, J. H. (1977). Why self-help? Americans alone with their diseases, 1800-1850. In G. B. Risse, R. K. Numbers, & J. W. Leavitt (Eds.), *Medicine without doctors* (pp. 31-48). New York: Science History.
Cheney, E. D. (Ed.). (1982). *Louisa May Alcott: Her life, letters, and journals.* Boston: Roberts.
Cott, N. F. (1983). *The bonds of womanhood: Women's sphere in New England, 1780-1835.* New Haven, CT: Yale University Press.
Dewey, M. E. (Ed.). (1871). *Life and letters of Catharine M. Sedgwick.* New York: Harper.
Douglas, M. (1966). *Purity and danger: An analysis of concepts of pollution and taboo.* London: Routledge & Kegan Paul.
Dwyer, E. (1987). *Homes for the mad: Life inside two nineteenth-century asylums.* New Brunswick, NJ: Rutgers University Press.
Faragher, J. M. (1979). *Women and men on the Overland Trail.* New Haven, CT: Yale University Press.
Farrell, J. J. (1980). *Inventing the American way of death, 1830-1920.* Philadelphia: Temple University Press.
Fee, E., & Fox, D. M. (1988). Introduction: AIDS, public policy, and historical inquiry. In E. Fee & D. M. Fox (Eds.), *AIDS: The burdens of history* (pp. 1-11). Berkeley: University of California Press.
Glenn, S. A. (1990). *Daughters of the Shtetl: Life and labor in the immigrant generation.* Ithaca, NY: Cornell University Press.
Grob, G. N. (1973). *Mental institutions in America.* New York: Free Press.
Goodfriend, J. D. (1987). *The published diaries and letters of American women: An annotated bibliography.* Boston: Hall.

Gubrium, J. F., & Sankar, A. (Eds.). (1990). *The home care experience: Ethnography and policy.* Newbury Park, CA: Sage.

Hampsten, E. (1979). *To all enquiring friends: Letters, diaries, and essays in North Dakota, 1880-1910.* Grand Forks: University of North Dakota.

Hinding, A., & Chambers, C. (1979). *Women's history sources* (2 vols.). New York: Bowker.

Hoffert, S. D. (1989). *Private matters: American attitudes toward childbearing and infant nurture in the urban north, 1800-1860.* Urbana: University of Illinois Press.

Katz, M. B. (1986). *In the shadow of the poorhouse: A social history of welfare in America.* New York: Basic Books.

Leavitt, J. W. (1986). *Brought to bed: Child-bearing in America, 1750-1950.* New York: Oxford University Press.

Leavitt, J. W., & Numbers, R. L. (1985). Sickness and health in America: An overview. In J. W. Leavitt & R. L. Numbers (Eds.), *Sickness and health in America: Readings in the history of medicine and public health* (pp. 3-10). Madison: University of Wisconsin Press.

Lensink, J. N. (1989). *"A secret to be buried": The diary and life of Emily Hawley Gillepsie, 1858-1888.* Iowa City: University of Iowa Press.

McMillan, S. G. (1990). *Motherhood in the old south: Pregnancy, childbirth, and infant rearing.* Baton Rouge: Louisiana State University Press.

Mitchell, L. S. (1953). *Two lives: The story of Wesley Clair Mitchell and myself.* New York: Simon & Schuster.

Moore, M. L. (1977). Nursing an aging mother. In G. Lerner (Ed.), *The female experience: An American documentary* (pp. 172-178). Indianapolis, IN: Bobbs-Merrill.

Motz, M. F. (1983). *True sisterhood: Michigan women and their kin, 1890-1920.* Albany: State University of New York Press.

Myerson, J., & Shealy, D. (Eds.). (1987). *The selected letters of Louisa May Alcott.* Boston: Little, Brown.

Osterud, N. G. (1991). *Bonds of community: The lives of farm women in nineteenth-century New York.* Ithaca, NY: Cornell University Press.

Premo, T. L. (1990). *Winter friends: Women growing old in the New Republic, 1785-1835.* Urbana: University of Illinois Press.

Reid, A. J. (1923). *Letters of long ago.* Caldwell, ID: Caxton.

Reverby, S. M. (1987). *Ordered to care: The dilemma of American nursing, 1850-1945.* New York: Cambridge University Press.

Rose, H. (1986). Women's work: Women's knowledge. In J. Mitchell & A. Oakley (Eds.), *What is feminism? A re-examination* (pp. 161-183). New York: Pantheon.

Rosenberg, C. E. (1979). Florence Nightingale on contagion: The hospital as moral universe. In C. E. Rosenberg (Ed.), *Healing and history: Essays for George Rosen* (pp. 116-136). Kent, UK: William Dawson.

Rosenberg, C. E. (1987). *The care of strangers: The rise of America's hospital system.* New York: Basic Books.

Rothman, D. J. (1971). *The discovery of the asylum: Social order and disorder in the new republic.* Boston: Little, Brown.

Ruddick, S. (1982). Maternal thinking. In B. Thorne (Ed.), *Rethinking the family: Some feminist questions* (pp. 76-94). New York: Longman.

Ryan, M. (1982). *Empire of the mother: American writing about domesticity, 1830-1860.* New York: Institute for Research on History and Haworth Press.

240   Documenting Women's Caregiving Experiences

Saum, L. O. (1975). Death in the popular mind of pre-Civil War America. In D. E. Stannard (Ed.), *Death in America* (pp. 30-48). Philadelphia: University of Pennsylvania.

Siegel, J. S., & Tauber, C. M. (1986). Demographic perspectives on the long-lived society. *Daedalus, 115*(1), 77-118.

Springer, M., & Springer, H. (Eds.). (1986). *Plains woman: The diary of Martha Farnsworth, 1882-1922*. Bloomington: Indiana University Press.

Starr, P. (1982). *The social transformation of American medicine: The rise of a sovereign profession and the making of a vast industry*. New York: Basic Books.

Strasser, S. (1982). *Never done: A history of American housework*. New York: Pantheon.

Tomes, N. (1984). *A generous confidence: Thomas Story Kirkbridge and the art of asylum-keeping, 1840-1883*. Cambridge, UK: Cambridge University Press.

Verbugge, M. H. (1979). The social meaning of personal health: The Ladies' Physiological Institute of Boston and vicinity in the 1850's. In S. Reverby & D. Rosner (Eds.), *Health care in America: Essays in social history* (pp. 45-66). Philadelphia: Temple University Press.

Vogel, M. J. (1980). *The invention of the modern hospital: Boston, 1870-1930*. Chicago: University of Chicago Press.

Waerness, K. (1987). On the rationality of caring. In A. S. Sassoon (Ed.), *Women and the state: The shifting boundaries of public and private* (pp. 207-234). London: Unwin Hyman.

Welter, B. (1964). The cult of true womanhood, 1820-1860. *American Quarterly, 18*, 151-174.

White, E. (1977). Memoirs of pioneer childhood and youth in French Corral and North San Juan, Nevada County, California. In C. Fischer (Ed.), *Let them speak for themselves: Women in the American West, 1849-1900*. Hamden, CT: Archon.

PART V

Writing and Recommending

15

Writing for the Right Audience

ANN DILL

Writing is generally a solitary activity done to complete a particular project. It is easy to forget that writing up research can also be experienced as a process of communion producing communication. While writing, the author vicariously encounters the people who provided information, this time from an analytic, geographic, and temporal distance. The author reviews the role performed as a researcher and the material collected while in the role. The intended audience forms a third party with whom the author communicates in the process of writing. Although the discourse and conventions of the audience may (or may not) have guided the research before this, they come forth now to shape both substance and style.

The role of author requires the ability to translate and mediate between the different parties, simultaneously being critic, astute observer, informed discussant, quizzical student, and even admiring advocate. This chapter examines the nature of these encounters, focusing first on the relationship between researcher and subject and then on relationships with different audiences for aging research. The aim is to encourage researchers to become aware of how writing in its own right expresses the research process, as well as to expand researchers' understandings of the applicability of their work.

Authoring and Authority

Independent of specific methods, a common objective of qualitative research in aging is to represent the social world experienced by older

243

people with authenticity, sensitivity, and fidelity. Incorporating and expressing the perspectives of the research participants are critical means toward this end. But what is it that justifies the authority of the researcher to voice these perspectives? And by what, or whose, criteria, can the result be fairly judged? These have been central questions and issues in the intellectual currents challenging the canons of positivist research that idealize the scientific method as "the paradigm of human knowledge" (Mitchell, 1979, pp. 144-145). Far from providing a transparently objective record, which positivists presume to be both goal and standard, the research act is now seen as producing an account mediated by the historical, political, institutional, and cultural contexts of analysis as well as the experiences of those subject to analysis (Marcus & Fischer, 1986; Silverman, 1989; Van Maanen, 1988).

Failure to be aware of this mediation can lead to two forms of interpretive error. One occurs when the researcher's own systems of meaning are imposed uncritically on the research material. Because qualitative research typically (though not always) focuses on the systems of meaning of the research subject, extreme error of this type is rare. Some systems of meaning appear easier than others to translate into terms significant to the researcher as well as the research participants, however. To represent an indigenous rhetoric or aesthetic may, for example, require using those rhetorical or aesthetic standards to frame and present the analysis. This demands stylistic skills arguably more complicated than those needed to describe cosmologies or kinship norms (Marcus & Fischer, 1986).

A second and related error derives from the rhetorical nature of the author's role. In asserting an interpretive stance (however cogent and well-reasoned), the author runs the risk of presuming to speak for, rather than about, the subject. The risk is heightened, and the stakes greater, when the subject is already at a status disadvantage. This has been particularly of concern in research on groups subject to Western political and economic domination, where the research report may become an act of "rhetorical totalitarianism" (Marcus & Fischer, 1986, p. 2; Said, 1979). Gerontology has similarly been charged with privileging its theoretical apparatus over the meanings and voice of the often so-called frail elderly themselves (Gubrium, 1993; Tornstam, 1992; Vesperi, 1985). Under any circumstance, the challenge for the author is to convey how the subjects' views may differ from, but be as valid as, the written analytic account.

Both forms of error warn against a more general fault line: overdetermined interpretation. This occurs when the researcher ignores factors other than those central to the theoretical model, treating them as extraneous "noise" while insisting on the model's analytic omnipotence. Understanding that the researcher is situated in a particular context implies that the resulting account is necessarily partial and tentative. To work from this understanding requires more than humility on the part of the researcher; it calls for an ability to seek, realize, imagine, and represent contradictory and confounding evidence. Taken together, these concerns underlie the questions raised above about the nature of the author's authority: What is it and from what claims does it arise? How is it evidenced in the substance and style of the written account?

Qualitative researchers and, in particular, ethnographers have proffered various responses and approaches differing in substance, style, and underlying philosophy.

The Realist Approach

One approach—the *realist* account (Marcus & Fischer, 1986; Van Maanen, 1988)—reaffirms many of the conventions of positivist objectivity by claiming authority on the basis of the scientific neutrality of the researcher. This approach holds that "time in the field" or an equivalent depth of exposure during data-gathering provides the grounding for the validity, scope, and accuracy of the author's interpretation. Topics of conceptual and disciplinary interest then guide the analysis and the written report (Van Maanen, 1988).

The following extract illustrates this approach and how it asserts the author's authority. It is taken from a paper first written for a professional audience (Dill, 1989) and presents an ethnographic analysis of hospital discharge planning for older persons to show how institutional structures, professional orientations, work requirements, and other contextual elements shape hospital staff's decision making. The analysis is meant to show how staff produce evaluations of patient attributes deemed relevant to discharge decisions. In this instance, the attribute in question is termed *decisional capacity,* or the patient's ability to make an informed, rational decision in his or her own best interest.

Viewed as part of the process of discharge planning, issues concerning the decisional capacity of the patient become socially constructed events, in which medical staff use models of decisional capacity in order to accomplish their work. It must therefore be determined how and when the patient's decisional capabilities come into question; which elements of those capabilities receive the focus of attention; and how understandings about the nature of those capabilities are achieved.

These processes are illustrated by the case of "Mr. Sellers," a 73-year-old man with peripheral vascular disease. Subsequent to two operations to improve circulation in his legs, the condition of Mr. Sellers' right leg deteriorated to the point that medical staff felt amputation was required. When Mr. Sellers refused to submit to this procedure, the vascular surgery staff requested a psychiatric consultation to document his capacity to make this decision. While the psychiatrist did ratify Mr. Sellers' mental capacity, the patient finally changed his mind and the amputation was performed. At the point when he was considered medically ready to leave the hospital, Mr. Sellers insisted on going home, refusing to consider other options such as a nursing home or rehabilitative unit.

Fulfilling Mr. Sellers' preference was complicated by two factors. First, he would continue to need regular physical therapy and extensive personal care; for example, two people were needed to move him from bed to chair, and one strong person to turn him at night to prevent bed sores. Medicare would cover payment for only a portion of these services, and only for a limited time. Then responsibility for securing and paying for them would devolve on Mr. Sellers and his wife.

This brought up the second complication: Mr. Sellers' wife. In the past, she had rejected and/or refused to pay for assistance provided by community agencies. Mr. Sellers had refused to become involved in these situations, saying his wife was in charge of the household and finances. The staff on Mr. Seller's unit attributed his wife's actions to psychological disturbance: they variously described her as agoraphobic, confused, paranoid and in other ways suffering from severe psychopathology. In turn, they evaluated Mr. Sellers as pathologically indecisive and dependent on his wife. Their major concern was that Mrs. Sellers would endanger her husband by compromising his care at home, and that Mr. Sellers would do little or nothing on his own.

Unit staff asked a geriatric psychiatrist for a consultation to re-evaluate Mr. Sellers' mental capacity. The psychiatrist's initial report was that, although Mr. Sellers' desire to go home might not be wise, his mental capability was sufficient that he should be allowed to make that decision. Following a visit with Mr. Sellers to his home, observing his interaction with his wife, the psychiatrist wavered on this view because of Mr. Sellers' evident dependency on an individual who appeared severely psychopathic.

The social worker formally assigned as the discharge planner on the case buttressed this perspective by asserting that his wife's opposition had been a major influence causing Mr. Sellers to delay in consenting to the amputation, ultimately resulting in the loss of a greater portion of his leg. This research-er's investigation of past records and interviews with other staff revealed, however, that Mrs. Sellers' opinion had not been a major factor in her husband's decision. In fact, he had not delayed a decision but had made an outright refusal of the proposed amputation.

Following almost three months of staff deliberations, Mr. Sellers was sent home after signing a "service contract" advising him of the risks he would face if the home care services that had been arranged were not provided. It was unclear that anything in his situation had changed at that point, other than that the staff had made up its collective mind to take this course of action, and then obtained Mr. Sellers' assent.

As written, the extract establishes authority in several ways. It fo-cuses on the beliefs, behaviors, and systems of meaning of hospital staff members to show how their evaluation of Mr. Sellers's mental capacity was conditioned by the medical work at hand. It thus uses detailed illustration of the generalized category of decisional capacity to evoke the typicality of a more general process of decision making; that is, it goes well beyond particulars (or the facts) to account for the attributed meaning of particulars. Although later sections of the paper further analyze both this category and process, the conceptual linkage between them is presumed in the way the report is constructed.

The author also achieves authority through narrative control, organ-izing the account to pose, discuss, and then resolve the question of how staff members construct mental capacity. Stylistic techniques reinforce this control. Use of the third person decreases the appearance of subjec-tivity. For example, consider the concluding statement: "It was unclear that anything in his situation had changed at that point." This phrasing asserts as facts that nothing had changed and that an objective observer (such as the researcher) would have detected this lack of change; to say in any way "it was unclear to me" would substantially reduce the statement's authority. Throughout this extract there is minimal presen-tation of self-reflective commentary, alternative perspectives, or areas not fully analyzed. For instance, the author does not wonder about the course of the analysis in the text, although she may privately do so.

Although realist accounts assert unquestioned interpretive authority, they also have increasingly acknowledged the constructed nature of that assertion. Some do this through vigilant documentation of methods and analytic procedures, seeking thereby to establish their reliability and validity. Others reflexively examine their own texts while attempting to explain how research subjects themselves account for their experiences. An example is Marjorie Shostak's *Nisa: The Life and Words of a !Kung Woman* (1981), a life history that, although focused on themes derived from the informant's perspective, considers how the text was influenced by the cultural and life-cycle differences between author and informant (Marcus & Fischer, 1986, pp. 57-59). More experimentally, some authors have organized their material according to the frames of reference and textual conventions of their research subjects, such as Michelle Rosaldo's (1980) choice to structure her analysis of maleness among the Ilongot (a headhunting hill tribe in the Philippines) around life-cycle experiences assessed by Ilongot men as critical to their social existence (Marcus & Fischer, 1986, pp. 59-61). The objective of these efforts remains, however, to produce a convincingly authentic representation.

The Confessional Approach

An alternative *confessional* approach (Van Maanen, 1988) differs primarily in viewing the research process as interpretive, rather than purely descriptive. Its focus is directly on how the researcher has come to understand and represent the topic at hand. There is thus considerable attention to how research data have been mediated by the researcher's own field experience as well as relationships with the subjects. The author does not attempt to establish, like the realist, that his or her analytic stance is omnipotent, merely that it is plausible.

In substance, this approach yields accounts depicting and demystifying the research process. Generally written in the first person, they cast the researcher in the role of student or translator of the cultural text. For example, rather than writing, "This researcher's investigation . . . revealed, however, that Mrs. Sellers' opinion had not been a major factor in her husband's decision. . . ," as in the above extract, the author might write, "Having heard the social worker and other staff implicate Mrs. Sellers in her husband's refusal to have surgery, I was very surprised when I read his chart and found that he seemed to have made up his mind independently of her opinion. This changed my view of the entire case." In this approach, the narrative follows the research process itself, documenting the researcher's preconceptions, mistakes, and bafflement as well as moments of rapport, understanding, and *epiphany* or sudden insights. The author appears willing to "tell all" in the interest of revealing the research that supports the analysis.

A great deal of methodological detail would have to be added to turn the story of Mr. Sellers into a confessional account, one that would reflect how the extract was written. What was the role of the author in the clinical setting? How was that communicated to and understood by different people there? How were the site and research participants selected? How was the "general" nature of discharge planning observed, recorded, and induced? Were there other cases in which decisional capacity became an issue? How were those similar to or different from the one described?

Answers to these questions might be regarded as minimal detail essential to convince the reader of the solidity of any research project. Moving toward truly confessional writing would require a focus on the interpretative process itself. For example, what uncertainties led the author to question the way the social worker was portraying Mr. Sellers's response to his surgery? How could the author be sure, at the end, that the staff had changed but Mr. Sellers had not? Providing this information would take the reader behind the mere facts to examine how the facts were interpreted.

The Impressionist Approach

Far different in intent is the last approach to issues of authority. Impressionist accounts represent the socially constructed nature of the research process and the knowledge it produces. In dramatic and sometimes allegorical form they tell of the researcher's experience of memorable events and personalities, representing general aspects of the subject under study through a particular, or even exceptional, "slice of life" (Van Maanen, 1988). In attempting that representation, the author is making a claim of considerable interpretive skill. Unlike the realist approach, the interpretation itself is not highlighted, however. Instead, the author allows multiple, often contrasting, analyses to emerge either directly, through the commentary of subjects, or indirectly by inviting the reader's participation in the analytic process, such as in Gubrium's (1992) presentation of equally authentic versions of separate parties to an event. The written account, like the research experience, is depicted with a sense of contingency; the absence of a claim of closure emphasizes the inherently partial nature of cultural analysis.

We can turn the foregoing extract into impressionist writing. For example, the contingency of hospital staff members' perspectives described in the fourth paragraph could be highlighted, showing how their views of Mr. Sellers were shaped by diverse conceptual frames, as the following sections suggest:

> [The social worker] feared that Mr. Sellers would face enormous risks at home if left in his wife's care. [She] expressed this fear through "worst case" scenarios . . . using statements such as the following: "[Mrs. Sellers] is not to be trusted to take over responsibility for his care. . . . Her need is to create crises and turmoil. . . . She will try to get him to do more than he can, like getting out of the wheelchair. . . . He's at very real risk as an [amputee] . . . he could get skin decubiti [open sores] bad enough that he could die." The nursing and rehabilitation staff said they doubted that Mr. Sellers would do very well at home. They almost uniformly described him as "lacking in motivation" to improve or take charge of his own situation. . . . [He] did not act like other patients in their experience who would participate more actively in their own care in order to facilitate their return home. (Dill, 1987, pp. 49-50)

As with the confessional approach, the author of an impressionist account assumes a personalized authority by constructing a report clearly derived from the researcher's place and experience in the course of research. As the above discussion suggests, however, this is a deliberately contested authority, and its purpose is not to assert that the author's actions conform to research standards but to question the subject-object distinction behind those very standards. The research work is depicted as coproduced, as when Vincent Crapanzano in *Tuhami: Portrait of a Moroccan* (1980) represents the mood and tone of an interview situation with such force that "the text itself resembles the fragmentary nature of the series of interactions that it describes" (Marcus & Fischer, 1986, p. 72). The written product likewise evokes the reader's sense of participation by drawing concretely on the flow of events and using rich, evocative description. Further, these are often tales of extraordinary events, startling the reader (as the author presumably was startled) into an altered understanding of the situation.

Impressionist accounts seek plausibility rather than accuracy, authenticity rather than representativeness. This is more than a case of alternative objectives. Writers using an impressionist approach make a different claim about the nature of social reality than those using confessional or realist approaches. The latter seek to convey literal accounts of a unitary social reality. The impressionist approach aims to represent that many processes coincide to frame what is real.

Organizing an impressionist account can be tricky. One stylistic device is to make the story chronological, showing at different points in time the perspectives of various actors. This in fact was done in a different version of Mr. Sellers's case (Dill, 1987), which was published in a journal oriented to aging practitioners. This version shows no overt conceptual analysis. Readers are instead invited to deduce the meaning of the account and compare their views with those of several commentaries printed separately. The story starts in the middle of the staff's decision making and then takes the reader through Mr. Sellers's home situation and previous care to the events shaping the ultimate discharge. Along the way, the written account presents the voices of different staff members in all of their confusion. Largely missing, however, is a direct account of Mr. Sellers's views or those of his wife. Moreover, the researcher is a "fly on the wall," trying to appear as neutral reporter. Adding the latter voices to the interpretive chaos would have made the story more truly impressionist.

Written accounts of qualitative research do not, of course, fall neatly into one or another of the three categories. Many accounts combine realist, confessional, and impressionist elements; others experiment with writing styles that in some ways transcend this classification. Viewing these as different answers to questions of written authority can be useful heuristically, however, particularly when considering which answers may be expected by different audiences.

Audiences in Aging Research

Since its beginnings as a formal field, gerontology has called for the contributions of multiple disciplines and perspectives. Potential audiences for qualitative research on aging span institutional boundaries among specialties as well as the conventions separating applied from basic inquiry. Knowing which audience to try to reach poses one challenge for the researcher; understanding how to do so becomes a second challenge.

One established figure in qualitative research counsels, "The best advice I have ever received (was) . . . to pick out a 'target reader' and write . . . for only one reader. Pick out some real person whom you know, then set down your materials so this person will understand what you are saying" (Spradley, 1979, p. 213). Fruitful as this approach may be, in the likely event that the identity of the target reader is uncertain, it may be useful to take a step back and clarify the purposes of the writing to be undertaken. Establishing the goals as well as target of the writing guides the writing style: whether to be descriptive or analytic, objective or prescriptive. These decisions also underlie the choice of the appropriate level of analysis, from individual or microlevel to macrosystemic. They may further determine which voices to bring forward and how explicitly to display them, thus dictating a choice among realist, confessional, or impressionist approaches. For example, a federal funding agency may expect realist writing even when an impressionist tale can be told about multiple perspectives.

Ultimately, these decisions guide the author toward a particular audience and the anticipation of the expectations and conventions that audience holds. In practice, of course, the author may not be free to determine the audience or writing may involve trade-offs among divergent professional and personal goals, as when the desire to reach a wide readership competes with the need for legitimation by disciplinary colleagues in determining writing style, substance, and potential sources of publication. Recognizing the multiplicity and diversity of audiences for aging research should, however, free the writer to experiment with different presentational frames. Some ways in which different audiences can engage the qualitative researcher will now be considered.

Interdisciplinary Writing and "Normal Science"

Having achieved considerable stature as a scientific enterprise, gerontology is now confronting critical theoretical challenges to its positivist underpinnings. Imported mainly from philosophy, anthropology, and humanist discourses, these critiques are gradually providing the basis for alternate formulations of concepts guiding understandings of aging and the life course (Cole, Achenbaum, Jakobi, & Kastenbaum, 1993; Moody, 1992; Tornstam, 1992). Qualitative research has much to contribute to this development because it seeks a deep and grounded exposition of alternative perspectives, problematizing the taken for granted.

This very nature can, however, make it difficult for qualitative work to find a warm reception within the aging field. To change a paradigm requires considerable intellectual freight, Kuhn (1962) reminds us, and gerontology has displayed a pattern of refashioning, rather than rejecting, existing theories despite accumulated contradictory evidence (Tornstam, 1992). This no doubt reflects a human tendency to avoid change as well as established institutional practices (Estes & Binney, 1989). It may also accrue from the same orientations that have broadened the scope and significance of the field; interdisciplinary and applied in nature, aging research seeks legitimation by adopting the paradigms and standards of normal, basic science.

Whatever the sources of their tenacity, the conceptual foreground of gerontology imposes certain expectations that the qualitative researcher cannot afford to ignore. Despite variability in technique and purpose, qualitative research methods share certain attributes that have both positive and negative consequences for responding to these expectations. First, the relatively unstandardized approach to data gathering and analysis allows the researcher to produce an account grounded in an intimate understanding of the study site. Although this can yield a rich and contextualized "inside view," it also generates criticism that the researcher may have been biased or that those studied may have been (intentionally or not) misleading. Often subsumed under the rubric of "reliability," these issues cut to the epistemological center of qualitative work.

Second, qualitative methods restrict the scope of the study site or population to that with which the researcher can have ongoing, intensive, in vivo encounters. This also is responsible for the depth and richness of the end product, as well as lending a sense of wholeness to the analysis. The concern here regards the relevance of study findings for other situations or populations. Beyond the statistical notion of generalizability, this issue queries the very typification of that which is studied: what type of setting, scene, event, or group does this one exemplify, and why?

A third feature of qualitative studies is the comparison and cross-checking of information obtained from diverse cases. This may involve contrasting the views of different individuals or the same person at different times. It is largely this comparative process, as well as the time and analytic energy it requires, that has given qualitative work the reputation of having high validity. Using multiple sources of data introduces the possibility of multiple biases, however, and complicates assessments of the strength and significance of findings. Application of statistical criteria can resolve these issues for some data sets (Brim &

Spain, 1974), but the challenge for all authors is to convince readers that they have refrained from an explanation better than that which the data really allow.

Although the writer can take different tacks in approaching these issues, responses to them should be explicit. Careful specification of research operations, informant-selection and site-selection criteria, and units of analysis will go far toward enhancing credibility (Eckert, 1988). Hypothesis testing is often more implicit than explicit in qualitative work; nonetheless, falsification procedures, such as negative case analysis, should be brought to light and, it is hoped, carefully documented.

In framing a response, it is reasonable to assert that the strengths of the methods used outweigh limitations on a particular point. It is often the case, for example, that qualitative work taps dimensions less amenable to quantitative measures or provides contextual information critical to the interpretation of those measures. In both instances validity is clearly enhanced so that the researcher is better able to make more specific generalizations, even if global generalizability is limited. An alternate justification is to offer a different standard or criterion. Impressionist accounts do this by promoting allegorical rather than statistical or even substantive significance. For example, in the classic and largely impressionist *Number Our Days,* Barbara Myerhoff (1978) describes conflicts among participants at the Aliyah Senior Citizens' Center not simply to reflect the everyday tenor of life there, but to underscore a central cultural idiom—"We fight to keep warm," as one informant puts it (p. 153)—life and conflict are inseparable. Confessional accounts warrant findings by giving reflexivity primacy over supposed objectivity, such as the same author's conclusion after several years of soul searching on the legitimacy of her inquiry: "In the end, the only acceptable answer I could find to the question 'Am I qualified to write this book?' was that my membership [her own Jewishness] and my affection were my qualifications. When I judge these people, I judge myself" (Myerhoff, 1978, p. 28).

The General Readership

The continuing dialogue within gerontology about its own scientific status should hearten qualitative researchers, encouraging them to test the limits of their understandings of research findings. Part of that testing can include the appeal to audiences broader than disciplinary colleagues. Attempting to write for the general audience may appear to be motivated more by personal (or financial!) reasons than professional ones. There are, however, distinct intellectual rewards to be gained here.

A major one contradicts usual concerns about being "too late" in one's work: finding belatedly that the central concepts revealed by qualitative research have already been explored (Lofland & Lofland, 1984). Tackling the translation from disciplinary to popular discourse may well involve reinventing core concepts, in the process extending their meaning and significance. Consider, for example, the description by Vesperi (1985) of older people in St. Petersburg, Florida, an ethnography that grew out of a series of articles for the local newspaper. To examine how social interactions undermine the status and self-esteem of older people, Vesperi applies the key anthropological concept of *reciprocity,* which denotes norms that one should make a return to others, in degree or kind, for goods or services given. Vesperi maintains that cultural biases, bureaucratic welfare procedures, and their own needs impede the ability of elders to "give back," transforming them into supplicants instead of active contributors to society. She documents attempts by elders to circumvent this transformation in order to maintain their dignity; for example, some try to assume control of interviews by social service workers by steering the discussion toward a more active, less needy phase of their lives. Ironically, these very strategies may inadvertently reinforce stereotypes about the elderly, such as a supposed tendency to wander in conversations. By showing the multiple levels at which reciprocity (or its absence) governs the everyday interactions of older people, Vesperi establishes an important link between interpersonal relations and identity issues in old age. The use of this example raises (and arguably answers) a critical question: What is the difference between popularized qualitative work and journalism? Whereas both seek to describe and explain social reality, the intent of qualitative research is more likely to be the elucidation of broader, conceptual issues.

When writing in the popular vein, however, the researcher does confront some journalistic conventions that both shape and respond to general reader expectations.[1] First, the structure of popular writing is more apt to place its important points and conclusions up front. Breaking news stories epitomize this; in fact, they "pyramid" their contents by condensing the who, where, what, when, why, and how in their first few sentences. Feature stories are probably closer in format to that of qualitative work, but they also quickly inform the reader why he or she should bother to continue reading. This results partly from editorial imperatives, such as the constraints on space that determine the ultimate length of a piece of writing. It also reflects the view that the reader will not long tolerate being left to wonder where a story is going. Regardless of the veracity of this view (which may merely reflect modern media sensibilities), it can support the qualitative analyst who chooses to underscore the purpose of an article succinctly at the outset.

A second journalistic convention is the use of the third person, with the author remaining hidden behind the text. In journalism, this accrues from a concern that stories appear objective. It also represents an effort to engage the reader directly with the subject matter under consideration, rather than with the narrator.

These conventions are obviously more compatible with realist than confessional or impressionist approaches. Given the inductive and personal nature of qualitative research findings, however, it may seem not merely artificial but invalid to present conclusions at the outset or to obscure the writer's identity. In that case, it is essential to devise alternate ways of engaging and convincing the reader. Vividness of language, metaphor, and detail can be paramount tools here.

Policy Makers

Although many discussions of social policy focus on specific legislative acts, policy making is in fact a multifaceted process. It begins with the identification of a social problem and vetting of alternative solutions. It continues through to the implementation and evaluation of specific regulations or programs (Rochefort, 1986). Qualitative research can contribute at any point to this dynamic.[2]

Several particular uses accrue from the written grounding of data in the perspectives of research subjects. These may yield information on the ways people who will be affected by social programs themselves define their needs, as well as their perceptions of the real-life costs, benefits, and risks attached to different programmatic structures. Knowing how these attitudes and values are likely to affect program participation and outcomes in practice is clearly of strategic significance for their planners. Qualitative work can also focus on actual responses to programs already in place or on the social context influencing their operations. Qualitative studies are especially apt at providing documentation of real-life facts of programs and should be incorporated into policy evaluation and redesign efforts.

In the area of policy, the writer must target the potential audience and appeal to its interests. This clearly requires an understanding of the salience of current policy issues and the ability to link in a convincing way what the research suggests to what the audience wants to do or is doing. Say, for example, that the audience is a particular federal agency. If that agency is developing a new policy initiative, then it may be most receptive to a reasoned, apparently neutral description of alternative approaches. If, on the other hand, it is attempting to build consensus or neutralize opposition to a particular program, it may seek expert opinion that is overtly persuasive. Knowing the agency's agenda can thus influence the tone and voice that dominate the report; appealing to that agenda may also require selective use of current buzzwords and punchlines.[3]

As must writing for the general reader, policy reports must hook the audience quickly. As one analyst puts it, "Most clients . . . are not interested, get distracted, and have short attention spans" (Meltsner, 1976, p. 237). It is essential to minimize detail and to avoid technical terms (or shift technical material to a later section or appendix). Tables or pictures can be useful to condense material, but their contents must be clear and informatively titled. Quotations, headings, underlining, and clear organizational structure add emphasis and increase the work's persuasiveness. The writer might even experiment with a question-and-answer format, briefly explaining major findings and recommendations and anticipating tough questions.

Holding the reader's interest is also easier with a coherent theme linking together the main sections of the report. This theme should justify the conceptual approach and research techniques. It should demonstrate emphatically how the design and logic of the research are relevant to the policy question being addressed. In short, it should establish that "the facts you select to describe the problem . . . lead to a single obvious solution" (Meltsner, 1976, p. 238).

Such brevity and singularity may pose a dilemma for the qualitative researcher used to writing monograph-length analyses of complex social processes. To achieve policy impact requires a certain commodification of research findings: an ability to single out the ideas that will communicate most clearly to the target audience. The researcher has already done this while conducting research by learning the rules for communicating with the people studied. All that is really required here is translating this skill to the policy domain.

Practitioners

Qualitative research can make much the same contribution to discussions of clinical practice as to aging policy. On the macrolevel, analysis of the social context of particular programs can call attention to broader structural and cultural factors impinging on practitioners. On the microlevel, qualitative work can identify the current parameters and limits of clinical practice, suggesting alternative directions (Bloor & McKeganey, 1989; Prior, 1989).

The researcher need not, however, share the ameliorist assumptions of practitioners in order to write for this arena. For example, by amplifying the voice of the service recipient, qualitative writing can provide information that practitioners want and need about lay perceptions of need, service provision, and treatment goals. Recent works illustrating this approach are Mitteness's (1987) analysis of the social construction of incontinence and Kaufman's (1988) comparison of the views of stroke patients with those of medical providers regarding which domains of their lives require medical intervention.

The writer who elects a more critical vein can treat problematically the concepts and assumptions underlying clinical practice. One format for achieving this is to reveal how the use of practice models comes to make sense within a particular context, as the description of Mr. Sellers' decisional capacity is intended to illustrate. Showing how service recipients themselves reject or rearticulate elements of those models can go even farther toward "unsettling" the polarities within clinical discourse (Silverman, 1989).

Getting these messages through to a clinical audience may again require some adaptation of writing style. Medical journals especially may require a more concrete framing of hypotheses and results than the qualitative researcher customarily constructs. The main issue, however, is to demonstrate convincingly that the findings are interesting and useful to practitioners in different practice sites. Striking a balance between realist and impressionist approaches to writing helps. Doing this requires succinct typification of the social processes and contexts at work, a productive phrasing of a critical stance, and real-life, native accounts.

An exemplar here is Cohen and Sokolovsky's (1989) *Old Men of the Bowery,* an ethnography of the social networks, life histories, and daily lives of skid-row residents. Viewing the world through the eyes of these men leads the authors to portray their actions as strategies for survival as well as behavior that puts them at considerable risk for physical and emotional ills. The authors devise recommendations for treatment interventions that are grounded in the worlds of their informants and illustrate the workings of an actual program based on those recommendations. That one author is an anthropologist (Sokolovsky) and the other a psychiatrist (Cohen) undoubtedly helped to produce a work that defined problems and solutions in terms that make sense both ethnographically and clinically. The lesson here for the single author is again that writing requires an act of brokerage, translating the findings and experience of qualitative research into the language and conventions of the audience.

Conclusion

The multiple perspectives of the experiences that are the purview of qualitative work intensify the dilemmas of attempting to translate between items of analytic interest and the expectations of audiences. This chapter has forwarded a view of the author as a broker among different discursive frames, considering ways of producing written accounts that are simultaneously authentic, conceptually interesting, and acceptable. The reader may well protest at the compromises and contradictions such a role implies; having to compress and commodify findings for a policy- or practice-related audience, for example, may seem a violation of the researcher's holistic approach or of the voice of the research subject.

One response to this is highly relativistic. The question of which perspective and whose writing is privileged is inescapable in the act of representation. As Silverman (1989) notes, following Foucault, "There is no 'discourse of truth' . . . knowledge is always implicated in power" (p. 42). Given this, the best course for the researcher may be to remain engaged in the unsettling business of questioning established assumptions and polarities, including the researcher's own, and to reflect this in writing.

More concretely, the multiple audiences available to qualitative aging researchers offer a reminder that no one written piece need be considered a final statement. Keeping this in view while writing can help reduce "the agony of omitting" (Lofland & Lofland, 1984, p. 138) inherent in fitting qualitative material into an overall structure. Different aspects and components of a study may be best displayed in different frames, much as a visual artist would construct a thematic series.[4] Contributing to diverse dialogues, an expansion of repertoire can help researchers refine their understandings of the meaning of their work. This then enhances the benefit for each party in the exchange of the writing process.

In opening up to diverse audiences, the writer in essence comes full circle in the research process. Once again, issues of meaning and procedure come to the fore, because the author must reformulate the purpose and substance of the written account. This may require new data-collection activities, such as content analysis of the publications or mission statements of groups representing the target audience. Ethical concerns emerge; for example, reaching an audience in a policy domain may push the author to assume a more prescriptive stance than he or she is comfortable with or to privilege the voice of the "expert" over that of informants. Dealing with these diverse issues while trying to produce readable prose requires analytic and management skills equal to any developed in previous research activities.

When it comes to the writing itself, as one cartoon figure fairly advises another, "Writing is simple. . . . First, you have to make sure you have plenty of paper . . . sharp pencils . . . typewriter ribbon. Then . . . roll a sheet of paper into the typewriter . . . and stare at it until beads of blood appear on your forehead" (in Klauser, 1987, p. 15). Fortunately for the many who share this sentiment, help has arrived in the form of various instructives on how to tap a creative free flow that links ideas to words (Klauser, 1987; Tarvers, 1988). Free writing (Elbow, 1975) and writing logs or journals (Maimon, Nodine, & O'Connor, 1989) may be particularly suitable for qualitative researchers because they mirror the problematizing and associative thinking processes used throughout the research.

Whatever techniques the author chooses, and whatever style, approach, and form of authority the author assumes, the goal remains the same: to create a shared reality—between author and audience—that fairly represents the reality coexperienced with the research participants. Attaining this goal requires nothing more or less than the reflexivity, analytic understanding, and communication skills inherent in successful qualitative research.

Notes

1. Much of this discussion is based on conversations with Tracy Breton, a journalist for the *Providence Journal-Bulletin*.

2. Often overlooked as outlets for policy-related pieces are the trade journals and newsletters of nonprofit groups such as the National Conference of State Legislators, the National Conference of Mayors, the League of Cities, the American Association of Retired Persons, the Urban League, the National Association for the Advancement of Colored People, and the Coalition for Human Needs.

3. For a thorough discussion of the tricky art of communicating within the political realm of bureaucracies, see Meltsner (1976).

4. The visual analogy was first suggested by sociologist and visual artist Joan Mancuso.

References

Bloor, M., & McKeganey, N. (1989). Ethnography addressing the practitioner. In J. F. Gubrium & D. Silverman (Eds.), *The politics of field research* (pp. 197-212). Newbury Park, CA: Sage.

Brim, J., & Spain, D. H. (1974). *Research design in anthropology*. New York: Holt, Rinehart & Winston.

Cohen, C. I., & Sokolovsky, J. (1989). *Old men of the Bowery*. New York: Guilford.

Cole, T. R., Achenbaum, W. A., Jakobi, P. L., & Kastenbaum, R. (Eds.). (1993). *Voices and visions of aging*. New York: Springer.

Crapanzano, V. (1973). *Tuhami: Portrait of a Moroccan*. Chicago: University of Chicago Press.

Dill, A. E. P. (1987). A safe plan. *Generations, 11*, 48-53.

Dill, A. E. P. (1989). *The ethnography and ethics of discharge planning*. Paper presented at annual meeting of American Anthropological Association, Washington, DC.

Eckert, J. K. (1988). Ethnographic research on aging. In S. Reinharz & G. D. Rowles (Eds.), *Qualitative gerontology* (pp. 241-255). New York: Springer.

Elbow, P. (1975). *Writing without teachers*. New York: Oxford University Press.

Estes, C. L., & Binney, E. A. (1989). The biomedicalization of aging: Dangers and dilemmas. *Gerontologist, 29*, 587-596.

Gubrium, J. F. (1992). *The mosaic of care*. New York: Springer.

Gubrium, J. F. (1993). Voice and context in a new gerontology. In T. R. Cole, W. A. Achenbaum, P. L. Jakobi, & R. Kastenbaum (Eds.), *Voices and visions of aging* (pp. 46-63). New York: Springer.

Kaufman, S. R. (1988). Stroke rehabilitation and the negotiation of identity. In S. Reinharz & G. D. Rowles (Eds.), *Qualitative gerontology* (pp. 82-103). New York: Springer.

Klauser, H. A. (1987). *Writing on both sides of the brain*. San Francisco: HarperCollins.

Kuhn, T. (1962). *The structure of scientific revolutions*. Chicago: University of Chicago Press.

Lofland, J., & Lofland, L. H. (1984). *Analyzing social settings* (2nd ed.). Belmont, CA: Wadsworth.

Maimon, E. P., Nodine, B. F., & O'Connor, F. W. (1989). *Thinking, reasoning, and writing*. New York: Longman.

Marcus, G. E., & Fischer, M. M. J. (1986). *Anthropology as cultural critique*. Chicago: University of Chicago Press.

Meltsner, A. J. (1976). *Policy analysts in the bureaucracy*. Berkeley: University of California Press.

Mitchell, G. D. (Ed.). (1979). *A new dictionary of the social sciences*. Hawthorne, NY: Aldine.

Mitteness, L. S. (1987). The management of urinary incontinence by community-living elderly. *Gerontologist, 27*, 185-193.

Moody, H. R. (1992). Gerontology and critical theory. *Gerontologist, 32*, 294-295.

Myerhoff, B. (1978). *Number our days*. New York: Simon & Schuster.

Prior, L. (1989). Evaluation research and quality assurance. In J. F. Gubrium & D. Silverman (Eds.), *The politics of field research* (pp. 132-149). Newbury Park, CA: Sage.

Rochefort, D. A. (1986). *American social welfare policy*. Boulder, CO: Westview.

Rosaldo, M. Z. (1980). *Knowledge and passion: Ilongot notions of self and social life*. New York: Cambridge University Press.

Said, E. (1979). *Orientalism*. New York: Random House.

Shostak, M. (1981). *Nisa: The life and words of a !Kung woman*. Cambridge, MA: Harvard University Press.

Silverman, D. (1989). The impossible dreams of reformism and romanticism. In J. F. Gubrium & D. Silverman (Eds.), *The politics of field research* (pp. 30-48). Newbury Park, CA: Sage.

Spradley, J. P. (1979). *The ethnographic interview*. New York: Holt, Rinehart & Winston.

Tarvers, J. K. (1988). *Teaching writing: Theories and practices*. Glenview, IL: Scott, Foresman.

Tornstam, L. (1992). The quo vadis of gerontology: on the scientific paradigm of gerontology. *Gerontologist, 32*, 318-326.

Van Maanen, J. (1988). *Tales of the field*. Chicago: University of Chicago Press.

Vesperi, M. D. (1985). *City of green benches*. Ithaca, NY: Cornell University Press.

16

Qualitative Evaluation and Policy

SHULAMIT REINHARZ

What do social programs, medical services, educational activities, and services for the elderly have in common? Typically, they are all the object of evaluation research at one point or another. Some are the object of continuous evaluation. They might be evaluated to determine what "consumers" think of the quality of the service delivered. They might be evaluated to identify problems in those services. Or they might be evaluated to find ways of cutting costs. Projects that deliver any kind of service to older people are thus likely to be associated with evaluation research.

In fact, a hallmark of modern society is its rationalization and bureaucratization, two factors that are intimately linked to a culture of evaluation. Not to evaluate is almost equivalent to being irresponsible or immoral in contemporary society. People are socialized even to have their bodies evaluated annually regardless of how they feel and irrespective of symptoms. Evaluation is thus applied to the past, present, and future and with what has occurred, what is in effect, and what will be.

To the extent that aging in contemporary U.S. society is associated with institutions (medical, financial, social, legal, and residential), it also will be embraced by the "culture of evaluation. It is important to understand how to undertake evaluations that serve the interests of older people as much as they serve the interests of the institutions designed to assist and protect elders. Evaluations themselves should be evaluated, because evaluations have considerable moral authority and thus social power. This chapter will describe a few efforts at evaluation, illustrating

the specific strengths of qualitative evaluation research and voicing
some warnings about the dangers of improper evaluation research.

Qualitative Evaluation Research:
Assets and Deficits

Evaluation research comes in many varieties, but they can be differ-
entiated in several ways: *process evaluation* versus *outcome evaluation*
and *qualitative* (i.e., descriptive, interpretive) versus *quantitative* (i.e.,
numerical, positivist). The variety also goes by different names. For
example, Egon Guba (1978) uses the term *naturalistic inquiry* in his
monograph on qualitative evaluation; Barney Glaser and Anselm Strauss
(1967) use the term *grounded theory* in their discussion. I agree with
Charles Reichardt (see Steinmetz, 1980): "Qualitative evaluation is an
umbrella term that covers a host of different definitions and additional
claims." Generally, however, qualitative evaluation is research undertaken to assess or describe a program, drawing on qualitative methods
to conduct the study. The assessors can be insiders or outsiders to the
program.

Qualitative research can take the form of a single case study (Reinharz, 1992, chap. 9) or a comparative analysis (e.g., Kayser-Jones
1981). According to experimental methodologist Donald Campbell
(1978), qualitative research looks for variation within its subject area,
uses retrospective reports to obtain time-series data of sorts, and collects
many global measures.

Qualitative evaluation research has the asset of providing the reader
with a record of the actual words and a description of the actual behavior
of the people involved in the service (Reinharz & Rowles, 1987).
Feminist scholars have pointed out the particular value of "giving
voice" to underprivileged, relatively powerless people to enable social
scientists to have a fuller understanding of social reality (Calasanti,
1992). Qualitative evaluation research is capable of doing this. An
example comes from the work of a gerontologist in New Zealand who
studied people who cared for relatives at home:

> Some people (for a variety of motivations/desires/guilt) did wish to care for
> their relatives at home, and on top of that there were some really positive
> experiences as well as the very negative ones. But what happened in the
> accounts was that these moments became typically submerged beneath the

realistic emphasis on the problems caring generated and the physical and emotional consequences. Those better moments were there, albeit not in all accounts, and I struggled to ensure that they did not get totally suppressed, to find ways of representing them which encompassed their presence and at the same time their precariousness. In a way, that was also one of the reasons for publishing the texts of the interviews, because a careful reading (not just skimming over) allows them to be remarked on. (Opie, personal communication, 8 March 1992)

Her work allows us to understand human behavior as deeply ambivalent rather than simple. Such research also has the assets of believability derived from the opportunity to read descriptions of observed phenomena and accessibility to the people studied (see Patton, 1980, who believes that they are "more communicable to staff").

This strength can be taken too far, however. If the researcher focuses on transmitting the voice of the people studied for the sake of authenticity, he or she may slip into thinking that what the people say is *the* reality rather than simply a view of their reality. All texts produced by an informant, observer, or interviewer are by definition constructions produced within specific historical, political, and cultural conditions.

Qualitative evaluation research also has the deficit of being time-consuming both to produce and to read, as well as less conventional or prestigious because of its "weakness of less systematized sampling, less standardized measurement, and less experimental control. Qualitative studies are also harder to focus directly for outcome evaluation" (Steinmetz, 1980, p. 55).

Aside from these possible deficits, data gathering for qualitative evaluation research has the problem of reactivity, although the asset here comes in allowing the researcher to utilize all of his or her interpretive skills, fortuitous experiences, and exploratory powers.

The emphasis in [qualitative research] is on naturalism and holism. To the fullest extent possible, one wants to draw conclusions from facts [that] were emitted spontaneously. Consequently observation is preferred to interviewing and open-ended interviewing is preferred to closed-ended interviewing. (Steinmetz, 1980, pp. 5-6)

Because of these characteristics, particularly skillful observers and interpreters such as Arlie Hochschild (1973), Jerry Jacobs (1974), Barbara Myerhoff (1978), and Kevin Eckert (1980) have ben able to produce powerful monographs about aging in a variety of community settings. These shaped readers' visions of how services and retirement communities should be organized for older people or how low-income neighborhoods unattractive to middle-class people *are* functional for low-income people.

Hochschild's study supports the policy of homogeneous housing arrangements, particularly with regard to low-income widows. Jacobs's study suggests that retirement communities must provide a wide range of medical and recreational services if they wish to be cut off from the larger community. Myerhoff's study suggests that community workers help people refashion religious rituals to combine what they remember from the past with what is possible in the present. And Eckert's study suggests a policy of urban retention of single-room occupancy hotels rather than widespread gentrification if older people are to retain a semblance of independence. Similarly, in the context of long-term care, Jules Henry (1963) provides us with an image of the horror of inadequate and unfeeling care in later life that leads to an increased awareness that such institutions need to be under strict supervision. Lee Bowker (1982) presents a model of humanized care that is not always available even to elderly people who are wealthy. He shows that care can be offered within either a medical or humane model and that the humane is almost always preferred.

Qualitative methods also may guide evaluations of programs designed to affect specific behaviors rather than the comprehensive environment such as those studies mentioned above. For example, nutrition researchers made the following comment:

> Methods of qualitative analysis are powerful and necessary tools for examining the meaning of dietary regimes as these are expressed through the experiences and reports of older people. There is no shortage of sophisticated techniques for analyzing nominal data (e.g., Reynolds, 1977), but decisions have to be made by investigators about linear or nonlinear measures of association. To acquire the type of information necessary to make an informed choice, investigators would be well advised to have a good grasp of the types of "data" used by the respondents themselves in making their decisions. As Keith (1986) notes, holistic and qualitative data are vital if robust explanations are to be formulated. (Hendricks, Calasanti, & Turner, 1988, p. 75)

Surprisingly, many, if not most, qualitative anthropological and sociological research studies contain within them an evaluation component, particularly an evaluation of a policy. These evaluations may concern a micropolicy implemented in a local program or a macropolicy that provides a set of ideas with which to guide national priorities. Embedding evaluation within qualitative research may, in fact, be the rule rather than the exception. Thus instead of asking whether qualitative methods can be used for evaluation research, we might ask if we can do qualitative research without simultaneously doing an evaluation! This linkage between qualitative research and evaluation may reflect the fact that the social sciences are rooted in social reform efforts and have been supported by governments interested in solving social problems.

An explicit example of the way evaluation research is incorporated almost inadvertently into sociological or anthropological qualitative studies can be found in the following statement by Vesperi (1985) that introduces her urban ethnography:

> The writing of this book fell naturally into two parts, in line with the ongoing development of my observations about St. Petersburg's low-income elderly. Part One is concerned with the symbolic processes whereby older people apprehend and subsequently accept, reject, or renegotiate a variety of messages about aging received from an urban community in transition. (p. 29)

Such a statement conveys the researcher's interest in theory. She continues as follows in implicating policy:

> Part Two explores the question of whether the goals of specific social programs aimed at low-income retirees reflect more accurately the needs of those who are served or the perceptions of whose who serve them. (p. 29)

The reverse process occurred in Joel Savishinsky's (1991) study of a nursing home. In this case, he began his research with the intention of evaluating a pet therapy program in a nursing home. Inadvertently, however, he broadened his concerns to include more theoretical questions. He explains this transition this way:

> While the animals provided the initial impetus for this work, they proved to be just the starting point for a widening circle of concerns and questions. The research soon moved beyond the initial focus on pet therapy to explore why elderly individuals had come to live at Elmwood Grove and how they felt about being there. (p. xiii)

Given the prevalent connection between qualitative research and evaluation, it was surprising to read earlier methodological analyses by

Knapp (1979) and Mullhauser (1975) that argued an intrinsic difficulty in doing ethnography for applied purposes such as program evaluation. An opposing and somewhat extreme view is voiced by Robert Broadhead (1978), who argues that qualitative research is almost intrinsically virtuous. He argues for "the replacement of quantitative methodology with qualitative methodology . . . [and] sees qualitative methodology as [virtuous because it is] unfunded, skeptical, muckraking" (Steinmetz, 1980, p. 8).

Yet quantitative evaluation research does have its assets: For example, quantitative evaluation research can provide handy and concise "bottom-line" information. Concise data are what administrators prefer.

Nonetheless, one has to be careful that the data on which these summaries are based are meaningful and not overly reduced for the purpose of cost-benefit analyses. This is not always the case. Studies done with the goal in mind of generating very clear bottom-line information are likely to lose sight of the complexity of social and psychological issues.

An example is provided by sociologist Jaber Gubrium, who used qualitative methodological techniques to answer the question, "How is care in a nursing home accomplished by those people who participate in its everyday life?" In his well-known study *Living and Dying at Murray Manor* (1975), Gubrium "documents the way in which the 'work' of everyday life in a nursing home is organized and conducted." After reading Gubrium's study of nursing home staff behavior, it would behoove all researchers to question the use of chart entries and records concerning patient status. Yet studies of nursing home outcomes are quite likely to use charts without questioning the procedures that led to entries being made. Gubrium describes in great detail the staff conferences that precede the writing of entries into the charts. Many such conferences end in vignettes such as the following.

Erickson: Well, people, we're out of time. Mrs. Singer, you'll see that our goals for Jeannette Bruska [which haven't been discussed] are placed in her chart.

Singer: Yes. (p. 69)

Quantitative research for evaluation purposes is typically not discussed in these terms. Rather than questioning the nature of the data themselves, quantitative evaluation research rests on the assumption that the quality of the data that are quantified is unproblematic. If the data are carefully checked as to their meaningfulness and are reduced into numerical forms, then clear assets can be derived from quantitative research. In the words of one analyst of evaluation research, "Quantitative methods have the advantage of being able to generate policy relevant statistics such as estimates of magnitude of effect and probability of effect" (Steinmetz, 1980 p. 55).

Being able to estimate the magnitude and probability of effect means being able to assess the power of a problem and to predict its future strength. These are very important attributes and have led to a state of affairs whereby quantitative evaluation research in aging has a predominant, even exclusive, place in discussions of research methods. For example, Maddox and Wiley (1976) offer no discussion of qualitative methods and devote their chapter entirely to quantitative strategies in every aspect of gerontological research. Similarly, a decade-old review (Steinmetz, 1980, p. 8) of the field found that "qualitative methodology is totally excluded from the journals (e.g., *Evaluation Quarterly*) and the handbooks (e.g., Sechrest et al., 1979) that cover the field." To reverse this trend and affirm the need to address the assets, specific texts have been devoted to the topic of qualitative evaluation in many different fields of inquiry, including gerontology (e.g., Fry & Keith, 1986), education (e.g., Schratz, 1993), and nursing (e.g., Parse, Coyne, & Smith, 1985).

Combining Evaluation Methods

A solution to the continuous struggle between advocates of qualitative and quantitative evaluation methods is the strategy of combining them. Such an approach is becoming quite popular even in common practices such as teacher evaluations or course evaluations. These evaluations typically use a combination of open-ended (qualitative) and closed information, for example, linking the question "What do students have to say about a teacher's performance?" with "How do students score a teacher?" In this case, students' written comments are thought to convey information about the meaning behind the numerical data. The challenge for the researcher is to find ways of integrating the information if they conflict (Connidis, 1983).

Another role for combining methods is to provide "contextual information [that] will make the quantitative data more interpretable"

(Steinmetz, 1980, p. 56). This idea of "meaning in context" is particularly important in terms of reminding us that evaluation of aging-related policy must be culturally specific. Policies and programs must be evaluated within their own cultural contexts rather than be generalized.

A further use is to provide an introduction to the quantitative study. Daniel Steinmetz (1980), for one, found an important place for qualitative evaluation by stressing that this type of research should precede the quantitative component.

> In the formative stage of program development, qualitative methodology has three major advantages. It is strong at discovering variables and processes. It is strong in generating insights about unfamiliar culture groups and institutional populations. This information can be used to design and implement programs for these populations. Qualitative methodology is also strong in informing interpersonal technologies and in developing the social skills of interpersonal practitioners. (p. 57)

Focus groups also can function effectively at the early stage of a project to gather qualitative information in precisely this way. At the same time, it is important to keep in mind that qualitative evaluation is not primarily a precursor to quantification (Gubrium, 1992; Reinharz, 1984).

Detailed Examples

The remainder of this chapter describes several examples of qualitative evaluation research: Mary Ann Wilner's (1987) study of support groups for older people or for the people who care for them; Barbara Willson's (1993) study of creating consumer-based definitions of "quality of care" among people over the age of 85 who require the services of home health aides; Margaret Ann Mahoney's (1990) "Women's Decisions About Life-Sustaining Interventions on Behalf of Patients With Alzheimer's Disease"; and Susan Sheehan's (1984) study of the transitional community placement program.

Wilner's Study

Mary Ann Wilner's (1987) study concerns self-help groups for the elderly. In the first group (the pseudonym is Georgetown), she observed how older people cope with old age and grapple with problems of memory loss and treatment by family and medical personnel. Her goal was to investigate how some elderly people use the self-help movement to deal with problems of growing older and being stigmatized in a youth-oriented society.

A second group she observed was a support group for members of families of Alzheimer's patients. While analyzing this group, she asked, "How have families of the cognitively impaired elderly turned to each other for support and sustenance?" Wilner's observations and participation in the groups led her to identify significant changes in the participants: "The most notable changes among the [Georgetown] group members were their enhanced self-esteem and ability to be assertive in the familial and professional worlds. This meant an increased ability to care for themselves."

For the Alzheimer's group, Wilner remarks,

Changes were subtle in the Alzheimer's group. Mere attendance at the meetings, implying an acknowledgment of the presence of the disease, reflected substantial change. Being able to make plans for moving the relative, when necessary, to a more appropriate caregiving environment was enormously significant. For example, Paula had spent her first several months in the group just determining if her mother had Alzheimer's disease. In less than six months, not only had she placed her mother in a rest home, but [also] she talked about the realization "that [her] mother will not live the rest of her life in a rest home either, but will have to be moved again to a more intensive care facility." (p. 158)

Wilner's observational study implied an evaluation of the groups and an evaluation of the program used by some agencies of providing groups for various issues connected with aging. Wilner concludes:

The Alzheimer's group seems to have prevented the premature placement of a relative in an institution. The discussions suggest that group members learned to make appropriate use of doctors, institutions, and social workers because they learned to use the group for the more basic information about the nature and management of the disease, and for necessary tension release and mutual support. (p. 158)

There are special difficulties inherent in research of this sort that does not use control groups and yet judges the efficacy of a particular group. On the other hand, Wilner comments:

There are serious ethical problems in imposing a controlled evaluation on this population. Caregivers of Alzheimer's patients find it difficult to follow directions of a group leader or even to listen to an informal talk about Alzheimer's. Imposing structured questionnaires, validated tests, and controlled interviewing would be disrespectful to these caregivers, and many of them would find it very difficult to respond. (p. 160)

In addition, Wilner raises and answers the question of the small numbers inherent in the nature of the support group structure, essentially arguing for a meta-analysis:

It is encouraging that findings from this research and a few other qualitative studies have replicated each other. Together these studies add up to a larger population. Their many similar findings contribute to the accumulating body of knowledge and add new information specific to the support group process and its effectiveness. (p. 160)

She adds:

A variety of qualitative studies and personal accounts have already revealed the enormous benefits gained by participating members. Significant changes—such as acknowledging the presence of the disease, being able to make plans for eventual institutionalization of the relatives, and learning to incorporate other family members in offering emotional support—are mentioned in each of the studies. . . . The groups are important in strengthening the morale, emotional well-being, and treatment skills of care-providing families. (p. 160)

Willson's Study

Barbara Willson's (1993) study stemmed from her concern that standards for evaluating home care were being developed exclusively by those who deliver the care rather than by those who receive it. Her literature review demonstrates that consumers of home health care are not partners in the search for standards of care. Instead, in association with care providers, experts set the standards. She argues that knowing what clients want would make for more satisfaction and more efficiency. She also mentions that a previous study showed that although patients want to receive "technological sophistication," nurses want to give "listening."

Willson's study used face-to-face contact between herself and users of home health care over the age of 85. Although she tried using a standardized scale to determine their evaluations of care, she found that the subset of older people she interviewed was unable to understand the questions or tired when attempting to do so. On the other hand, through careful communication with these people, she was able to conduct open-ended conversations and obtain the information she needed. This information in turn allowed her to understand how a diverse group of frail elderly evaluate home care in general and their own home care in particular.

Mahoney's Research

Margaret Mahoney's (1990) research falls into the domain of new questions that have arisen about how relatives will deal with a terminally ill loved one whose life is sustained artificially by machines. Specifically, her research "examined how wives of Alzheimer patients made their decisions about the use of life-sustaining interventions on behalf of their husbands" (p. 1). In addition to learning how the wives made the decisions, Mahoney's research enabled her to learn if the procedures established in the hospital were helpful to the wives. In this sense, her study can be interpreted as qualitative evaluation of a policy. Specifically, the wives (or other relatives) had to choose from among five levels of care: (a) aggressive medical care, (b) complete medical care without cardiopulmonary resuscitation (CPR), (c) no CPR and no transfer to an acute-care setting for high-technology interventions, (d) no treatment of intercurrent illnesses except in a palliative way, and (e) supportive care without use of invasive medical interventions such as and including feeding tubes.

Mahoney's study relied on a content analysis of the records kept after she had observed conferences to examine the correspondence between actual behavior and charted information. She examined the words used in decision making, the frequency of choices made, and the possible conflicts occurring between the surrogate's decision and the staff decision.

Sheehan's Case Study

Susan Sheehan is a Pulitzer Prize-winning journalist whose book *Kate Quinton's Days* is a case study of the life of one Kate Quinton during her 80th year, from February 24, 1982, to February 24, 1983. On the first day recorded in the book, Kate Quinton lay in a bed at Lutheran Medical Center in Brooklyn, New York, having been admitted some six weeks earlier. As she was improving, and ignoring her objections, hospital social workers tried diligently to have Kate admitted into a nursing home, despite the shortage of beds in "good" homes. At the last moment, however, Kate became a participant in an alternative program called Transitional Community Placement. This arrangement had been established to enable aged people to be cared for in their own homes. Sheehan's book documents precisely what happened to Kate Quinton and took place around her as she became a recipient of that program's services. Through the vehicle of a case study, the reader obtains a qualitative evaluation of a program designed to serve a special subgroup of older people.

Conclusion

Because gerontology is a relatively young field, traditions about how to do research and evaluation studies are not yet set in stone. It is therefore possible to set expectations for qualitative evaluation studies. As in feminist research, an extremely useful one should be the pertinence to the reader of hearing the voices of people rather than have them buried in administrative categories (Gubrium, 1993). A second expectation can be that because qualitative research methods allow for human interaction, they also are useful for keeping the program evaluator honest rather than just efficient. Qualitative research usually raises questions in the field about the nature of various types of data collected. Such questions can also be an expectation of qualitative evaluation research in gerontology. Undoubtedly there are several others, including the search for complexity and the bridge to everyday practice.

If we can establish a set of expectations in gerontological research, it is also important not to replicate the hostility that exists in so many fields between qualitative and quantitative research approaches. Perhaps the field of gerontology can provide both older people and their researchers with new opportunities and a new vision based on productive cooperation in the area rather than exclusionary practices.

References

Bowker, L. H. (1982). *Humanizing institutions for the aged.* Lexington, MA: Lexington.

Broadhead, R. S. (1978). *An interactionist approach to evaluation research.* Paper presented at American Sociological Association Meeting, San Francisco.

Calasanti, T. (1992). Theorizing about gender and aging: Beginning with the voices of women. *Gerontologist, 32*(2), 280-282.

Campbell, D. T. (1978). Qualitative knowing in action research. In M. Marsh, P. Brenner, & M. London (Eds.), *The social contexts of method* (pp. 184-209). London: Croon Helm.

Connidis, I. (1983). Integrating qualitative and quantitative methods in survey research on aging: An assessment. *Qualitative Sociology, 6*(4), 334-352.

Eckert, K. (1980). *The unseen elderly.* San Diego, CA: Campanile.

Fry, C. L., & Keith, J. (Eds.). (1986). *New methods for old age research: Strategies for studying diversity.* New York: Bergin & Garvey.

Glaser, B., & Strauss, A. (1967). *Discovery of grounded theory: Strategies for qualitative research.* Hawthorne, NY: Aldine.

Guba, E. (1978). *Toward a methodology of naturalistic inquiry in educational evaluation.* Los Angeles: University of California (Center for the Study of Education).

Gubrium, J. (1975). *Living and dying at Murray Manor.* New York: St. Martin's.

Gubrium, J. (1992). Qualitative research comes of age in gerontology. *Gerontologist, 32,* 581-582.

Gubrium, J. (1993). Voice and context in a new gerontology. In T. R. Cole, W. A. Achenbaum, P. L. Jakobi, & R. Kastenbaum (Eds.), *Voices and visions of aging* (pp. 46-63). New York: Springer.

Hendricks, J., Calasanti, T. M., & Turner, H. B. (1988). Foodways of the elderly: Social research considerations. *American Behavioral Scientist, 32*(1), 61-83.

Henry, J. (1963). *Culture against man.* New York: Vintage.

Hochschild, A. (1973). *The unexpected community.* Englewood Cliffs, NJ: Prentice-Hall.

Jacobs, J. (1974). *Fun city: An ethnographic study of a retirement community.* New York: Holt, Rinehart & Winston.

Kayser-Jones, J. S. (1981). *Old, alone and neglected: Care of the aged in Scotland and the United States.* Berkeley: University of California Press.

Keith, J. (1986). Participant observation. In C. L. Fry & J. Keith (Eds.), *New methods for old age research: Strategies for studying diversity* (pp. 1-20). New York: Bergin & Garvey.

Knapp, M. S. (1979). Ethnographic contributions to evaluation research: The experimental schools program evaluation and some alternatives. In T. D. Cook & C. S. Reichardt (Eds.), *Qualitative and quantitative methods in evaluation research* (pp. 77-90). Beverly Hills, CA: Sage.

Maddox, G., & Wiley, J. (1976). Scope, concepts and methods in the study of aging. In R. H. Binstock & E. Shanas (Eds.), *Handbook of aging and the social sciences* (pp. 3-34). New York: Van Nostrand Reinhold.

Mahoney, M. (1990). *Women's decisions about life-sustaining interventions on behalf of patients with Alzheimer's disease.* Unpublished manuscript, Brandeis University, Waltham, Massachusetts.

Mullhauser, F. (1975). Ethnography and policy-making: The case of education. *Human Organization, 34,* 311-315.

Myerhoff, B. (1978). *Number our days.* New York: E. P. Dutton.

Parse, R. R., Coyne, A. B., & Smith, M. J. (1985). *Nursing research: Qualitative methods.* Bowie, MD: Brady.

Patton, M. Q. (1980). *Qualitative evaluation methods.* Beverly Hills, CA: Sage.

Reinharz, S. (1984). *On becoming a social scientist: From survey research and participant observation to experiential analysis* (2nd ed.). New Brunswick, NJ: Transaction.

Reinharz, S. (1992). *Feminist methods in social research.* New York: Oxford University Press.

Reinharz, S., & Rowles, G. (Eds.). (1987). *Qualitative gerontology.* New York: Springer.

Reynolds, H. T. (1977). *Analysis of nominal data.* Beverly Hills, CA: Sage.

Savishinsky, J. S. (1991). *The ends of time: Life and work in a nursing home.* New York: Bergin & Garvey.

Schratz, M. (Ed.). (1993). *Qualitative voices in educational research.* London: Falmer.

Sechrest, L., et al. (1979). *Evaluation studies review annual* (Vol. 4). Beverly Hills, CA: Sage.

Sheehan, S. (1984). *Kate Quinton's days.* New York: New American Library.

Steinmetz, D. (1980). *Qualitative methods in evaluation: A literature review.* Unpublished manuscript, Department of Sociology, University of Michigan, Ann Arbor.

Vesperi, M. D. (1985). *City of green benches: Growing old in a new downtown.* Ithaca, NY: Cornell University Press.

Willson, B. (1993). *Perceptions of quality home health care among home care recipients 85 years and older and their providers.* Unpublished manuscript, Brandeis University, Waltham, Massachusetts.

Wilner, M. A. (1987). The transition to self-care: A field study of support groups for the elderly and their caregivers. In S. Reinharz & G. Rowles (Eds.), *Qualitative gerontology* (pp. 147-162). New York: Springer.

Author Index

Subject Index

definition of, 38
Etic data, 219

Felt age:
  as emic theme, 220-221
Fieldwork:
  contributions of to aging research,
    156-160
  definitional labor in, 156
  definition of, 155
Fieldwork, group and institutional, 155-
  169
  as unique opportunity for study of ag-
    ing, 169
  California Department of Aging pro-
    ject, 161
  example of in Alzheimer's day care
    centers, 160-169
  limits to researcher's insights from, 156
  researcher's role in, 155
Fieldworkers, 43-47
  and training efforts of staff, 93-94
  as advisers, 47
  as culture brokers, 116
  as group facilitators, 46
  as recruiters, 46
  as social workers, 47
  as trainers, 46
  ethnic disparity and, 43-44
  generational disparity and, 44-45
  multiple roles of, 46-47
  role blurring and, 45-47
  social status disparity and, 45
Free writing, 260

Gillespie, S., 233, 234, 235
Grounded theory, 264
Guided conversation, 106, 111

Harvard adolescence study, 112
Hermeneutic circle, 213
Hermeneutic phenomenological, 218, 219
Hermeneutics, 212
Human Relations Area Files (HRAF),
  111, 113, 115
Human science research:
  as philosophical grounding for analyz-
    ing personal journals, 212-213

doing, 212-213
object of, 212
philosophical tradition of, 212
preferred methods of, 212-213
products of, 224
source of, 212

In-depth interviewing, 123-136
  appropriate responses in, 130
  building and maintaining relationships
    in, 126-135
  empathetic listening in, 130, 134
  interview guide in, 123, 124, 126-135
  listening in, 133-135
  nature of collaboration in, 127-130
  open-ended questions in, 125
  rapport and trust in, 130-132
  research questions in, 123-126
  respectful probing in, 130
  tactful probing in, 130
In-depth interviews, 82
  emotion in, 127
  pacing of, 132
  paradoxical quality of, 128
  preparation for, 132-133
  spacing of, 132
  style of, 127
Interdisciplinary writing:
  and "normal science," 252-254

Jackson, N., 235
Joyce, J., 192

Kincaid, G., 234

Life histories, 82
Life satisfaction:
  as outcome variable, xii
Life stories, 137-152, 192
  as social constructions, 138-139
  conception and use of, 140
  definition of, 137
  nature and use of, 138-139
  subjective nature of, 138
  use of to address patterns of socio-
    structural relations, 139
  use of to discover objective facts of in-
    dividual's life, 138

About the Contributors

Emily K. Abel is Associate Professor of Public Health and Women's Studies at the University of California at Los Angeles. Her most recent books are *Circles of Care: Work and Identity in Women's Lives* (1990), coedited with Margaret K. Nelson, and *Who Cares for the Elderly? Public Policy and the Experiences of Adult Daughters* (1990). Abel is writing a history of family care for the sick and disabled in the United States from 1850 to 1950.

Judith C. Barker currently is in the Division of Medical Anthropology, Department of Epidemiology and Biostatistics, University of California at San Francisco. She has considerable experience in studying health care and social support issues among ethnic minorities in the United States and abroad. Her interests are aging, chronic illness, risk-taking behaviors, home health care, and social organization. Her recent work has focused on the daily management of illness in a variety of community and institutional settings.

Harry J. Berman is Professor of Child, Family, and Community Services at Sangamon State University in Springfield, Illinois, where he teaches courses on life span development and aging. He has written several articles on the analysis of personal journals in later life and is completing a book on the subject. He also has conducted research on relations between adult children and aging parents, retirement decisions, and the turnover of nurse aides in nursing homes. He is coeditor of *Successful Nurse Aide Management in Nursing Homes* (1988).

Ann Dill teaches social gerontology and medical sociology at Brown University. She trained in the Rutgers-Princeton program in mental health research, sponsored by the National Institutes of Mental Health. She has conducted studies of community-based care systems of the elderly, the chronically mentally ill, individuals with AIDS, and others with long-term needs. Her current research includes an ethnographic analysis of perceptions of those systems by their clients, as well as a comparative study of changes in social welfare for the elderly in the former Yugoslavia.

Lucy Rose Fischer is Research Investigator in Geriatrics at Group Health Foundation in Minneapolis. She has written three books: *Older Volunteers: A Guide to Research and Practice* with K. B. Schaffer (1993), *Linked Lives: Adult Daughters and Their Mothers* (1986), and *Older Minnesotans: What Do They Need? How Do They Contribute?* with D. M. Mueller, P. W. Cooper, and R. C. Chase (1989). Fischer has published many articles and reports on intergenerational family relationships, informal caregiving, paid home care, volunteering, and qualitative research methods.

Jaber F. Gubrium is Professor in the Department of Sociology at the University of Florida. He has conducted research on the social organization of care in diverse treatment settings from nursing homes and physical rehabilitation to counseling centers and family therapy. His continuing fieldwork on the organizational embeddedness of social forms serves as a basis for the development of an interpretive comparative ethnography. He is the editor of *Journal of Aging Studies* and author of *Living and Dying at Murray Manor* (1975), *Oldtimers and Alzheimer's* (1986), *Analyzing Field Reality* (1988), *The Mosaic of Care* (1991), and *Out of Control* (1992). His recently coauthored book with J. Holstein, *What is Family?* (1990), presents a social constructionist approach to family life.

J. Neil Henderson is a Medical Anthropologist at the Suncoast Gerontology Center in the University of South Florida Medical Center in Tampa and is a faculty member in the Department of Psychiatry and Department of Community and Family Health. He has conducted qualitative research in nursing homes and implemented Alzheimer's disease support groups in African-American and Hispanic communities in Tampa and Jacksonville. He continues to do research on ethnic minority aging, Alzheimer's disease, ethnic-specific caregiving, service utilization, and dementia care units in nursing homes.

James A. Holstein is Associate Professor of Sociology at Marquette University. His research brings an ethnomethodologically informed constructionist perspective to a variety of topics, including mental illness, social problems, family, the life course, and dispute processing. He is coeditor of the research annual *Perspectives on Social Problems*, coauthor (with J. Gubrium) of *What Is Family?* and *Constructing the Life Course*, and author of *Court-Ordered Insanity*. He recently has coedited (with G. Miller) *Reconsidering Social Constructionism* and *Constructionist Controversies*.

Dale J. Jaffe is Associate Professor of Sociology at the University of Wisconsin, Milwaukee, where he also serves as chair of the graduate program and the university-wide undergraduate certificate program in aging. His interests are in the areas of the sociologies of aging, health and illness, and qualitative methodology. He is the author of *Caring Strangers: The Sociology of Intergenerational Homesharing* (1989) and editor of *Shared Housing for the Elderly* (1989). He currently is writing a book on the experience of Alzheimer's disease based on four years of ethnographic fieldwork in group homes.

Sharon R. Kaufman is a Medical Anthropologist with expertise in identity development in late life, adaptation to illness, changing values in health care, and the culture of medicine. She is Associate Research Anthropologist with the Institute for Health and Aging in the Department of Social Behavioral Sciences and the Medical Anthropology Program at the University of California at San Francisco. She has conducted research with well and chronically ill elderly, physicians, and other health care professionals.

Jeanie Kayser-Jones is Professor in the Department of Physiological Nursing and is affiliated with the medical anthropology program at the University of California at San Francisco. She has published *Old, Alone and Neglected: Care of the Aged in the United States and Scotland* and numerous articles in nursing, gerontology, social science, law, and medical journals. She has lectured extensively in the United States and abroad on the care of the institutionalized elderly. Currently she is principal investigator on a National Institute of Aging study of eating and nutritional problems in nursing homes.

Jennie Keith is Centennial Professor of Anthropology and Provost at Swarthmore College. Her research has focused on the meanings of age in different societies. Related fieldwork has been conducted in retirement communities as well as through Project AGE, a crosscultural comparative study that she codirected with Christine Fry.

Barbara A. Koenig is Senior Research Scholar and Executive Director of the Stanford University Center for Biomedical Ethics. She has received several research grants from the National Institutes of Health, including one to study cultural pluralism and ethical decision making. She has published articles on death and dying, AIDS, and physician response to new and lethal infectious diseases, and she has written two books, *The Meaning of AIDS* (with E. T. Juengst) and *The Technological Imperative in Medical Practice.*

Mark R. Luborsky is Senior Research Scientist at the Philadelphia Geriatric Center. He has received grants from the National Institutes of Health and private foundations to study sociocultural, ethnic, and personal meanings in relation to mental and physical health, disability, and rehabilitation. He has published widely and is past president of the Association for Anthropology and Gerontology.

Karen A. Lyman is Professor of Sociology and administers the gerontology program at Chaffey College in California. She also is a Research Associate at the University of Southern California's Gerontology Research Institute. She has conducted a comparative field study of eight Alzheimer's day care centers, the results of which have been published in *Day In, Day Out With Alzheimer's: Stress in Caregiving Relationships* (1993) and in numerous articles. Her current interests include dementing illnesses from the perspective of afflicted patients.

Eleanor M. Miller is Associate Professor of Sociology and Assistant Vice Chancellor for Equal Opportunity at the University of Wisconsin, Milwaukee. She is author of *Street Woman* (1986) and coeditor of *The Worth of Women's Work: Synthesizing Qualitative Research* (1987). Her interests include feminist social theory and method, gender, and deviance.

Linda S. Mitteness is Associate Professor and Interim Chair of the Division of Medical Anthropology, Department of Epidemiology and Biostatistics, University of California at San Francisco. Her main interests are in the experience of illness, especially the management of multiple chronic conditions in later life. Her recent research has included the management of urinary incontinence by both relatively healthy and frail elderly, the management of smoking by patients in a skilled nursing facility, patient adaptation to lower limb amputation, and family members' perceptions of safety issues in caring for relatives with dementia.

Shulamit Reinharz is Professor of Sociology at Brandeis University. She was a Research Scholar at the Brookdale Institute of Gerontology in Jerusalem and has been coeditor of the journal *Qualitative Sociology.* She is the author of numerous articles in social gerontology, qualitative methodology, and women's studies. She has written *Feminist Methods in Social Research, Aging on the Kibbutz, On Becoming a Social Scientist,* and *Psychology and Community Change* and coedited *Qualitative Gerontology.*

Robert L. Rubinstein is Director of Research and Senior Research Anthropologist at the Philadelphia Geriatric Center. He has conducted field research in Vanuatu in the South Pacific and in the United States. His interests include culture and aging, older men, home environments of older people, qualitative methods, and health and aging. He has published numerous articles and books on aging, including *Elders Living Alone* and *Singular Paths.* He currently is working on a book on the aging body in cultural perspective.

Andrea Sankar is Assistant Professor of Anthropology and Director of the medical anthropology program at Wayne State University, Detroit. She has written many articles on health care and the aged, is the author of *Dying at Home: A Guide for Family Caregivers* (1991), and is coeditor (with J. Gubrium) of *The Home Care Experience* (1990). Her research includes studies of high-tech home care, community care for HIV-positive persons, and theory in gerontology. With Frances Trix, she has written *Going Beyond the Polls: A Cultural Analysis of the Hill/ Thomas Hearings.*

J. Brandon Wallace is Assistant Professor of Sociology at Middle Tennessee State University in Murfreesboro. He is interested in life stories as a method for studying the experience of aging and life change and has used these stories to address topics such as the social nature of reminiscence, gender differences in late life, the process of placing a family member in a nursing home, and changes in the experience of pregnancy and childbirth in the past 50 years. He also is interested in the act of narration itself, especially the conditions that shape narrative practice.